Oil

Resources

Peter Dauvergne & Jane Lister, *Timber*

Michael Nest, *Coltan*

Elizabeth R. DeSombre & J. Samuel Barkin, *Fish*

Jennifer Clapp, *Food*

David Feldman, *Water*

Oil

GAVIN BRIDGE AND
PHILIPPE LE BILLON

polity

First published in 2013 by Polity Press

Polity Press
65 Bridge Street
Cambridge CB2 1UR, UK

Polity Press
350 Main Street
Malden, MA 02148, USA

ISBN-13: 978-0-7456-4925-2
ISBN-13: 978-0-7456-4926-9(pb)

A catalogue record for this book is available from the British Library.

Typeset in 10.25 on 13 pt FF Scala
by Servis Filmsetting Ltd, Stockport, Cheshire
Printed and bound in Great Britain by the MPG Books Group

For further information on Polity, visit our website: www.politybooks.com

Contents

List of Figures, Tables, and Boxes   vi
Acknowledgments   viii

Introduction   1

1 The Nature of a Political Resource   5

2 Capturing Oil   35

3 Marketing Oil   69

4 Securing Oil   93

5 Developing Through Oil   125

6 Governing Oil   153

7 Better and Beyond: The Future of Oil   180

   Notes   206
   Selected Readings   226
   Index   235

Figures, Tables, and Boxes

FIGURES

1.1 World oil production and price (1900–2011)   10
1.2 Major international oil trade flows (2011)   18
1.3 Oil consumption, OECD vs. non-OECD   21
1.4 The politics of the hydrocarbon chain   28
2.1 A generalized oil-production network   36
2.2 Variation in production costs by type of oil source 57
3.1 Oil price, volatility, and US recessions (1945–2011) 71
3.2 Futures and options contracts for oil and other
     commodities (1993–2010)   89
4.1 Maritime choke points   106
4.2 Chinese oil production and consumption
     (1965–2010)   117
5.1 GDP, HDI, and poverty levels among oil
     producers   142
7.1 Urban population densities and ground
     transportation emissions per capita   199

TABLES

1.1 Reserves, production, and consumption, leading
     countries (2010)   12
1.2 Unconventional oil reserves   16
2.1 Top 15 integrated oil companies (2010)   40

2.2   The supermajors' dwindling control over world oil   55
4.1   Main internationally disputed oil areas   95
4.2   Energy security criteria by resource type   99
4.3   Gasoline taxes or subsidies for selected countries   115
5.1   Distribution of cash flow from oil sector   137
5.2   "Government take" from oil revenues   140
5.3   Secessionist conflicts in oil-producing countries   149
6.1   Main positions on oil governance   156
6.2   Oil and energy-related international initiatives and organizations   163
7.1   Adaptation strategies for selected regions   186

BOXES

1.1   Conventional versus unconventional oil   14
2.1   China's national oil companies   44
2.2   From the "Seven Sisters" to "Big Oil"   49
2.3   The rise and fall of production sharing agreements   59
2.4   Royal Bank of Scotland: "the oil and gas bank"   64
3.1   Compartmentalizing the market – China's loans-for-oil   91
4.1   Revisiting the "oil weapon"   108
5.1   The oil we eat: petroleum in the geopolitics of food production   127
5.2   Swapping "oil for nature" in Ecuador   134
5.3   Petrodollars   139
5.4   Oil revenue transparency   148
6.1   Deregulation and oil price speculation   174

Acknowledgments

In writing this book we have accumulated a series of debts for information, assistance, and time freely given. Sara Elder, Sotonye Godwin-Hart, and Knut Kitching provided excellent research assistance, and comments and assistance on an initial draft from Nadia VonBenzon and Guy Leung were most helpful. We thank Nick Scarle in the School of Environment and Development at the University of Manchester and Eric Leinberger at the School of Geography of the University of British Columbia for their work preparing the maps and graphics. We appreciate the comments and suggestions of the anonymous reviewers who read the full draft and engaged with our argument. Less directly – but no less significant – are the conversations and collaborations with colleagues near and far whose knowledge and perspectives have helped shape our account. We also warmly thank Louise Knight and David Winters for inviting us to contribute to this series and for enabling us to give shape to the final product. Finally, we both thank our families.

Introduction

Oil pulses through our daily lives. It is the plastic we touch, the food we eat, and the way we move. Oil powers our cars, chainsaws, and tanks. Yet six generations back, oil was a bit player in an emerging lubricant market where it competed with the rendered bodies of whales, lizards, and fish. Oil's brief and startling career – from small-town hustler to global kingpin – is one of spectacular boom and bust, extremes of wealth and poverty, and environmental ills ranging from local spills to global climate change. During the twentieth century, this complex hydrocarbon has been pulled from the earth and spread far and wide. The worlds made by and through oil, however, are anything but uniform. The international oil trade links every country on earth, but only a handful of countries hold the lion's share of known reserves. Every minute, millions of dollars change hands through the oil markets as crude is bought and sold, but oil itself moves through pipelines and in tankers at a comparatively medieval pace. Oil provides an unprecedented freedom from geographical constraint for those who can access it, yet its record of pollution and distorted development cripples the lives of many others.

Creating wealth and power from oil is quite a trick. Crude hides below ground and must be hunted and captured. This raw oil is frequently in the wrong place – miles from markets, in places difficult to access or already used by others. Unlike the subterranean lakes of the imagination, crude inhabits tiny gaps in ancient sediments and often must be compelled to the surface. In the ground, oil takes on characteristics of time and place – local variations in viscosity and the content of metals and sulfur, for example – that must be erased by refineries if oil is to behave as required in engines, power stations, and production lines. In the search for value, refineries create fresh distinctions between grades of oil and different types of petrochemicals, producing a catalogue of products tailored for hundreds of specific uses. Most of these products are flammable, noxious, and difficult to contain, but must be transported, stored, and distributed widely if demand is to be created and sustained. Most oil is burnt to provide mobility via land, sea, and air, but the by-products of this combustion can be directly hazardous to health and livelihoods. Exchanges and final markets help lubricate the global movements of oil, yet speculation over oil's *future* price can disrupt existing patterns and rates of oil movement by driving wild swings in price. There is, then, a savvy to the business of making money from and through oil that extends beyond oil's *physical* properties to the economic and political structures that take shape around it. The popular fascination with oil's tycoons, barons, and sheiks – Getty, Rockefeller, Abramovich, or the Sultan of Brunei – acknowledges how oil's value can be captured to remarkable effect. Beyond the palaces, yachts, and gleaming towers, oil's many other landscapes also reveal how its value evades a large proportion of the population in many oil-rich countries.

If we think of oil at all, we tend to think of it as a gift of nature – a natural endowment bequeathed by geology and time. Oil is indeed a legacy from the past, an accumulation of carbohydrates and proteins from the bodies of algae and plankton that has been trapped and cooked underground. But to think of oil in this way is misleading, as it gives nature too much of a hand. Where, how, and when oil moves within modern economies has little to do with nature or geology. The way we use it, who can afford it, where it is extracted, and even how we know how much is in the ground are determined by the actions and interactions of some of the most powerful actors and institutions in the global economy. Because decisions about finding, moving, and using oil bring together groups of people with different interests and agendas, oil is unavoidably political. Oil may be drawn from the earth but it is a very social resource.

This point is important for understanding what we mean in this book by the "politics" of oil for two reasons. First, the political character of oil is a normal and continuous state of affairs and not an aberration or interrupting event. We aim in this book to show how the politics of oil are changing, rather than to suggest oil is now becoming political (it has always been so). Second, we take the politics of oil to mean more than a zero-sum game over a fixed and declining resource – a scramble at the end of the "Age of Plenty" for nature's unclaimed gifts. Instead, the politics of oil concerns the relationships of competition, conflict, and cooperation that define the social and geographical distribution of the various "goods" and "bads" that can be produced through oil. In the twentieth century, the politics of oil was about the management of abundance, state power, and market growth. The legacy of this "Age of Plenty" includes declining conventional oil reserves, volatile prices, climate change, and major political and economic distortions in most oil-rich countries. Our argument in this book is that a new geopolitics of oil is now emerging, centered on changes in the availability, accessibility, affordability, and acceptability of oil. The dynamics of competition, conflict, and cooperation associated with this new geopolitics point to the imperative for more effective global oil governance.

Our goal in the chapters that follow is to highlight the critical relationships – among states, firms, and society – that are key to understanding oil's geopolitics, and their relationship to changes in the availability, accessibility, affordability, and acceptability of oil. It is not the characteristics of individual actors that matter to us, but the dynamic relationships among them and what these relationships mean for the governance of oil. In chapter 1 – "The Nature of a Political Resource" – we explore the origin of oil's extraordinary utility and its potential for social conflict. We review the state of global oil reserves after more than a century of exploration and the shifting character of contemporary demand. Chapter 1 introduces five fundamental tensions that underpin the oil sector and that together make up the geopolitics of oil: these are then explored in chapters 2–6. In chapter 2 – "Capturing Oil" – we examine the structure, connections, and interactions between different parts of the production and consumption chain for oil. We move from a physical, metabolic process of refining crude to an understanding of the distribution of value along the chain. Chapter 3 – "Marketing Oil" – focuses on the politics of value creation, contrasting efforts to create new markets with contemporary attempts to reduce demand. In chapter 4 – "Securing Oil" – we explore the political geography of oil's winners and losers, and ask for whom oil is secure. Chapter 5 – "Developing Through Oil" – examines the social and environmental challenges associated with oil dependence. Chapter 6 – "Governing Oil" – shows how oil is in need of global governance, explains why and proposes reforms to existing institutions. Chapter 7 – "Better and Beyond" – summarizes the "new reality" of oil as an apparently intractable challenge: efforts to sustain supply in the face of rising demand appear to only further exacerbate the economic, social, and environmental ills associated with capturing, producing, and consuming oil. We conclude that there is an imperative for better oil governance, and identify four priorities for improving oil's economic, social, and environmental impacts and, in the longer term, moving beyond oil.

CHAPTER ONE

The Nature of a Political Resource

"Oil" is a catch-all term that covers a diversity of liquid hydro-carbons. The starting point for most of these is "conventional" crude oil, a form of oil sufficiently liquid to be pumped directly out of the ground and rich enough in carbon-hydrogen atomic linkages to be directly refined. Conventional crude fueled the remarkable expansion of oil production and consumption during the twentieth century but growth in the last decade has stalled, and is increasingly giving way to 'unconventional' sources. These are mostly hydrogen-enriched synthetic crude recovered from sand and rock containing bitumen and liquids associated with natural gas production; together these account for 5 percent of global oil production and could rise to 10–20 percent by 2035. The origins of oil and the chemistry of crude formation might seem of little relevance for understanding the politics of oil. However, the conditions under which oil forms are key to understanding both the extraordinary utility that modern societies have found in oil and fundamental questions of control. They determine the character of crude, the uneven distribution of oil resources at the global scale, and the costs and risks of turning raw resources into valu-able products. Oil forms via the decomposition of organic (carbon-based) matter under conditions of heat and pressure – a process akin to "slow cooking," more properly known as "diagenesis." Most of the oil being extracted today was formed between 200 and 2.5 million years ago. The processes that break down organic matter and lead to the formation of oil typically occur at temperatures between 75°C and 150°C, and in most settings these conditions are found 2–3.5 kilometers below the surface. This creates an "oil window": above it, temperatures are too low for oil to form; below it, the longer hydrocarbons are broken down into shorter chains, producing natural gas instead of oil. A particular combination of physical conditions is needed if these hydrocarbons are to concentrate together rather than simply disperse. Oil forming in an organic-rich source rock needs a porous "reservoir" rock (typically sands, sandstone, or limestone) into which it can migrate and accumulate, and an impermeable seal or cap that prevents oil from moving further. Because the conditions for the formation of oil are not found everywhere, crude oil is variable in its physical and chemical properties and unevenly distributed in the earth.[1]

Crude oil is primarily carbon, atoms of which are locked together with hydrogen in different arrangements to form "hydrocarbon" molecules. As with other "fossil" fuels, the carbon atoms in crude oil are an underground stock accumulated over millions of years via the global carbon cycle. Pumping, refining, and burning crude oil returns these carbon atoms to the surface – ultimately in the form of carbon dioxide emissions to the atmosphere. In this way, the global oil industry acts as a carbon conveyer, moving carbon stocks from below ground into the atmosphere. And because the rate at which carbon flows to the surface is much greater than the return flow – via the decomposition of organic matter or the deliberate capture and storage of carbon dioxide – the oil industry is deeply involved in the atmospheric accumulation of carbon dioxide and climate change.

The way in which carbon and hydrogen are combined varies, so that crude oil is made up of many different types of hydrocarbon molecules. The larger the number of carbon atoms that make up a molecule, the heavier the hydrocarbon:

from gaseous methane and ethane with one and two carbon atoms respectively, through liquid gasoline with 7–10 carbon atoms per molecule, to highly viscous bitumen with more than 35. Crude oil also contains other materials, including sulfur, nitrogen, metals, and salts. Because it is a natural material that reflects the conditions of its formation, the quality of oil in underground reserves is highly variable. Among the most significant forms of variability are: density (oil with more hydrogen is lighter and has a lower specific gravity); sulfur content (a higher content characterizing "sour" from "sweet" crudes); viscosity (how readily it flows); and acidity and the presence of metals. Oil is a liquid hydrocarbon. The rather obvious fact that oil flows is significant, because – unlike gas or coal – it can be moved over distance with comparatively few energy and labor inputs. It can be pumped across continents, into storage tanks, and into engines. Underground, oil is a liquid that is often under pressure, and under the right conditions it travels to the surface without lifting. On the other hand, this flow character lends oil an unruliness – a capacity to flow beyond control – that requires capital, equipment, and skill to contain.

For thousands of years, societies have found utility in these physical and chemical properties of crude, including waterproofing for boats, as a mechanical lubricant and as a medical ointment. Today, crude's value lies in its role as a chemical feedstock and fuel. The diversity of hydrocarbon molecules – and the relative ease with which they may be split, combined, and re-engineered – provides a rich storehouse of potential petrochemical combinations with which to manufacture new materials, including plastics, synthetic fibers, and a range of chemicals. One of every 15 barrels of crude oil (i.e. 6 percent) is used in this way as a feedstock for the production of petrochemicals.

It is as a fuel, however, that most crude oil is used.

Combining hydrocarbon molecules with oxygen – as in combustion – releases large amounts of energy as heat and light. Oil packs a greater energy punch than coal or natural gas: nearly twice as much as coal by weight, and around 50 percent more than liquefied natural gas by volume. The practical effect of this greater "energy density" is that oil has unrivaled capacities as a transportation fuel. The amount of oil required to move a ton or travel a thousand kilometers is less than for other fuels, allowing expanded mobility and geographical flexibility. The replacement of coal (through steam) by oil (diesel, gasoline, kerosene, and marine fuels) in transportation, which occurred for the most part in the first half of the twentieth century, reflected the greater energy services that oil could provide. The higher energy density of oil changed the economies of scale required for crossing space, allowing the size of vehicle units to fall – from the train and tram to the automobile – and an increase in the power output for a given size or weight of engine. Oil's energy density enabled the evolution of the *internal* combustion engine (where oxidation/combustion on a small scale released a sufficient amount of energy to enable the direct movement of a piston), as opposed to the much larger, *external* combustion engines associated with steam power. Oil was not the first fossil fuel to have significantly shrunk distance: the introduction of coal-fired steamships in the second half of the nineteenth century drove down shipping costs and further facilitated long-distance trade in bulk commodities like wheat and wool. But oil consolidated this process and drove it further: from cars and airplanes, to diesel and bunker fuels for ocean shipping. In the US today, three-quarters of all petroleum is used as transportation fuel. As a fuel, oil is burned in a variety of forms. These include gasoline and jet fuel at the lighter end of the spectrum; heavier diesel fuels, heating oils, and bunker fuels for shipping; and, heaviest of all, petroleum coke which is used as a fuel in steel smelting and cement production.

Oil's high energy density and liquid properties mean the "gap" between the amount of energy expended in gathering a barrel of oil, and the amount of energy that the barrel can release, can be very large. Harnessing this "energy surplus" has enabled large gains in labor productivity over the last hundred years, as oil-based machines replaced human labor and facilitated growing economies of scale. The energy surplus available through oil has enabled industrial economies to overcome declining resource quality and the exhaustion of local stocks, expanding in turn the output of food and raw materials. The average energy surplus available through oil has been declining, from around 100:1 down to 30:1 over the course of the twentieth century, with some deep-water crude and unconventional oil sources now as low as 5:1. This declining ratio demonstrates the gradual deterioration of "energy returns" as investment has increasingly become geared toward accessing harder-to-reach conventional oil deposits or hard-to-upgrade unconventional sources.[2]

The condition of the resource: growing uncertainty, declining quality

Over the last 150 years around 1.3 trillion barrels of oil have been extracted from the earth, over half of it since around 1989 (see Figure 1.1). At the same time, global oil reserves have grown: world reserves grew by 38 percent between 1990 and 2010 and now stand at 1.4 trillion barrels. The clue to this apparent paradox is that reserves (unlike the total planetary resource) are not fixed, but are shaped by geological knowledge, technology, political factors, and the economics of production. As oil companies probe the earth, they produce not only oil at the top of the well but also new reserves

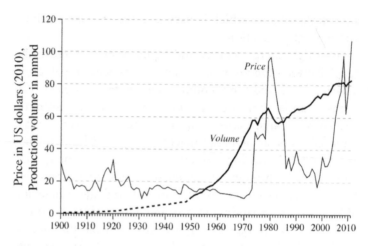

Sources: BP Statistical Review 2011, US Department of Energy, World Oil 1948 Atlas.

Figure 1.1 World oil production and price (1900–2011)

at the bottom. For most of the twentieth century, exploration activity and investment in existing fields "produced" reserves faster than they were recovered, and most of the world's largest fields – the "supergiants" that continue to supply today's demand – were discovered between the 1930s and 1960s. While exploration and technological change continue to "produce" reserves, there are three significant changes.

First, finding new reserves of "conventional oil"– the type of crude oil that has underpinned twentieth-century growth – is proving increasingly difficult. Outside the Organization of Petroleum Exporting Countries (OPEC), the growth of conventional reserves has slowed to a standstill and there is increasing uncertainty over the ability to expand production from known reserves in the Middle East. The Reserves/ Production Ratio – which captures this dynamic of depletion and replacement – grew during the 1990s from 30 years to

around 45 but has been flat since 2000 despite a significant
rise in the price of oil. A handful of countries control the
lion's share of the gold-standard conventional crudes that
have underpinned economic growth in the twentieth century
(see Table 1.1). The center of gravity of global reserves of conventional oil continues to be the Middle East with 54 percent
– 800 billion barrels – of proven reserves, although its dominance has been falling (see p. 15). The future of conventional
oil will remain the Middle East, but it is clouded by uncertainties over the real volume of reserves, political factors, and
rising domestic oil consumption. Saudi Arabia has continued
to declare about 260 billion barrels of conventional crude oil
reserves since 1989 while maintaining, apparently with some
difficulty, production of around 10 million barrels per day
(mmbd) in recent years. At 155 billion barrels, Iran supposedly
holds among the world's largest reserves and, despite doubts
about many upward revisions, there remains much potential
given major political constraints on production growth since
the 1980s. Iraq reassessed its reserves upward to 146 billion,
assuming higher oil recovery rates. With the end of hostilities
and major investments, its production could double to about
6 mmbd by 2020, a far cry from the Iraqi government's initial target of 12 mmbd by 2017. The Persian Gulf is not only
a major repository of oil, but it also enjoys some of the lowest
production costs and is relatively close to major markets, with
Europe, India, and China all within two weeks of tanker travel
or less than 6000 km of pipelines. The reserve-holding states
of this region – and their custody of a high proportion of the
world's high-quality oil resources – are one of the distinctive
features of the political economy of oil.[3]

    Second, the quality of reserves is changing. As the highest-
value light crudes are depleted, the physical and chemical
profile of reserves is shifting toward heavier, poorer-quality
oils that are more costly to extract and refine and which are

Table 1.1 Reserves, production, and consumption, leading countries (2010)

Oil reserves			Oil production			Oil Consumption		
Country	Amount (billion barrels)	Cumulative percentage of global	Country	Amount (thousand barrels daily)	Cumulative percentage of global	Country	Amount (thousand barrels daily)	Cumulative percentage of global
1. Saudi Arabia	264	19	1. Russia	10,270	13	1. US	19,143	21
2. Venezuela	211	34	2. Saudi Arabia	10,007	25	2. China	9,057	32
3. Iran	137	44	3. US	7,513	34	3. Japan	4,451	37
4. Iraq	115	53	4. Iran	4,245	39	4. India	3,319	41
5. Kuwait	102	60	5. China	4,071	44	5. Russia	3,199	44
World total	1383	100	World total	82,095	100	World total	87,439	100

Source: Data from BP Statistical Review 2011 (includes NGLs, 26.5 billion barrels of bitumen for Canada, and 94.2 billion barrels of extra-heavy oil for Venezuela).

associated with higher greenhouse gas (GHG) and other emissions. Within the broad category of conventional oil, average sulfur content is rising as poorer-quality crudes are brought into production, and there is a shift toward heavier crudes overall to match growing oil demand. There is also a turn toward so-called "unconventional" sources of crude (see Box 1.1). Although these do not have the premium characteristics of conventional crude, they are expected to account for around 15 percent of consumption by 2035. The growth of unconventional reserves challenges the primacy of Saudi Arabia in global reserves, with Canada, Venezuela, and Russia holding major reserves in heavy oil and bitumen, and the US and China in shale oil (see Table 1.2). Alberta's "tar sands" lead the global production of unconventional oil, with production recently increasing to 1.3 mmbd and planned projects reaching 4 mmbd by 2020, while Venezuela's unconventional oil production has stagnated at 0.5 mmbd but could reach 2 mmbd by 2020. Because unconventional sources are essentially "under-cooked" relative to conventional oil – their long hydrocarbon molecules have not been broken down into shorter ones – significant inputs of energy, hydrogen (in the form of natural gas), and water are needed to both extract and upgrade them. Unconventional oil reserves are very large but the energy demands and environmental burdens are high, characteristics that are highlighted by opposition to the Alberta tar sands.

Third, in the search for new reserves, the "frontier" of extraction is changing. This includes the Arctic, the ultra-deepwater environments offshore (i.e. over approximately 1,500 meters of water depth), as well as areas with limited state capacity and where the governance systems and civil society are in a fledgling condition. These "unconventional" locations are increasingly a feature of the international political economy of oil. Production from ultra-deepwater

Box 1.1 Conventional versus unconventional oil

Variation in the physical, chemical, and energy properties of crude oil mean that some sorts are more highly prized than others. "Conventional oils" have lower densities than "unconventional" sources of oil, and thus flow more easily out of reservoirs. They also produce more of the highest-paying fractions of oil such as gasoline, with most oil refineries set up to handle conventional crude. This in turn has made conventional oils the target of exploration and the bulk of global supply. The gold standard is a light, "sweet" (low sulfur) crude, such as Bonny Light from Nigeria. At the other end of the conventional oil spectrum are the heavy, "sour" crudes like Arab Heavy from Saudi Arabia. Between light and heavy are so-called "benchmark" conventional crudes like West Texas Intermediate and Brent Blend.

The term "conventional" recognizes explicitly the boundaries of current practices and also points to the significance of recent changes. Sources once seen as "unconventional" are now an increasingly significant component of overall oil supply, enabling the production of liquids to continue to expand to meet rising demand and delaying the point of decline. These unconventional sources include, in order of decreasing ease of production, extra-heavy crudes (mobile at reservoir conditions, Venezuela's Orinoco Delta), bitumen (mobile only if reservoirs heated, Canada's Athabasca), and oil shale (non-mobile requiring mining or fracturing of source rock, US's Green River Formation), and the use of coal-to-liquids technology. Unconventional oil production faces stiff public opposition, in response for example to groundwater contamination and potential seismic impacts associated with underground fracturing (or "fracking") using toxic solvents and explosives. Pressed by international oil companies and industry organizations, the US Securities and Exchange Commission changed its accounting rules in 2008, allowing companies to book unconventional deposits as proven reserves. A more encompassing definition of "unconventional" oil considers not only the physical and chemical characteristics of oil, but also the broader geographical context. The political scientist Michael Klare, for example, refers to "extreme energy" to capture how the search for the sorts of oil to which we have been accustomed – and upon which current infrastructure and trade relations are premised – means oil producers are increasingly exploring and developing oil in unconventional operating environments.[4]

environments in Brazil, the Gulf of Mexico, and the Gulf of Guinea has been growing over the last decade. The explosion on the Deepwater Horizon drilling rig in 2010, and the subsequent uncapped flow of crude from the Macondo oil field around 1,500 meters below the sea surface, indicate the risks and challenges of sourcing supply from unconventional environments.

The production of oil is necessarily linked to reserves, but the geographies of production and reserves do not neatly map onto one another. If the development of oil followed a strictly economic logic, in which the largest, low-cost reserves were exploited preferentially, then production would converge on the comparatively low-cost reserves of the Middle East where break-even costs are lower than US$10 per barrel. Production followed this trend between 1955 and 1975 as a result of attractive economic conditions and the introduction of super-tankers that drove down the cost of moving crude oil to markets. However, the nationalization of production by large resourcing-holding states during the 1960s and 1970s – and dramatic spikes in the price of oil that these states achieved through coordinated action in the Organization of Petroleum Exporting Countries – drove new oil-field development in the UK, Norway, Alaska, Nigeria, the Gulf of Mexico, Angola, and Russia. This pattern of geographical diversification away from the Middle East has continued with the collapse of the Soviet Union, so that the geography of production is now significantly less concentrated than that of reserves: the Middle East accounts for 54 percent of reserves but only 31 percent of production. The development of unconventional sources continues this trend of diversification away from the Middle East, such as the 1.6 mmbd (equivalent to Qatar) currently produced from bituminous sands in Canada, or the 0.5 mmbd (equivalent to Sudan) from the Bakken shale in North Dakota. In 2011, the president and CEO of Saudi Aramco, Khalid al-Falih, acknowledged the "more balanced geographical distribution of unconventionals" was reducing demand for growth in conventional output from the Middle East. Unconventional oil production is itself spatially concen-trated (partly due to the geography of the resource base, but also to the massive infrastructure required to upgrade uncon-ventional sources to liquids). However, further development

Table 1.2	Unconventional oil reserves			
	Extra-heavy oil	*Bitumen*	*Shale*	*Total*
US	–	11	1086	1097
Canada	–	350	3	353
Venezuela	300	–	–	300
Russia	–	53	178	231
China	1	1	220	222
DR Congo	–	–	64	64
Kazakhstan	–	63	–	63
Brazil	–	–	53	53
Australia	–	–	34	34
Morocco	–	–	34	34
EU	2	2	28	32
Rest	–	11	35	46
Total	303	491	1735	2529

Value represents best estimates of Ultimately Recoverable Resources (URR) in billion (or giga) barrels.

Sources: S. H. Mohr and G. M. Evans (2010), "Long-term prediction of Unconventional Oil Production," *Energy Policy* 38(1): 265–76; World Energy Council, *2010 Survey of Energy Resources.*

of unconventional oil sources – particularly oil shales which are widely distributed – could see this degree of concentration decline.[5]

The shape of demand: lighter, cleaner, Asian

Overlaid on the highly uneven geography of global oil reserves is a different pattern of industrial development and economic growth. Simply put, the centers of greatest demand for oil do not coincide with reserves. Demand varies widely among countries (and within them). The US consumes 21 percent of world production yet has only 2.4 percent of reserves and 4.5

percent of the population. Consumption is around 100 barrels per day per thousand people in the Gulf Emirates, 68 in the US, 29 in the UK, 6 in China, and less than 2 in Kenya. For both individuals and countries, the price of oil can be an obstacle to participating in "demand." The discrepancy between these two different geographies, between where oil is found and where it is required, underpins several significant features of the global political economy of oil as outlined below.[6]

First, imbalances in consumption and production are the basis for international oil trade: close to 7 of every 10 barrels produced is exported and imported, a movement of over 53 mmbd and the largest component of world trade (see Figure 1.2). There are net outflows of oil from the Middle East, North and West Africa, Latin America and Russia, and net inflows into East Asia, Europe, and the US. Second, the number of consuming countries is much larger than those holding reserves – every country consumes oil to some degree while there are many without significant reserves – and consumption is less concentrated on a country basis (see Table 1.1). As a consequence, the market power of consuming countries is weak in relation to the small number of countries that control reserves and there is significant competition among importing states for access to supply. This underscores the need for countries with limited reserves but large and/or growing demand to reduce the risk associated with this relatively weak market position. The strategies available indicate the political choices at stake. Supply risk can be reduced through an increase in the intensity of domestic drilling; by diversifying the locations from which oil is imported; strategic investment partnerships with oil exporters to "lock-in" supply outside of the market; the use of direct military or paramilitary force to control production and supply routes; or via domestic policies that reduce demand and facilitate a transition away from oil.

Third, at the global scale, demand for oil continues to rise.

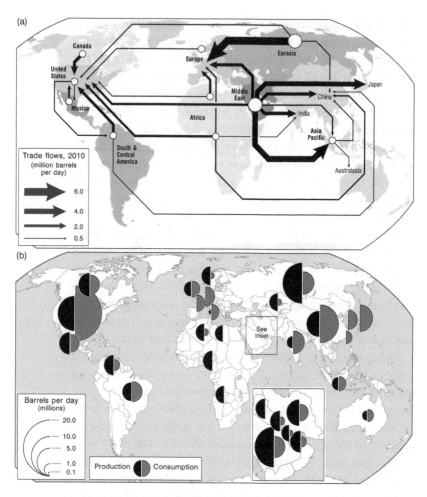

Source: Authors, based on data from BP Statistical Review 2011

Figure 1.2 Major international oil trade flows (2011)

Consumption of oil grew by 14 percent in the last decade, despite an economic recession in the last three years. But global growth obscures a significant geographical shift in *where* oil is being consumed. As the world economy's center of gravity shifts away from North America and Europe toward Asia and the Pacific, so market growth – and overall demand – has tilted decisively to the East. In China and Vietnam, for example, 10 percent more oil was consumed in 2010 than in the previous year. Some of this shift in oil demand is the result of Organisation for Economic Co-operation and Development (OECD) countries outsourcing manufacturing to take advantage of lower production costs. Many of the products manufactured in these lower-wage economies are ultimately consumed back in OECD countries, although the GHG emissions associated with their production are attributed to the place of manufacture. This problem of "embedded carbon" is substantial – the carbon embedded in China's exports is estimated to be twice as large as the UK's carbon emissions – and an important factor in assessing responsibility for oil-related GHG emissions.

China's demand for oil outstripped its domestic capacity in 1993 and since then it has been a significant importer and an increasingly assertive presence in the search for access to new reserves. The shift in the center of gravity for oil demand is associated with a shift in bargaining power among importing states – notably between the US and China – and with the development of new strategies by importing states for the acquisition and/or control of nondomestic sources of oil. Within former oil-exporting states like Indonesia, domestic growth and the development of a middle class has absorbed production and changed the direction of flow: since 2005, Indonesia has imported more than it exports. Consumption is also rising in other large producing and exporting states: Saudi consumption increased by 60 percent between 2000 and 2010. By contrast, in Europe oil demand peaked prior to the recession and is expected to continue to fall as a result of slow economic growth, climate regulation, and high prices influenced by the comparatively high taxes on fuels. Oil demand in non-OECD economies has steadily risen and is predicted to pass that of the OECD in the next couple of years (see Figure 1.3). The result is that "rich countries are not setting the rules on either the demand or the supply side of the equation anymore."[7]

Fourth, there is also a shift in the nature of demand toward the lighter fractions available from the refining of crude oil that are used as transportation fuels (diesel, gasoline, jet fuel) and away from heavier heating oils. Within growing markets, this is associated with an emerging middle class, growing car ownership, and air travel. Within mature markets, the shift reflects a substitution by natural gas in heating and power sectors and increasing regulation of air quality. The changing nature of demand is creating a growing "quality gap" between the direction of the market for petroleum products and the increasingly "hard-to-get" and lower quality raw materials available to the oil industry. The gap can only be met by "upgrading" the resource, implying greater inputs of energy and rising costs (often despite efficiency gains). In addition, the shift of oil into transportation and out of the power sector decreases the ease with which emissions from the burning of oil and petroleum products can be captured, ensuring a collision between "car culture" and climate change.

Fifth, the models of development that embedded oil within industrialized economies in the postwar period, later replicated in most parts of the world, took little account of the "externalities" of gathering and processing oil, turning it into durable plastics and emitting carbon dioxide and other pollutants during the combustion phase. Environmental regulation and an increasing awareness of both climate

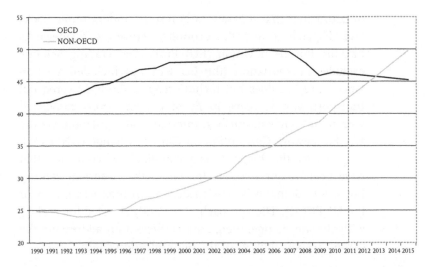

Source: Authors, based on data from BP Statistical Review 2011 (authors' estimate for 2011–15)

Figure 1.3 Oil consumption, OECD vs. non-OECD, in mmbd

change and the wider consequences of oil development now influence the accessibility of oil reserves (e.g. environmental considerations), the price and demand for oil (e.g. via "green" taxation of fuels and carbon accounting) and the acceptability of current practices of oil extraction and use. Peak demand – rather than supply – is a reality in the OECD while "demand destruction" is increasingly a policy objective as part of broader efforts to decarbonize economies as a response to climate change. The mismatched geographies of oil production and consumption also raise challenging questions about responsibility for the carbon dioxide emissions associated with oil. Current approaches point to the responsibility that consumers have at the end of the carbon chain (via the regulation of emissions) rather than to the countries or companies that separate carbon from underground stocks and dispatch it into the economy. However, frameworks like the European Union (EU) Emissions Trading Scheme exclude transportation (the EU ETS has included aviation since 2012 but does not include road or diesel-powered rail transport) and so leave many of the emissions associated with oil untouched. Further, international regulation, via the UN Framework Convention on Climate Change (UNFCCC), emphasizes the historic responsibilities of countries that have been major markets for oil in the twentieth century but where demand is now in decline (Annex 1 countries of the UNFCCC). The approaches currently adopted for dealing with climate change, then, are insufficient for addressing the carbon responsibilities of the oil-production chain.

Actors: states, firms, and civil society

The landscape of actors in and around oil is complex, and we examine this in more detail in chapter 2. Key actors are states, firms, and civil society organizations. Here we highlight the way these are involved with oil and point to significant emerging issues.

Oil resources are embedded – literally – in the territorial framework of states. In most jurisdictions (although not all, such as nonfederal lands in many US states) oil resources are owned by national governments. Physically, legally, and culturally, oil is frequently understood as part of the "body" of the nation, so that national interests can play a decisive role in decisions about the production of oil. For states that host large oil reserves, oil can be seen as a route to modernization and development. The record on this is remarkably mixed and the state's ownership of resources can be a means for those in power, or close to government, to capture public wealth for private gain. Many states holding large reserves have also sought to capitalize on their ownership position and become drillers, refiners, and marketers of oil via the formation of national oil companies.

The consumption of oil is also closely tied to state-level policies. Tax revenues from fuel sales, the sensitivity of economic growth to oil prices, and the geopolitics of energy security ensure that national governments have a keen interest in the accessibility and affordability of oil. High taxes on oil consumption allow some importing states to get more revenues from oil than exporting ones. National security and the ability to project "hard power" are also significant concerns for import-dependent states, as military flexibility and muscle are premised on a suite of petroleum products. National military institutions are concerned about the stalling of conventional supply and increasing competition for reserves. States also play a significant regulatory role in occupational health, safety, and the environment. National governments, then, play a larger role in oil than in many other resource sectors. An important distinction is between states that are net importers of oil and those that export. These two groups face each other on different sides of the oil market, although there is also a mutual dependency around price as higher prices for oil (which benefit exporters) can erode markets as importers reduce demand and substitute other energy sources. Tensions over price and the security of supply historically led these two groups of states to form their own "clubs" to protect their interests, in the form of the Organization of Petroleum Exporting Countries (OPEC, created in 1960) and the International Energy Agency (IEA, created in 1974).

States may own most of the world's oil, but it is companies that search for, develop, refine, and market it. The international, vertically integrated oil firm – headquartered in the US or Europe and with extractive and marketing arms around the world – is the iconic actor, its capacity to regulate the flow from reserves to markets giving it historically a dominant position. Firms like Standard Oil and Shell defined the shape of the industry from its beginnings and into the postwar years and for this reason have become known as "the majors" or, more prosaically, "international oil companies" (IOCs). Today, "the majors" is something of an anachronism. IOCs remain among the ranks of the leading producers, but the nationaliza-tion of their crude oil assets by many reserve-holding states in the 1950s and 1960s removed their control over supply. Exxon, for example, holds the most reserves of any IOC yet ranks only fourteenth worldwide with 1 percent of global reserves. State-owned, national oil companies (NOCs), head-quartered in some of the most significant oil-exporting states, decisively entered the field in the 1960s and 1970s. Building on their ownership of low-cost reserves, many of these firms have developed extensive, vertically integrated networks of distribution to markets in Europe, the Americas, and Asia. NOCs produce close to three-quarters of the oil extracted each year. Saudi Aramco, the world's largest integrated oil com-pany in terms of annual output, produces around 10 percent of the world's crude and NOCs head the world rankings of oil companies by operational (as opposed to financial) criteria.

   This distinction between IOCs and NOCs has historically been important for understanding competition over access to resources and markets. IOCs have been understood as "resource-seeking" (in order to supply their downstream refineries and "home" markets) while NOCs have been seen as "market-seeking" (looking for external markets to absorb their exports). However, this dichotomy is increasingly insuf-ficient for grasping the global political economy of oil, for four reasons. First, the distinction typically highlighted the way NOCs operated to a national political logic rather than commercial objectives. But NOCs are an increasingly diverse

group: for many state-owned firms, the level of state ownership has been reduced over time via public offering with the
state retaining a controlling share, and a few have technical
and commercial capabilities on a par with the IOCs. Second,
IOCs and the large reserve-holding NOCs are increasingly in
cooperation with one another in the development of the more
challenging fields. Third – and most significantly – a number
of NOCs have emerged from Asian economies that are not
market-seeking but resource-seeking. Firms like the Korea
National Oil Company, the Oil and Natural Gas Corporation
(India) (ONGC), China National Offshore Oil Corporation
(CNOOC), and PetroChina are state-owned firms: as important as their "national" ownership, however, is their strategy
of transnationalization and their competition with the IOCs
for access to resources. Fourth, with slowing rates of growth
and declining margins in the historically large markets of
Europe and North America, many of the IOCs are engaged in
"market-seeking" activity. This includes shifting their assets
to sell into the growing Asian markets while also moving
more heavily into growing segments of the US and European
markets such as natural gas.

Civil society, a collective term for the nongovernmental and
noncorporate organizations and institutions that have come
to play an increasingly significant role in public advocacy,
has emerged as an important actor in the political economy
of oil. Working through the medium of information and harnessing public concern to bring pressure on corporations and
governments, civil society organizations have turned a spot-
light on oil. Organizations like Global Witness, Oil Watch,
PLATFORM, Publish What You Pay, and Revenue Watch
Institute draw attention to the unsavory political bargains created in and around oil and the importance of transparency
in furthering human rights and reducing corruption. Other
groups emphasize the *development challenge* of oil. The strong

association between oil extraction and persistent poverty (the "resource curse") in parts of Africa, Latin America, and the former Soviet Union has sharpened the question of who benefits from oil and how oil extraction may be harnessed for sustainable forms of economic and social development. Still other civil society organizations highlight oil's environmental deficits, from groundwater pollution and habitat loss to climate change. In short, civil society organizations have not only identified and publicized many of the negative externalities of oil production and consumption but have also *contested* them. Their argument, in effect, is that oil is failing in significant ways to meet broad social goals. The ways in which we access, process, and use oil, they claim, are unacceptable and something must be done.

Summary
As a result of a prodigious growth in the production and consumption of oil over the course of the twentieth century, the resource base is changing. The quality of crudes is declining: the oil added to new reserves is generally "dirtier" (in terms of energy needs and carbon contribution), more costly to extract, and located in environments that push the envelope of design and implementation. There are also uncertainties over the size of available reserves, creating concerns that the historic pattern of supply growing to match demand may no longer hold. Against this background, world demand continues to grow, driving prices and speculation about future supplies. Growing domestic demand in Asia is behind the emergence of new, state-controlled transnational firms seeking resources beyond domestic territory to supply home markets. And growing domestic demand in major oil-exporting countries suggests that their "surplus" for export will be increasingly squeezed. The trillion barrels of oil produced to date has not only driven growth and productivity in industrial economies

but has contributed to the accumulation of carbon dioxide in the atmosphere, generated water and air pollution, and conspicuously failed to create a basis for social development in many oil-producing economies. This, then, is the context that defines the contemporary politics of oil.

The geopolitics of the hydrocarbon chain

The geopolitics of oil is the struggle to define who wins and who loses as oil moves from underground reserves to the point of consumption. We refer to this as *"geopolitics"* for two reasons. First, the "hydrocarbon chains" that ferry oil from its underground reserves into the engines of cars, cargo ships, planes, and tanks, and that transform crude into carbon dioxide, are fundamentally geographical. Oil moves across space and at key points is claimed in different ways by national governments and other interests – as a resource, as a traded good, as a source of tax revenue, as a set of development possibilities, and as environmental burdens to be allocated and addressed. Second, power and control in the oil sector are, by and large, about the control of particular spaces: the dominance of the Middle East over conventional oil reserves; the ability to exclude "foreign" firms from domestic markets; the emerging capacity of governments to regulate access to the atmosphere as a dumping ground for greenhouse gases; or the capacity to close a key pipeline or tanker route. Struggles over oil often revolve around particular sites, although their outcomes can influence the entire oil sector.

Distributional questions – who wins, who loses – are at the heart of the geopolitics of oil. Importantly, these extend beyond the traditional question of oil supply to encompass issues of resource access, value creation, price, revenue distribution, and the allocation of responsibility for pollution. In each of these cases, the things that people struggle over

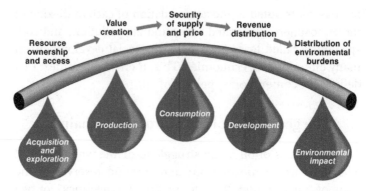

Figure 1.4 The politics of the hydrocarbon chain

– the object of politics – are different: what unites them, however, is a common set of distributional concerns that center on the management and performance of the hydrocarbon commodity chain. Schematically, then, we can think of these different distributional questions as five sequential "cuts" through the hydrocarbon chain, each associated with a distinctive phase in the chain (see Figure 1.4). We expand briefly below on each of these cuts and the geopolitical issues associated with them.

Laying claim to other people's oil: resource acquisition
Because most oil resources are owned by governments, negotiations over resource access are typically between the host state and a company seeking resources. The relationship arises because of a mutual dependence: for resource holders, the value of the resource is dependent on it being extracted and sold; and firms without access to their own resources depend on gaining access to resources owned by others. The object of politics is typically the terms of access, and the arrangements for sharing the revenues and rents that result

from oil development. These tensions are seldom resolved in any final way: indeed, the agreements made between investing firms and resource-holding states have been characterized as an "obsolescing bargain" because of the way in which, when oil begins to flow, there is pressure from resource holders to renegotiate terms agreed at the outset of oil development. More generally, the historical pattern is that periods of relatively liberal resource development – in which the balance of power tilts in favor of the investing firm – are followed by periods of resource nationalism in which the resource-holding state seeks to assert its authority and wrest back some of the value that had previously been awarded to the firm. The struggle to locate oil reserves and secure exclusive control provides much of the drama in the history of oil development. From the colonial "concession" to production sharing agreements (PSAs) and service contracts, rights of access take a variety of forms. Today, transnational state-owned firms – like PetroChina and Petrobras – are in competition with the IOCs that produce much of the world's oil but which control a relatively small proportion of world reserves. For both IOCs and the transnationalizing NOCs, access to "other people's oil" is an imperative. Both sets of companies call on the political resources of "home" states for support, so that a landlord–developer relationship evolves into a relationship between states. We examine the geopolitics of "capturing" resources in more detail in chapter 2.

Getting a cut: value distribution
Once oil has been captured through an access agreement, the next step in the hydrocarbon chain is production. In physical terms, this is the transformation of crude into a series of products for sale to market. However, the object of politics is the way economic value is distributed along the various parts of the production chain during this conversion of crude into

different petroleum products. There are many elements to
this, but four – concerning companies, consumers, governments, and investors – are particularly significant. First, the
logic of capturing value across the production process underlies the vertically integrated character of both IOC and NOC
firms, which allows the capture of profits in both the upstream
and downstream reaches. Nationalizations by reserve holders
in the 1950s and 1960s challenged the capture of value by
IOCs and sought instead to retain it within the framework of
NOCs. A further issue over the distribution of value concerns
efforts by oil exporters to "upgrade" their part of the hydrocarbon chain by moving into downstream processing. Second,
the distribution of value to end consumers versus producers
revolves around the crude oil price. If producers can secure
control over a significant proportion of supply, they are able
to exert an upward effect on prices. Rises in price erode value
for consumers but, as long as production costs do not also
rise, they increase value for producers. The erosion of value
can be particularly acute for *poor* importing states, and high
oil prices have significant implications for their development.
OPEC's actions in the 1970s demonstrated the ability of
producers to club together to control supply for short periods of time, although this was undermined by diversification
of supply and competition within OPEC for market share.
Third, consuming governments also siphon value from the
hydrocarbon chain via the taxation of fuels. In Europe, this
"tax wedge" is large and has become a target for political protests from road users. Fourth, the ownership of "paper oil"
– the trading of oil futures without the intention of taking
physical delivery – allows financial managers to capture value
from, and create, shifts in price. Against a background of
anticipated supply shortages and growing Asian demand, the
role of speculation in driving price is now a major concern
for oil importers and consumers. We examine the question

of the distribution of value, with a particular focus on price, in chapter 3.

No surprises: securing flow
A third "cut" across the hydrocarbon chain highlights the question of securing the flow of oil between *net exporters* of oil, countries that produce more than they consume, and *oil importers* that do not produce any or enough oil for domestic demand. This is a relationship based on the physical movement of oil via trade and a reciprocal flow of revenue, and the mutual needs of importing and exporting states for reliable trading partners. The object of this relationship is the security of supply. The vulnerabilities and strategic opportunities created by flows of oil and money are at the core of international geopolitics, and structure the domestic politics of large exporting and importing states alike. Both the US and China, for example, are major producers of oil but these countries consume over twice the amount available from domestic supply. The consistent shortfall in domestic production relative to domestic demand in these countries exerts a significant influence on their foreign policy: whether via oil diplomacy, development-for-oil deals, or the projection of military force, the need of large oil-importing states to secure sufficient extraterritorial supplies of oil is a key feature of the global economy. On the other side of the coin, Russia is also one of the world's major oil consumers – it ranks fifth in the world in terms of its annual consumption of oil – but it produces around three times as much oil as it consumes and so is a leading exporter. Large exporters are also concerned about energy security, which for them means a concern about the loss of markets to new entrants, via the corrosive effect of high prices on demand, or regulation of carbon. We examine this dynamic of securing supplies and markets in chapter 4.

Avoiding the curse: modernization and development
A fourth cut illuminates the question of how oil contributes
to economic and social development. It centers on the relationship between the national and regional governments of
oil-producing and -exporting states and their peoples, and the
extractive firms that pump, refine, and export crude. Oil often
fuels dreams of development, yet the reality of modernization
through oil frequently falls short. Tensions revolve around the
management, or squandering, of oil revenues, the creation of
oil dependency, and the challenges of the so-called "resource
curse" – that countries with abundant natural resources tend
to have worse development outcomes than those with limited
endowments. At a national scale, it is useful to distinguish
between so-called *high absorbing* states, like Norway, Saudi
Arabia and Venezuela, that do better at incorporating oil revenues into their economies; and *low absorbing* states, such as
Angola, where governments lack the capacity to handle the
large and volatile revenue streams associated with oil exports.
    A critical question is how revenues are distributed geo-
graphically, and across different social classes and ethnic
groups. The issue here is the extent to which communities that host oil wealth are compensated for its extraction
and the social, economic, and environmental dislocations
this can cause. Tensions frequently arise between a central
government (the owner of oil underground) and regional governments that administer lands and other resources in the
area of oil development.

Accounting for nature: pollution
The fifth and final cut centers on the politics of emissions
from the hydrocarbon chain. These occur all along the chain
in the form, for example, of local groundwater contamination, ocean pollution, habitat loss, urban smog, and global
climate change. Critical questions are the distribution of these

pollutants – where they go and whom they affect – and the allocation of responsibility for addressing them. A growing alliance of civil society organizations and some governments are calling oil companies to account by demanding they address historic responsibilities for pollution (e.g. Chevron in Ecuador). Others seek moratoria or bans on drilling in sensitive environmental settings such as the Arctic. Increasingly, however, it is around the role of the hydrocarbon chain as a carbon conveyor – transforming fossil stocks of carbon into atmospheric carbon dioxide – that the politics of pollution revolve. The question of responsibility here is particularly significant. Conventional approaches highlight carbon emissions rather than the throughput of fossil fuels in the economy. An alternative approach, however, is one that seeks ways to prevent oil being extracted in the first place by generating revenue streams from the protection of habitat or foregone carbon emissions. We explore the politics of development and environment in chapter 5.

Conclusion

In the twentieth century, oil politics centered on the management of abundance, state power, and market growth. The remarkable energy surplus made available through oil transformed the experience of space and time for many of the world's population during that period; for many others, it fostered dreams of economic and social transformation. Today, the legacies of this "Age of Plenty" include volatile prices, dwindling conventional oil reserves, climate change, and enduring poverty in many oil-rich countries. Our goals in this chapter have been to identify those characteristics of the contemporary oil sector that differentiate it from the "Age of Plenty"; establish how these are linked to previous waves and historic practices of oil-fueled development; and indicate how these conditions add up to a new geopolitics of oil. Deteriorating resource quality and growing uncertainties over reserves, the rise of consumerism in Asia, the internationalization of state oil firms, and the tentative emergence of nonfossil alternatives to oil are signs of an industry being reordered by a range of powerful forces. The following chapters are organized around five critical tensions that are currently shaping the sector: the geopolitics of resource access; volatility of oil prices; security of supply; the possibilities of development through oil; and the environmental consequences of oil production and consumption. The future of oil will be determined through the ways these conflicts are addressed. In the pages that follow, we show how this new geopolitics is bringing into question commonplace assumptions about the governance of oil, while also raising fundamental questions about who now governs oil and for whom.

CHAPTER TWO

Capturing Oil

Oil is a resource both familiar and strange. To fill up at the local gas station is also to become entangled in concerns about national security, drill rig safety, Arctic sea-ice, financial speculation, and indigenous rights. Oil brings together worlds that appear normally quite separate and mixes them up, so that establishing where oil begins and ends has become increasingly difficult. This churning together of different issues is a feature of contemporary oil politics and, in particular, of the efforts by companies, governments, and NGOs to allocate responsibility along the production chain – for transportation choices, greenhouse gas emissions, long-term energy supplies, or the promotion of development and human rights in oil-producing countries. To begin to untangle the contemporary politics of oil, this chapter introduces the "global production network" of firms and states through which oil is located, extracted, refined, and distributed. We outline how economic relationships at the heart of this network are structured by the politics of competition and cooperation. We focus on "classic" actors – oil companies and national governments – and questions of resource sovereignty and access that defined much of the politics of oil in the twentieth century. But we also identify other actors – like the financiers that bankroll oil exploration – which are increasingly scrutinizing (and being scrutinized for) their involvement in carbon-intensive and socially disruptive activities. A key feature of the contemporary politics of oil, we argue, is the way

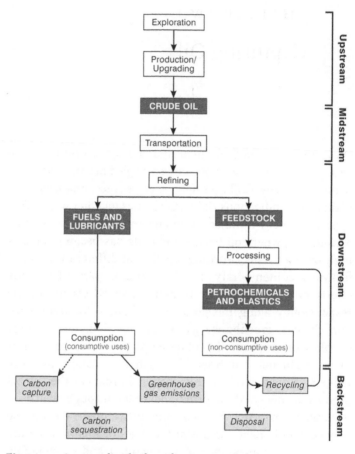

Figure 2.1 A generalized oil-production network

actors and spaces that conventionally have lain outside of oil
are now drawn within it.

As a first step, Figure 2.1 illustrates a generalized global
production network for oil. The foundation of this network is
the flow of crude oil. Crude is "captured" from the environ-

ment via the "upstream" phases of exploration and production at the top of the diagram; it moves through the so-called "midstream" phases of crude oil storage and transportation; to the "downstream" phases of refining, distribution, and the consumption of oil products at the bottom of the diagram. We also add a fourth phase – which we coin "backstream" – to refer to the return flow of waste products and emissions to the environment. These backstream flows occur all along the production network but, for clarity, only those associated with the post-consumption phase are shown in Figure 2.1. They include waste plastics, GHG emissions to the atmosphere from combustion and – potentially – deliberate strategies of carbon capture (via sequestration in plants or carbon capture and storage) that aim to "close the loop" and return carbon to the ground.

States and *firms* dominate this network, and relations among them produce tensions critical to the geopolitics of oil. The most significant are the tensions among major oil-importing states (such as the US, China, and the EU) over crude oil supplies; competition for production volumes and market access among leading oil-exporting states (such as Saudi Arabia, Russia, and Iran); rivalry among oil firms over project opportunities, and between resource-seeking companies and reserve-holding states over conditions of access; and the tension between oil exporters and oil importers over the volume, price, and reliability of supply.

States: oil landlords, national champions, and regulators

National governments play a significant role in the production network for oil, as landlords, national champions, and regulators.

Oil landlords

Around the world, it is mainly governments that own oil resources: private landowners or communities may own the surface, but oil underground belongs to the state. The state has an interest in generating economic rent from its resources and, in pursuit of this objective, allows firms to develop them under particular conditions. For example, in the UK, oil and gas resources are owned by the national government ("the Crown") under the Petroleum Act of 1934, with the Crown dispensing licenses to firms to search for and produce oil and gas on land and under the sea. The US constitutes a rare exception: an entrenched ideology of private property and a history of early oilfield development at a time of economic liberalism have ensured oil resources are not reserved to the government except on federal lands.

Because oil resources are typically state owned, national political considerations play a critical role in governing who can have access to them (domestic versus foreign firms), which resources are available for extraction and where (subject, for example, to environmental and resource conservation criteria), and the financial and other conditions attached to access (royalty payments, requirements on domestic employment or downstream processing). The principle of state sovereignty over oil resources developed gradually during the twentieth century. In many instances the nationalization of oil resources has been part of a broader struggle for economic and political self-determination. In Mexico, for example, the post-revolution Constitution of 1917 vested ownership of mineral resources in the national state and subsequently provided a foundation for the expropriation of international oil company assets by the Cardenas government in 1938. The principle that states should have sovereignty over natural resources within their territory became an international political claim in the 1950s, in the context of decolonization and the ambition of newly independent states for self-determination and protection against "economic colonization" by western states or companies. In oil-exporting countries with a long history of involvement by foreign-owned oil companies – such as Mexico, Venezuela, and Iran – there is a potent collective memory of the historical struggle to wrest control of "national" oil resources out of foreign hands. A consequence is that oil reserves around the world are legally and culturally embedded within national territories and subject to national political considerations. From the perspective of oil-importing states (and investing firms), this means that a good deal of the oil they seek is subject to foreign control.[1]

National champions – exporting states
States are major players in the global oil industry via their equity participation – in whole or in part – in NOCs, within which the state combines its role of landlord with that of an investor. Where it has responsibility for production decisions (either on its own or as part of a joint venture), the NOC also acts as the operator. Of the top 50 oil and gas companies by volume of production, over half are majority state-owned. National oil companies dominate the control of world oil reserves: the top 10 reserve holders are all NOCs headquartered outside the OECD economies and account for nearly 80 percent of oil reserves (see Table 2.1). This dominance of state-owned firms in reserves and production is all the more striking, given the general retreat of the state from the economy in many countries since the 1980s, including the privatization of many state-owned natural resource companies. Not all state-owned oil firms are alike, however, and it is useful to draw a distinction between the NOCs of countries that hold large oil reserves and which are significant oil exporters (such as Saudi Aramco, Venezuela's PdVSA, the National Iranian Oil Company, Kuwait Petroleum Corporation or Libya's

Table 2.1 Top 15 integrated oil companies (2010)

Reserves (billion barrels oil equivalent)		Production (million barrels per day)		Market capitalization (billion US dollars)	
Saudi Aramco	300	Saudi Aramco	11.0	Saudi Aramco	781
National Iranian Oil Company	289	National Iranian Oil Company	4.0	Pemex	412
Gazprom	168	Kuwait Petroleum Corporation	3.7	PdVSA	388
Qatar Petroleum	162	ENI	3.6	Kuwait Petroleum Corporation	378
Iraq National Oil Company	133	Exxon	3.3	Exxon	316
Abu Dhabi National Oil Company	124	Shell	3.3	CNPC	303
Kuwait Petroleum Corporation	108	Iraq National Oil Company	2.7	Gazprom	271
Petroleos de Venezuela SA	104	Chevron	2.7	Petronas	232
Nigerian National Petroleum Corporation	64	Petroleos de Venezuela	2.6	Petrobras	229
National Oil Company of Libya	47	Abu Dhabi National Oil Company	2.6	Sonatrach	224
Sonatrach, Algeria	38	PetroleosMexicanos	2.5	NIOC	220
Chinese National Petroleum Corporation	31	BP	2.4	BP	219
ExxonMobil	22	Nigerian National Petroleum Corporation	2.3	Shell	209
Lukoil	20	Libya NOC	2.1	Chevron	138

Sources: Forbes, Fortune, and company websites.

National Oil Corporation) and state-owned firms from countries that are significant oil importers (such as PetroChina, India's ONGC, or the Korean National Oil Company).

For countries holding large oil reserves, taking an ownership stake in the production of oil has typically been a political response to perceived exploitation by the international oil companies that have historically controlled production in these countries. Mexico was the first major producer and oil exporter to nationalize production when, in 1938, it expropriated the assets of Standard Oil of New Jersey and Shell and established the national oil company, Petroleos Mexicanos (Pemex). National governments in the Middle East first became equity participants (as opposed to simply acting as landlords and concessionaires) as a result of competition among the international companies for access to their reserves, with national shares in concessions established as part of the access bargain. An influential deal in 1957 between the Italian company ENI and the National Iranian Oil Company created an exploration and production company that was jointly owned and managed by ENI and the Iranian government.

Nationalization hits a high-water mark in the 1970s. Iraq nationalized the Iraq Petroleum Company in 1972, while in the same year OPEC required that all operations in Kuwait, Qatar, UAE, and Saudi Arabia have a 25% government share which would then rise over time – Saudi Aramco increased its share to 60% in 1974 and 100% in 1980. Malaysia set up the state oil company Petronas in 1974, replacing lease agreements with Shell and Exxon with production sharing contracts in which the state company had majority control; and Venezuela nationalized oil production in 1976 with the creation of PdVSA. The UK, Canada, and Norway also established national petroleum corporations in the 1970s following sharp price rises. Canada's PetroCanada was set up by the Trudeau government in 1975 to address federal concerns that oil development in the province of Alberta was governed by American interests and was not capturing sufficient benefits for Canadians, but it was gradually privatized between 1991 and 2004. To capture value from the newly developing North Sea fields and ensure supply, the UK and Norway created national oil companies – the British National Oil Corporation (BNOC) and Statoil – in the early 1970s. BNOC was abolished by the Thatcher government in 1985. The French government long participated in the capital of its "national" oil companies – Elf (50%) and Total (30%) – but sold its shares in the early 1990s and now receives very little revenue. In contrast, the Norwegian government maintains a 67% share in Statoil, which is listed on the Oslo and New York stock exchanges. The Norwegian government has annually received an average of US$3 billion in dividends from Statoil over the past five years, on top of revenues from Norwegian oil fields that it channels into a Norwegian pension fund worth US$573 billion by 2011.

The relative power of large reserve-holding NOCs within the oil production network is closely linked to their "spare capacity" – the ability to crank production up in the face of rising demand to restore market balance. Since the 1970s, Saudi Arabia (and OPEC more generally) has played a critical role in regard to this "capacity cushion." In the 1970s, for example, Saudi Arabia expanded production threefold – from 3 mmbd to over 10 mmbd in 1981 – establishing the country's dominance as the world's primary exporter and its key role as a "swing producer." OECD countries (and the US in particular) have frequently appealed to Saudi Arabia to expand production when markets are especially tight: such as in mid-2008 when the US begged the Kingdom to increase production as prices reached US$140 per barrel; or in early 2012 when importers of Iranian oil, most importantly China, gained reassurances from the Saudi regime that it could make up for the loss of Iranian exports under a western embargo. However, some oil analysts have expressed concern about the erosion of OPEC's spare capacity (from a high of 14 mmbd in 1985 or 23 percent of global demand to only 0.5 mmbd or less than 1 percent of global demand in 2004) and cast doubt on the ability of Saudi Arabia to extend production above 10 mmbd, despite investment in new projects. These uncertainties suggest to some oil analysts the possible eclipse of Saudi Arabia as a swing producer and that control of supply has passed out of the hands of OPEC. While Russia, the world's largest producer, has publically toyed with the idea of becoming the world's new swing producer, there are both technical and political challenges to the country taking on this role. It is clear, however, that Saudi Arabia and Russia now compete directly for access to Asian markets and that, as it is not part of OPEC, Russia's market strategy is not constrained by agreements with other oil producers to reduce production when prices are low.[2]

National champions – importing states

Although NOCs are most closely associated with oil-exporting countries – as "agents of the landlord states" – a handful of state-owned oil companies headquartered in *oil-importing* states in Asia have become a key feature of the contemporary political economy of oil. Over the last decade, state-owned companies from South Korea, India, and China have made equity investments overseas in upstream oil projects with the aim of securing access to new oil reserves, mirroring a strategy adopted by Japan's National Oil Company in the 1970s. Chinese state firms have participated in overseas energy ventures since 1993, reflecting the country's low reserves/ production ratios and the apparent peaking of domestic production at a time when consumption of oil has been rising dramatically as a result of rates of economic growth of up to

Box 2.1 China's national oil companies

China has three state-owned national oil companies. The largest one, China National Petroleum Company (CNPC), emerged from the Ministry of Petroleum in the late 1980s. Since 1998, it has been organized as a fully integrated oil company, and by 2011 was involved in 60 projects in around 25 countries. CNPC's biggest subsidiary – PetroChina – is the largest producer of oil and gas in China, has been active in upstream ventures overseas since 1993, and publicly traded in New York and Hong Kong since 2000. PetroChina tripled in value following its flotation on the Shanghai stock market in 2007 and became the world's first trillion-dollar company. Holding equity positions in overseas projects, CNPC also undertakes service contracts, including in Iran and Iraq (with BP to develop the Rumaila oil field and with Total and Petronas to develop the Halfaya field).

Sinopec is the second largest NOC in China and, like CNPC/Petrochina, is also an integrated producer. Historically a refining and marketing company, Sinopec continues to dominate China's downstream sector but has also been active internationally in upstream projects since 2002. Sinopec is now involved in 36 projects in 20 countries including Saudi Arabia, Iran, Kazakhstan, and Nigeria. CNOOC is the third largest NOC in China and specializes in offshore exploration and production, where most of China's conventional oil growth potential lies, but has now over 20 percent of its reserves overseas thanks mostly to mergers and acquisitions. These three Chinese NOCs account for about 10 percent of China's oil imports in the form of "equity oil" produced from their overseas operations. The amount of "equity oil" produced by Chinese NOCs overseas is rising fast, but it is not clear whether it is politically controlled (via a quota that NOCs must send back to the Chinese market) or subject to commercial considerations (sold into the most profitable markets). The IEA suggests equity oil is relatively independent of political control and finds, for example, that oil produced by Chinese NOCs in the Americas is sold into local markets rather than being channeled back to China. Chinese national oil companies have a number of competitive advantages over IOCs when it comes to securing access, including lower reputational risk from working in countries with poor human rights records, access to preferential credit from state banks, and ability to offer "oil-for-infrastructure" barter deals.[3]

10 percent per year (see Box 2.1). In what the Chinese refer to as the "going out" strategy, Asian NOCs have increasingly targeted international resources and, with access to cash, have been able to purchase new properties and acquire equity stakes. Chinese NOCs alone spent US$30 billion in mergers and acquisitions in 2010, with half of this in Latin America (including Sinopec's acquisition of a 40 per-

cent stake in Repsol-YPF's operations in Brazil), while the Korea National Oil Company, for example, purchased Dana Petroleum, which has upstream operations in the North Sea and Africa, for US$3.7 billion. Overseas equity participation has emerged as a core strategy for Chinese NOCs, which now have equity shares in oil and gas production in 20 countries (the majority concentrated in Kazakhstan, Sudan, Venezuela, and Angola).[4]

These deals are significant for several reasons. First, they highlight the inadequacy of the "NOC versus IOC" dichotomy that has been used to characterize the politics of oil since the 1970s. These state-owned firms are acting more like the international oil companies than conventional NOCs in that they are "resource-seeking" rather than resource-holding. Second, the emergence of transnational state-owned oil producers changes the dynamics of competition among traditional IOCs (and raises the price) for access to oil reserves. Third, as highlighted by the struggle between Chevron and the Chinese National Offshore Oil Company (CNOOC) for Unocal in 2005 – CNOOC trumped Chevron's bid with a US$18.5 billion offer for Unocal but withdrew in the face of US political pressure – the emergence of well-funded NOCs from "rising powers" intensifies competition among oil-importing states. Finally, these new resource-seeking NOCs also highlight the lack of an equivalent "national champion" among OECD countries and the limits of an energy security strategy predicated on markets alone. The question of whether the United States should develop a national oil company to address energy security concerns has been raised (not as a serious proposal, but as a way of querying whether the investment strategies of US-based international oil companies still serve national energy security interests). It is increasingly clear that the traditionally dominant markets of the OECD have lost control over *both* oil supply and demand: whereas the former

slipped away in the 1960s and 1970s with the nationalization of resource-holding states and the formation of OPEC,
the growth of Asian demand and the emergence of resource-
seeking, state-owned firms from Asian economies are steadily
ensuring the latter.[5]

Regulators
States impose a series of conditions on the production and
consumption of oil through their role as regulators and taxation authorities. Governments have responsibilities for the
protection of worker safety and the environment, for example, via their accession to international commitments (e.g. UN
Framework Convention on Climate Change) and through the
passage and implementation of national laws. The *Deepwater
Horizon* spill in 2010 highlighted the role of a US federal government agency, the Minerals Management Service (MMS),
in setting the conditions for oil exploration and production in
the Gulf of Mexico, and the thin line that separates an enabling
regulatory environment from lax safety and environmental
legislation. The MMS combined responsibility for both regu-
lating the oil industry and collecting royalties on behalf of the
government. Reorganization of the MMS in 2010 sought to
address this conflict of interest by separating safety oversight
from royalty collection.

Some of the fiercest political battles around oil are fought
over whether oil companies should have access to wilderness
or other protected lands, and the location of oil-related infrastructure (refineries, pipelines, terminals). Rising concerns
about energy security have increased the domestic political
pressure on national governments in net oil-importing states
to open up acreage for development and diversify sources of
supply. In the US, for example – where the slogan "drill, baby,
drill" was mobilized by Republicans in debates over energy
security during the 2008 election campaign – domestic access

issues include coastal drilling in California and Florida and in the Beaufort and Chukchi Seas in the Arctic and continuing calls to open up federal lands in western states for oil exploration. In many countries – including developing economies seeking to harness national resources for development – sustained high oil prices are creating powerful incentives to modify previous commitments on the conservation of forest and marine environments and the rights of indigenous peoples, and to encourage new exploration.

Governments, then, exert a key influence on where companies can explore for oil, the conditions under which they may do so, as well as the broader balance of incentives for transitioning away from oil or acceding to its incumbency. In addition, national political objectives may lead governments to impose restrictions on where companies can operate overseas and the practices that are acceptable when they do. The US, for example, imposed sanctions on Libya over the country's suspected terror links from the 1980s until 2004, requiring US companies to suspend operations in the country and sever all direct contacts. The US government has also prohibited all US persons from dealing with Sudan's oil sector since 1997, including Southern Sudan, on grounds of its link to terrorism and human rights abuses. Sanctions were also imposed on Iran in 1995, blocking direct access for US oil service companies to Iran's oil sector. The US government extended sanctions in 2010 to penalize any company selling gasoline to Iran or investing in the country's refining capacity, and both the US and the EU deepened the sanctions regime further in 2012. National variations in anticorruption legislation and standards of corporate transparency also exert an influence on where and how companies can operate. The US Foreign Corrupt Practices Act, for example, makes it a crime for companies to bribe foreign officials and there are a number of cases of oil companies being charged under this act. National legal codes can also provide leverage for groups concerned about the environmental and human rights implications of oil development. Since the late 1990s, church organizations, NGOs, and public interest groups have used the extraterritorial reach of the US Alien Tort Claims Act to challenge oil companies through US courts for human rights violations in Nigeria, Sudan, and Myanmar.[6]

States also condition the rate of oil consumption through taxes on fuel sales and subsidies to oil producers and consumers. Although crude oil is a globally traded commodity with prices quoted internationally, the price of petroleum fuels to final consumers varies greatly from one country to another. These differences are due primarily to different degrees of taxation by national governments. We examine this significant question of taxation and subsidy in more detail in chapter 4.

Firms: integration, independents, and the precariousness of "Big Oil"

Large, vertically integrated companies operating in multiple geographical locations play a dominant role in the global oil production network. Although there are no technical reasons to combine the upstream, midstream, and downstream phases within one organization, integration reduces the exposure of upstream and downstream operations to supply disruption and the volatility of oil prices. Integration enables firms to achieve economies of scale and geographic diversification simultaneously: this is why the production network for oil is both geographically extensive (many different oil fields, broad geographic spread of consumers) and, at the same time, organizationally concentrated.

The established multinational giants – such as Exxon, Shell, BP, Chevron, and Total – have a major market presence through their branded products and are among the world's

Box 2.2 From the "Seven Sisters" to "Big Oil"

The dynamic of collaboration and competition is neatly captured in the now obsolete designation Seven Sisters, which came to define the major international oil companies in the 1950s that mostly originated from the break-up of Standard Oil. Enrico Mattei, public administrator of the Italian state oil company ENI, coined the term to deride the cartel of western oil companies that kept at bay emerging competitors and maintained pressure on Third World producing countries. ENI was excluded from the cartel, which controlled eight of every ten barrels produced outside the communist world and North America. At a time when the US State Department sought to upturn the nationalization of western oil companies in Iran by boycotting Iranian oil output, Mattei successfully broke the Seven Sisters' control over Middle East concessions by agreeing to a deal more favorable to Iran – 75/25 rather than the standard 50/50 – and thereby contributing to the growing assertiveness of resource holders toward international oil companies. In the 1990s, Big Oil came to replace Seven Sisters as a shorthand for western corporate oil power, but the term misrepresents an industry now dominated by national oil companies holding the world's largest reserves. Nonetheless, Big Oil continues to capture something of the consumer's experience of the industry, as well as that of communities living in proximity to oil infrastructures, and to suggest that the actions of oil companies (on pricing, access to reserves, labor regulation, and environmental legislation, for example) are guided more by common cause than by competition.[7]

largest companies by market capitalization (see Table 2.1). Up until the 1960s, the control of these firms over both the world's major oil resources and downstream markets gave them a commanding position within the oil network and a powerful influence over price, underpinning their designation as "the majors" and, more derisively, the "Seven Sisters" (see Box 2.2). The nationalization of upstream assets, however, reduced their control over supply while the growth of so-called independents (nonintegrated oil firms) and the entry of Soviet oil into western markets further reduced their degree of control. Mergers and acquisitions in the 1980s and 1990s, however, mean that these firms have grown substantially in size. Today, seven "supermajors" (Exxon, BP, Shell, Chevron, ConocoPhillips, Total, and ENI) continue to be among the largest and most profitable oil producers, although their holdings of global oil reserves are comparatively small.

The majors no longer have a monopoly on vertical integration. Today, the largest oil companies in the world are integrated, state-owned companies. The top five companies in 2011 – based on a combination of reserves, production, refinery capacity, and sales volume – are Saudi Aramco, the National Iranian Oil Company, Exxon, Venezuela's PdVSA, and the China National Petroleum Corporation (see Table 2.1). There are also a small number of relative newcomers to the ranks of vertically integrated, globally operating firms, such as China's Sinopec, Repsol YPF of Spain, OMV of Austria, and Russia's Lukoil.

The "midstream" segment of transportation and storage is less concentrated than either production or refining. There are a great many firms in this part of the production network, and their tankers, terminals, pipelines, and storage farms are critical links in the oil network. Revolutionary changes in shipping technologies have enabled the progressive expansion of crude oil trade. Oil is now one of the most significant commodities in world trade, with three of every five barrels of oil produced being exported. The very large crude carrier and ultra-large crude carrier were developed in the 1960s and 1970s respectively to ship oil from the Middle East to Japan and the US: the latter are the largest vessels in the world, with a capacity of up to 550,000 dwt, and can carry around 2 million barrels of oil. The geography of trunk routes and chokepoints associated with tanker traffic and pipelines affords tremendous opportunities for control while, at the same time, creating vulnerabilities. Exports from Kuwait, Iraq, Saudi Arabia, the UAE, and Iran mean that over 15 mmbd flow through the Strait of Hormuz, around a third of all seaborne oil trade. A similar amount flows through the Strait of Malacca between the Indian and Pacific Oceans and is a critical chokepoint in the trade of oil to Asia: over three-quarters of China's oil imports (3.1 mmbd) flow through the Malacca Strait. Meanwhile in the Turkish Strait or Bosphorus, difficult navigation and heavy traffic raise additional environmental and safety issues that affect the flow of oil from the Caspian Basin to western and southern Europe. The concentration of flows through these chokepoints means that the prospect of interruption is a major concern for oil-importing states and a critical influence on oil prices.

In comparison to the midstream sector, the downstream refining sector has few actors and ownership is much more concentrated. Refining is the gateway for crude oil to end markets, and a major bottleneck in the production chain. Because refineries tend to be located closer to markets than to sources of supply, they exert a critical influence on market access. Refineries are also vast, complicated pieces of equipment which each day transform a stunningly large quantity of concentrated energy and chemical diversity. Refineries sit astride the flow of oil and face both ways: they are, in effect, caught in a "squeeze" between the availability and quality of crude (chapter 1) and the balance of demand for different petroleum products. The availability of sweet (i.e. low sulfur) crude is declining worldwide, but the trend downstream is for greater regulation of product quality (a reduction in allowable sulfur in fuels, ethanol blending, addition of oxygenates, and removal of lead) and for an increasing proportion of refinery output to be geared toward transportation fuels. As a result of this squeeze, the highest margins are made by refineries with sophisticated technology that can handle heavy, sour crudes and produce a full range of product outputs.

Worldwide, there are over 650 refineries with a total capacity of around 88 mmbd. Refinery capacity has been growing and shifting eastwards, with most investment taking place in growing Asian markets. The trend has been for average refinery size to rise over time, and for investment to be made in complex cracking and hydrocracking technology rather than the simpler hydro-skimming technology. The average refinery size in the US, for example, has grown threefold since the late 1960s (from 42,000 bpd in 1969 to 133,000 bpd in 2008) and over half the country's refineries have closed in the last 30 years, leaving 140 in 2010. In established, mature markets, such as Europe and North America, there is overcapacity in refineries and pressure on margins is particularly tight. There is little investment in new refineries, although capacity expansions have occurred at existing sites, and refinery owners have been seeking ways to divest non-core capacities, including partial shutdowns and the conversion of refineries to storage depots (in part, to defer expensive closure costs). These refineries in core markets can be attractive assets for upstream producers outside the region with "equity crude." In 2010, for example, PetroChina bought into the refining business of UK-based INEOS, gaining access to the Grangemouth (Scotland) and Lavera (France) refineries, and in 2011, Shell sold the UK's second largest refinery (Stanlow) to Essar Energy, an India-based integrated oil and gas producer.

Upstream independents

Oil producers that do not own downstream assets are referred to as "independents." Independent producers have had a substantial international presence for many years: US foreign policy actively encouraged the entry of independents into Saudi Arabia in the 1950s to work alongside Aramco (a consortium of four US majors) where they contributed to the declining control of the majors over world oil output. Today, independent upstream producers are key actors in the development of new oil basins around the world, with many active in several "frontier" oil provinces, at the same time following the liberalization of investment regimes in the 1990s. For example, Vancouver-based Africa Oil recently conducted exploration drilling in Puntland, Somalia, while Oslo-based DNO has begun production in Iraqi Kurdistan, which was both more secure and open to business with foreign oil companies than the rest of Iraq. Often the "first movers" into new or high-risk areas, the practices of independent oil firms in acquiring access to land and establishing a precedent for oil-field development are frequently the focus of social concern. The Canadian-headquartered Talisman Energy, for example, came under sustained criticism from NGOs and human rights campaigners following its purchase of assets in Sudan in the late 1990s, which it subsequently sold to ONGC in 2003.

Independents are in competition with integrated firms for access to resources and are an important part of the more general "squeeze" of the once-dominant majors. There are also synergies between them and integrated firms, as a spate of mergers and acquisitions among the "majors" over the last 20 years has left the largest integrated firms now very large indeed. To replace the amount of oil these firms extract each year requires searching for – and finding – substantial reserves. This has created an opportunity for independent firms to focus on finding and producing from smaller targets that, while still large in an absolute sense, are not on the radar screens of the majors. Companies like Tullow Oil and Cairn Energy, the two largest UK-based independents, have carved out positions by focusing on assets the majors overlooked. Tullow Oil was set up in 1985 to work over oil and gas fields left behind by the majors in Africa and is now the largest, independent oil company operating in Africa. Cairn Energy has grown over the last 25 years on the back of discoveries it made in Rajasthan – where it followed unsuccessful work by Shell – and is now at the center of a landmark "Arctic battle" over the conditions under which the offshore waters of Greenland will be opened up to oil development. Independents are also involved as partners with integrated firms, such as the relationship between US independent Devon Energy and the part state-owned Brazilian producer Petrobras in the Gulf of Mexico. The upstream assets of independents have been key targets for acquisition by Asian state-owned, integrated firms.

The precariousness of Big Oil
For all their swagger – both real and attributed – the super-majors are in a surprisingly precarious position. The essence of the problem, and one of the defining elements of the contemporary political economy of oil, is twofold: these giant firms which dominated the oil sector for much of the twentieth century are now shut out from the world's largest and lowest-cost conventional oil reserves and, as a consequence, are finding it increasingly hard to replace upstream assets; and their downstream assets in refining and marketing are in the wrong place as the center of demand shifts to Asia.

For integrated and independent producers alike, an important measure of commercial health is the ability to locate new oil reserves to replace the oil extracted during production. Reserves replacement is a key element of corporate strategy in the upstream sector and translates directly into corporate financial performance. For international oil companies, reserves replacement has become an increasingly challenging task. Replacement of reserves has lagged behind production since the mid-1990s. In the ten years to 2006, the top five supermajors replaced only 82 percent of production on average and lagged behind a group of 20 smaller US-headquartered companies. The reasons for this underperformance in reserves replacement are complex, as the size of a company's reserves are influenced by oil prices, levels of expenditure on exploration and development, and the

Table 2.2 The supermajors' dwindling control over world oil				
Control by "Seven Sisters" (%)	1953	1972	2006	Overall loss (%)
Concession Areas	64	24	7	89
Proven Reserves	92	67	5	95
Production	87	71	15	83
Refining Capacity	73	49	26	65

Source: Reproduced from Bridge and Wood, 2010; data from Nitzan and Bichler (2002, p. 219); citing Jacoby (1974); data for 2006 compiled from Petroleum Intelligence (2007), PFC Energy (2007), and Jaffe and Soligo (2007).

formal definition of "reserves" as laid down by, for example, the US Securities and Exchange Commission. However, a critical factor is that 80 percent of the world's conventional oil resources lie outside the control of these firms. The reassertion of national ownership and restrictions on equity participation by foreign firms mean that the ability of international oil companies to access and control these sources is severely constrained. On top of these national controls, domestic political restrictions – on participation in Iran and Sudan, for example – hamper the ability to access relatively low-cost crude from these significant conventional reserves. Table 2.2 shows how the supermajors lost control of about 83 percent of their market share over concessions, reserves, production, and refining markets worldwide since the 1950s.

Negotiating access: resource-holding states versus resource-seeking firms

Resource-seeking NOCs, independents, and majors face a fundamental challenge: the oil they seek belongs to someone else. As they do not own resources on their own account, these companies need to negotiate terms of access with national governments. The politics of resource access center on the relative power of the resource-holder and the operating firm, as these influence the acreage available to resource-seeking firms and the terms under which access can be acquired. At the center of this struggle is the division of rent. Here the balance of power changes with ups and downs in the price of oil, whether projects are exploring for oil or in production, and in response to broader shifts in approaches to economic development and role of the state. As a consequence, the politics of access are never settled (even when they are formally agreed) and are among the most contentious aspects of the oil production network.

A critical issue that has thrown resource-seeking NOCs and majors into direct competition is that the bulk of the world's low-cost, conventional oil reserves is in the hands of resource-holding national oil companies which restrict equity participation by foreign firms. The "ultimate prize" is the Middle East, which holds the bulk of the world's remaining conventional oil with around 800 billion barrels or 55 percent of the world's proven reserves. Figure 2.2 illustrates how the Middle East and North Africa enjoy some of the lowest production costs: the region's conventional oil resources are located at the bottom of the international cost curve, with production costs of between US$10 and US$25 per barrel. Furthermore, the region is in a relatively central position vis-à-vis the major European and Asian markets, and it has well-developed if vulnerable pipeline and shipping transportation infrastructure. Yet, since nationalization in the 1960s and 1970s, foreign companies have been restricted from taking equity positions in developing the fields of the region's largest reserve holders (Saudi Arabia, Iran, Iraq, and Kuwait). Oil companies currently work with these national champions as service providers – via technical service contracts – but it is on a fee-for-service basis which excludes them from sharing in the revenue from oil production.[8]

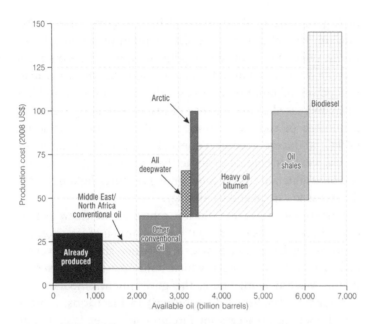

Source: Modified from International Energy Agency (2012), Resources to Reserves 2012.

Figure 2.2 Variation in production costs by type of oil source

Diversification and liberalization

After nationalization evicted the multinationals from their historic concessions in the Middle East, resource-seeking firms took up equity positions elsewhere. This diversification opened up new petroleum provinces like the North Sea and the Alaskan North Slope outside of OPEC, while oil companies also worked with national producers in OPEC countries, like Indonesia and Nigeria, through joint venture agreements. In Nigeria for example, Shell and Chevron operate onshore in the Delta through joint venture agreements concluded with the Nigerian National Petroleum Corporation in the wake of Nigeria's nationalization of oil in the 1970s. From 1986 onward, low oil prices – and the adoption of neoliberal economic policies in many developing and transition economies – created a new set of political conditions in which the relative power of oil-importing countries and resource-seeking firms increased at the expense of resource-holding states. In a number of significant resource-holding states (including OPEC producers such as Venezuela and Nigeria), terms of access were redesigned to attract new investment in the context of heightened competition among resource-holding states for access to capital and technology.

Agreements on access did not return to the freewheeling days of the concession era, but did give much greater control to investing firms and provided a greater share of revenue and profits. In Venezuela, which holds the largest reserves in the western hemisphere, the government embarked on the *Apertura Petrolera* ("oil opening") in the 1990s, a process of opening up access for foreign companies to carry out exploration and development activity. From 1992 onward, the state company PdVSA concluded a series of "operating agreements" with foreign firms to reactivate old fields, undertake exploration, and establish "strategic associations" with companies like Exxon and ConocoPhillips for the development of the unconventional "heavy oil" resources of the Orinoco Delta. These agreements were a special form of service contract that shared profits with investing firms and, as described by the then President of PdVSA, were a step toward the privatization of the state company's upstream and downstream operations. In Russia and the Caspian basin, governments encouraged foreign investment in oil and gas through production sharing agreements that allowed 100 percent foreign ownership (see Box 2.3). In sub-Saharan Africa, the 1990s and early 2000s saw a ramping up of production as the majors, independents, and resource-seeking NOCs concluded similar

Box 2.3 The rise and fall of production sharing agreements

Production sharing agreements (PSAs) are contractual arrangements between host governments and investing firms. PSAs originated in Indonesia in the 1960s, but their application expanded greatly during the low price environment of the 1990s where they were the tool of choice for governments in transition and developing economies to attract capital and technology to the petroleum sector. By one estimate, "nearly half of the countries with petroleum potential" had concluded PSAs by 1994. In seeking to encourage investment, PSAs are underpinned by a view of oil as "just another commodity" that should be subject to contractual arrangements around investment rather than as a special type of exhaustible asset for which the landowner should receive compensation. PSAs enable 100 percent foreign ownership and exemplify a "non-proprietorial" type of access regime as it is the profitability of investment – rather than the "government take" – that is the overriding consideration. In this regard, they have been seen by critics as a "return" to the concession era. Under a PSA, investing companies carry the risk of exploration and project development. As the name suggests, production is shared between the company and host state, with the company first recovering its costs through the sale of oil, and then sharing in subsequent profits. The calculation of costs is critical as budget revisions during project development can translate into significant delays before the host country receives revenues.

   PSAs have been renegotiated as part of a growing "resource nationalism" on the part of reserve-holding states. In 1997, the Kazakhstan government signed a PSA with a consortium of nine international oil firms led by ENI for the development of the Kashagan oil field in the Caspian. In 2005, with oil prices at a much higher level and a change in national strategy, the government changed its PSA legislation to require 50 percent equity participation by the state oil and gas producer in new projects, and since 2007 it has sought to renegotiate the terms of the PSA. The Russian government signed its first PSA in 1994 for the Sakhalin 2 project, giving 100 percent ownership to the three project partners, Shell, Mitsui, and Mitsubishi. After a series of interventions by the Russian government, the state-producer Gazprom took a majority stake in the project in 2006. At about the same time, the Russian government also rewrote its law on the subsoil in a way that increased government control over foreign participation in oil projects.[9]

production sharing agreements with governments in Angola, Guinea, Chad, Sudan, Nigeria, and São Tomé. When Shell moved offshore to develop deepwater resources in Nigeria in the 1990s, for example, it was not through a joint venture agreement with the state producer, but via a production sharing contract that gave the company 100 percent equity participation.[10]

Resource nationalization and the new squeeze on access
The situation has changed considerably over the last decade. Rising oil prices since 2000 have emboldened reserve-holding states to set new conditions of equity participation and renegotiate the terms of existing projects, pushing IOCs toward more marginal, costly, and environmentally risky projects. In countries like Russia, Kazakhstan, Ecuador, and Venezuela that once were regarded as bright spots for investment by international oil companies, the "access bargain" has come under strain. In Africa, Russia, Central Asia, and Latin America, governments have reasserted their position as resource-owners, increasing their equity participation and renegotiating the terms of existing projects with the result that a number of firms have left the field. In Venezuela, for example, the Chavez administration amended the Hydrocarbon Law in 2002 to increase state control and reduce private participation to a minority stake within the structure of a joint venture. This transformed the agreements signed under the *Apertura* and has led to PdVSA taking full control of the strategic associations in the Orinoco.

The reassertion of "resource nationalism" is squeezing resource-seeking firms, and comes at a time when conventional oil production in non-OPEC countries appears to have peaked, and when many of the conventional reserves that have been among the majors' core assets – in the North Sea, Alaska, and the Gulf of Mexico, for example – are experiencing decline. For the majors and independents, competition to secure "equity oil" and to gain a toehold in the Middle East (via service contracts) has increased with the entry since the 1990s of resource-seeking NOCs. State-owned and well resourced, these new transnational NOCs are encumbered by fewer "home country" restrictions on access (to Sudan and Iran, for example) and are able to cut bilateral deals with governments on infrastructure and economic development that the majors and independents cannot.

The result of this squeeze is a new geography of investment. Shut out of the lowest-cost reserves in the Middle East and with governments changing the terms of access to other key reserves of conventional oil, firms increasingly are seeking to access conventional oil in unconventional locations. These include deepwater offshore environments where the costs of producing a barrel of oil are in the range US$40–65, such as in Brazil, the Gulf of Mexico, the Gulf of Guinea, and the South China Sea. They also include the Arctic regions of Norway, Greenland, and North America, as well as the similarly challenging environments of the South Atlantic where costs can range from US$40 to US$100 per barrel (see Figure 2.2). At the same time, firms are turning to unconventional resources in accessible and relatively stable jurisdictions, such as the bituminous sands and oil shales of North America, which have similar production costs to the deepwater and Arctic but where potentially recoverable reserves are larger. Firms have lobbied hard to have unconventional oil resources counted as bookable reserves, and they make up an increasingly significant proportion of corporate reserves: between 2005 and 2009, Exxon, Shell, Total, and ConocoPhillips gained between 26% and 71% of their liquid additions to reserves from bituminous sands. Companies have also significantly increased the percentage of gas in their portfolio. Exxon's US$41 billion purchase of the unconventional gas producer XTO in 2009 enabled it to post a 200% replacement ratio that year when, without the deal, the company's reserve replacement rate would have been only 45%. There is mounting concern among environmental and human rights NGOs and some financial institutions that the squeeze on reserves is pushing oil companies into "marginal" fields and toward lower-quality resources that have much higher environmental and financial risks.[11]

Extending the network

The production network we have outlined so far captures some of the most significant relations among states and firms. A critical aspect of the current political economy of oil, however, is the way the boundaries of this network are being challenged. The business of producing oil has become increasingly entangled with broader social issues like climate change, human rights, and financial speculation. NGOs and some governments are requiring oil companies to account for their contribution to social goals which extends well beyond producing, refining, and marketing oil. Increasingly, shareholder value is tied to a company's performance on environmental and social grounds: the BP Deepwater Horizon explosion, for example, decreased the market valuation of BP by US$100 billion. More generally, oil companies' records on the environment and working with communities can influence their ability to acquire licenses to operate in new areas. BP is reported to have lost out in bidding rounds for the Greenland offshore in 2010 because of its record in the Gulf of Mexico.

At the same time, the identity of established actors is being renegotiated – and along with it, a sense of their responsibilities and accountability. Some oil companies, for example, are reinventing themselves as "energy companies" as the role of oil in their portfolios declines. As BP has found, however, moving "beyond petroleum" is exceedingly tricky, as the resource base moves from conventional oil to heavier hydrocarbons and exploration and production take place in more environmentally sensitive, politically troubled, and technologically challenging places. For companies like BP, Shell, and Exxon, diversification beyond conventional oil has involved decisive moves into unconventional fossil fuels (such as bituminous sands and shale gas) and other forms of high-cost "extreme energy" (deepwater, Arctic) that dwarf their investments in lower-carbon alternatives. A recent study suggests that for every dollar the oil industry invested world-wide in renewable fuel development (corn ethanol, sugar cane ethanol and other biofuels: total US$3.9 billion), it spent nearly US$50 developing bituminous sands (US$190 billion), and US$500 on oil exploration and production overall (total US$2,090 billion; all figures between 2006 and 2010).

The identity of "national" oil companies is also increasingly fluid, as many turn to transnational investment strategies to develop their upstream and/or downstream assets or adopt part-privatization programs. As they outgrow the geographical scale by which they have conventionally been defined, transnational state-owned corporations are sharpening the question of how and for whom petroleum development is governed. At the same time, commercial banks and international financial institutions (IFIs) are becoming ever more entangled in conflicts over the environmental, developmental, and human rights performance of the oil production network. Many projects demand multibillion dollar investments that are beyond the capacity of even oil majors to finance via the balance sheet. Construction of the Baku–Tiblisi–Ceyhan pipeline, for example, involved 15 commercial banks, seven export credit guarantee agencies, and three IFIs which together provided loans worth 70 percent of the US$4 billion project cost. The business opportunities presented by new oil projects have led banks like the Royal Bank of Scotland to specialize in the sector, which has in turn exposed it to significant criticism from environmental and human rights groups (see Box 2.4). In response to such pressure, IFIs like the World Bank and the

Box 2.4 Royal Bank of Scotland: "the oil and gas bank"

RBS is one of the five largest lenders in the world and the primary UK bank financing the extraction of fossil fuels. While all major banks are involved in oil and gas to some extent, RBS styled itself publically as the "oil and gas bank" from 2000 and sought to become a leader in the sector through its involvement in structuring loan agreements and providing credit across the production network, from upstream extraction to downstream refining and distribution. Projects involving the bank include bituminous sands in Canada and Madagascar, oil development in Peru and Uganda, and frontier projects in Greenland. In 2007, RBS dropped its slogan after a concerted effort by NGOs to make the connection between hydrocarbon extraction and climate change. Between 2001 and 2006, RBS agreed 30 oil and gas project finance details, provided over US$10 billion in oil and gas loans, and was adviser to or otherwise involved in projects worth over US$30 billion. Fossil fuel projects financed by RBS were estimated in 2005 to account for nearly 37 million tonnes of CO_2, equivalent to a quarter of UK emissions. RBS was bailed out by the UK taxpayer in 2008 to the tune of £48 billion. NGOs have continued to pressure the bank, arguing that the public character of the bank's ownership (85 percent is currently owned by the taxpayer) requires a higher standard of operation. In 2010, the NGOs World Development Movement, Platform, and People and Planet launched a legal challenge (which was rejected) to the bank's lending to oil, gas, and coal projects, arguing that the UK Treasury had not properly assessed the environmental consequences of injecting public money into the bank.[12]

European Bank for Reconstruction and Development (EBRD) have adopted procedures for assessing the environmental and social impact of project financing. A growing number of commercial banks have adopted the Equator Principles which, like the IFI procedures, require an evaluation and benchmarking of environmental and social impacts. The development of these environmental and social standards by banks has provided NGOs with a degree of leverage over oil development projects that they may not have via national political channels or the oil companies themselves. A sustained campaign by environmental groups over the social, environmental, and developmental impacts of Shell's Sakhalin-2 project in Russia, for example, targeted a loan decision by the EBRD as a way to influence aspects of project development. Funded by state banks and without making recourse to IFIs, NOC investments typically lack an analogous point of leverage for NGOs.[13]

The "politics of oil," then, increasingly revolves around the relationships between firms and states and entities *outside* the formal production network, and the way these new relationships have begun to transform the identity of core actors. Nowhere is this clearer – and the implications for responsibility and accountability potentially greater – than in the effort by NGOs (and some governments) to reframe the production and consumption of oil as part of the global carbon cycle.

Carbon conveyer

The business of extracting, processing, and consuming oil is part of a much broader global carbon cycle. From this perspective, the oil production network (see Figure 2.1) is a highly effective carbon conveyer, transferring "fossil" carbon from one site of long-term storage (underground) to another (the atmosphere). The problem, of course, is that the rate at which oil production and consumption mobilizes carbon stores that have accumulated underground over millions of years far exceeds the rate of the "return flow," by which carbon dioxide is sequestered and stored by photosynthesis and/or carbon burial. The contemporary politics of oil increasingly center on oil's contribution to the atmospheric accumulation of carbon dioxide. The prospect of global climate change means carbon abundance – rather than oil scarcity – is emerging as the critical constraint on the oil production network: mobilizing the amount of carbon locked up in proven oil reserves would push the world well beyond the 450ppm CO_2 threshold accepted by the UNFCC as a tipping point for dangerous climate change. Potential emissions from the world's proven oil reserves are estimated to be around 620 GtCo2, while the *entire* carbon budget (including coal and gas) for the period 2011–2050 has been calculated at 565 GtCo2 if the world is to avoid a 2°C rise in temperature. From this perspective, much of the carbon locked up in proven reserves – and on the balance sheets of publicly listed oil companies – is "unburnable."[14]

There are two important points here. First, the "free" services of the atmosphere in absorbing carbon and other by-products from the combustion of oil are integral to the way the production network functions. The current organization of the network, the rate at which oil flows within it, and the distribution of power along it are predicated on the availability and accessibility of the atmosphere as a carbon dump. The politics of oil, then, are increasingly bound up with the politics of pollution and climate change, as traditional concerns about depletion and energy security become paired with new concerns about greenhouse gas emissions and debate over critical threshold concentrations of carbon dioxide in the atmosphere.

Second, concerns about climate change – and the contribution of oil to aspirations for sustainable development more generally – incorporate a number of new actors into the production network. These include a wide range of NGOs and civil society organizations, as well as international governance bodies like the UNFCCC so that the production network for oil is entangled with, and increasingly shaped by, concerns over its implications for the environment and development. At the same time, carbon credits, carbon trading, and physical carbon capture and storage are also introducing nontraditional corporate actors and spaces (such as carbon sinks) into the global oil production network. Parallel to the processes of oil discovery and enclosure which mark the upstream end of the oil network, the identification and enclosure of downstream carbon "sinks" create significant new opportunities for value capture. For oil producers, for example, serious efforts to stem the accumulation of atmospheric carbon raise the interesting prospect of them becoming stewards of underground carbon stocks rather than extractors of oil (see chapter 6). For oil-exporting governments – and companies holding marginal, high-cost reserves – concerted moves toward a low-carbon energy future may leave them holding assets of *declining* value.[15]

Carbon trading shifts the accumulation of value further downstream toward a new class of "end user," those actors who own or control carbon sinks. Interaction between the "old" (fossil fuel) and "new" (trading and offsetting) carbon economies is producing a longer and more complex production chain for oil/carbon whose implications for development are currently unclear. One indication of what may be in store is the way some "old carbon" producers are experimenting with ways to protect the value of their oil assets by, for example, bundling carbon and carbon offsets together in their wholesale operations, providing the infrastructure for retail consumers to offset their emissions, or highlighting the potential for retooling reservoirs and infrastructure of depleted oil fields for carbon capture and storage. The largest regional development effects, however, are likely to be associated with the transfer of value toward those actors (states, firms) that own or control carbon sinks. Depending on the price for carbon, the value of these transfers could rival those associated with massive transfer of value from oil-consuming economies to oil-producing economies following the price rises of 1973 and 1979 (estimated at 3 percent of global GDP). The economic geographies to which exchanges of carbon credits and carbon finance give rise are still emerging. Like the OPEC revolution, however, opportunities for accumulation via the enclosure and trade of carbon sinks are likely to produce a new global geography of uneven development associated with the role of the oil production network as a carbon conveyer.

Conclusion

This chapter has illustrated how, while global and uneven in its distribution, oil is a highly *integrated* industry. We introduced the notion of a global production network to demonstrate how components of the oil sector are connected, and the relations of power among them. Although the sector has been operating for well over a hundred years and, by many measures, is a mature industry, it is also highly dynamic. Organizational shifts in the global production network for oil mean that some of the categories used to describe/define the industry and its geopolitics are now of limited utility. The politics of oil continue to center on the dynamics of competition (for access to both reserves and markets), concentration of ownership and control, and the distribution of value within the production network. Importantly, however, they increasingly encompass actors and institutions beyond the conventional network of production, refining, and marketing and extend to the implications of the production network for development, the environment, and social justice.

CHAPTER THREE

Marketing Oil

Oil's startling career over the last 150 years – from a bit player in the lighting market to a ubiquitous fuel and feedstock – can be explained only in part by reference to its mercurial properties (its energy density, fluid character, and great abundance). The *desire* for oil – the great pull that draws crude to the surface at the rate of about 85 mmbd – has been manufactured over time. In this chapter, we explore how the dramatic growth of oil consumption in the twentieth century has rested on the standardization of oil products, the cultivation of new markets, and the creation of scarcity in the face of sometimes overwhelming abundance in order to secure the profitability of production. We examine how oil is bought and sold, and the reasons for increasing price volatility over the past decade.

Like measurements of blood pressure or temperature, oil prices are a "vital sign" of the economy, a core metric by which the capacity of the economic body for reproducing itself is assessed. Tracked through benchmark crudes at international exchanges and prices posted at local gas stations, the "price of oil" is one of a select group of metrics that inform the daily routines of many people on earth. The central place oil prices occupy in the public imagination reflects the tight link between the price of oil and economic growth and the proliferation of oil within social routines (particularly around mobility). It also reflects how localized events – from strikes and other stoppages to extreme weather and geopolitical conflict – translate into price signals that are rapidly trans-mitted around the world via an integrated global oil market (and vice versa). Swings in price cause value to "slosh" back and forth from one end of the oil production network to the other: a rise in oil prices distributes value away from consum-ers and toward producers, while a fall in prices increases the value of oil to consumers at the expense of producers. A good deal of the politics of oil centers on the strategies of producers and consumers to influence the distribution of value to their advantage and to exert a measure of control over price.

Pricing power has migrated over time, from multinational oil firms to the oil-exporting states of OPEC and more recently to the financial markets. As oil prices have become increas-ingly volatile, the question of who controls price and where pricing power now lies has sharpened. In practice, the volatil-ity of oil prices is similar to that of many other commodities, yet oil is integrated into personal, corporate, and national economies like no other. For oil producers, high prices and volatility risk the possibility that consumers will switch from oil to cheaper, more reliably priced fuels. For oil consumers, volatile prices raise concerns about the security of supply and create a drag on economic growth, as in the US (see Figure 3.1), while the decreasing affordability of oil can leave poor consumers unable to access the energy services (such as heat-ing and transportation) that oil provides.

A prolonged tightening in the oil market since 2002 appears to mark the end of an "Age of Plenty," and a transition from an era in which demand for oil sets the bounds of supply to one in which oil's availability is significantly constrained. Price volatility, the failure of high prices to drive sufficient new investment, and the influence of speculators on price for-mation powerfully suggest that the political institutions – like OPEC and the IEA – whose interactions have historically gov-erned the price of oil are no longer effective. Both producers

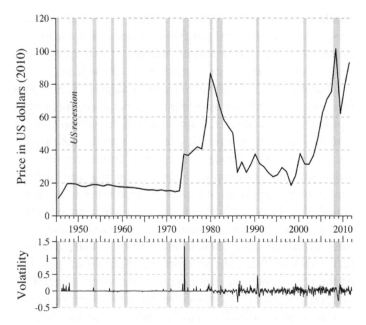

Sources: Federal Reserve Bank of St Louis (WTI monthly price volatility), and NBER (recession periods in gray).

Figure 3.1 Oil price, volatility, and US recessions (1945–2011)

and consumers, it would seem, have lost the capacity to control oil's price.

Standardizing products

The modern economy of petroleum rests on a basic yet quite remarkable fact: the machines, products, and devices that consume oil do so without regard to wide geographical variations in the local availability and quality of crude oil. The unprecedented personal mobility that cars and airplanes provide, for example, arises from their ability to travel across vast swathes of space without loss of function. This fundamentally geographical experience – of freedom from local constraints imposed by the quality and/or quantity of resources – is a key part of the experience of modernity, whose icons are the automobile and airplane and other technologies of time-space compression. While we tend to think of enhanced mobility as a product of great design, a key aspect of the design of these machines is their optimization for very specific fuel inputs. Such narrow specialization in regard to inputs requires the production of an external world outside the machine that can continuously supply these inputs, if function is to be maintained. The "globalization" of travel and trade is underpinned by the simultaneous specialization and standardization of fuels. Standardization, then, is one of the essential conditions that makes the international economy of petroleum possible. At the end of the nineteenth century, the world's largest oil company, Standard Oil, promoted itself by reference to this crucial aspect: initially, standardization assured customers using its fuel that kerosene lamps would be less likely to explode and set the house on fire.

Standardization also underpins the basic exchange at the heart of market trade, both for crude oil and petroleum products. Light or heavy, sweet or sour, crude oil itself is a highly variable commodity. If buyers and sellers are to agree terms, this variability of crude presents a potential problem. Some guarantees of product quality and consistency – against the reality of variability – are needed if buyers are to be certain of what they are acquiring. In the very early days of oil, guarantees on product quality were obtained directly as buyers would sample the product prior to purchase. However, this requirement for direct knowledge limits the ability to buy oil sight-unseen and constrains the pool of potential buyers. Getting oil to travel and reach a wide market, therefore, required a way of guaranteeing that the quantity and quality of the product would not vary but would be the same regardless of location. A first element of "standardization," then, was around quantity, and the emergence of the 42 gallon (159 liters) Standard Oil Blue Barrel (bbl) as the unit of measurement for a material that changes volume with temperature and evaporates (changes in volume of up to 5 percent are acknowledged in large trades).

A second element of standardization of crude oil is around quality. Variations in density, viscosity, sulfur content, distillation temperature profile, and a number of other characteristics now define more than 200 different grades of crude, which are identified by the names of key oil fields. These variations are significant because they influence the range of products that can be won from crude through refining. Given this degree of natural variation, trade in oil is facilitated via a pricing system that ties prices to one of a handful of "benchmark" crudes. Variations in quality from these benchmarks then attract a premium or discount for any given crude, producing a spread of prices and price differentials that are themselves wrapped up into financial contracts and traded on the futures and derivatives markets.

Downstream from the refinery, standard-setting organizations play a significant role in creating conditions that enable trade in refined oil products. These include international organizations like ASTM International (formerly the American Society for Testing and Materials) and the International Organization for Standardization, military organizations like NATO and the US Air Force, national and regional standards (such as Europe's EN228 standard for gasoline), as well as some corporate standards. These standards are fundamental to international petroleum sales. They enable buyers and sellers to understand quantity and quality without direct knowledge of the product, allow shortages in one area to be met by other sources of supply, increase competition among refineries and distributors, and help push for cleaner fuels standards. The significant role that environmental standards will play in making future fuel markets is exemplified by the EU's Fuel Quality Directive, which has set specifications on fuels in the interests of protecting health and the environment since 1998. Expansion of the Directive to promote lower-carbon fuel sources, by assigning greenhouse gas values to different renewable and fossil fuels, has been vigorously resisted by unconventional oil producers (which would be given a higher greenhouse gas value), and most particularly by representatives from Canada's bituminous sands industry. A similar low-carbon fuel standard introduced by California in 2007 was blocked in the courts in 2011 by a challenge led by the National Petrochemical and Refiners Association.[1]

Managing abundance

Scarcity is a central storyline in the unfolding drama of oil since the late nineteenth century. However, for much of the twentieth century, a primary issue for the oil industry was how to make oil scarce in the face of prodigious abundance so as to ensure profits from its production and distribution. Overproduction has dogged the oil industry for most of its history. This dynamic is now changing, however. Physical and institutional constraints on new supply have eroded spare capacity in the oil production network, while global demand for oil continues to grow. The result is a tightening of the oil market, heightened concerns about supply security, and increased price volatility. At the same time, higher prices for oil – and growing public concern about some of the products and by-products of crude oil production and refining – indicate the possibility of an alternative trajectory in which it is demand for oil that peaks rather than supply, as part of a broader energy transition. There is already evidence for this alternative scenario within Europe, although both the scale of transition and the pace of change are limited relative to the growth in worldwide oil demand.

Shutting oil in: proration and spare capacity
Strange as it may seem in a contemporary context, the politics of oil have frequently centered on how to "shut in" production and limit the rate at which oil flows onto the market, so as to avoid the depressing effect of excess supply on price. The enormous volumes of oil brought to the surface during the US oil booms of the early twentieth century, together with a highly fragmented pattern of ownership that undermined efforts at coordination, overwhelmed regional markets and created major problems of storage, waste, and damage to property. The practice of "proration" (proportional distribution) was introduced, first in Oklahoma in 1915 and then in other states, with the aim of preventing oversupply and waste. In these states, a government agency allocated allowable production to individual producers in the name of resource conservation. Until the early 1970s and the exhaustion of US spare capacity, the Texas Railroad Commission effectively controlled the rate of US oil production and domestic prices through its proration of the most significant oil-producing state in the country. Although the official role of proration orders was resource conservation and the prevention of waste, its influence on price stability served the interests of large oil producers.[2]

The international oil markets presented a similar collective action problem of managing excess capacity to avoid potentially ruinous competition. From the 1920s onward, a series of agreements among the majors sought to contain the potential for "destructive competition" over supply while at the same time securing their upstream and downstream positions against a growing group of independent oil companies and alternative sources of supply (see Box 2.2 on the Seven Sisters). The "Red-Line Agreement" in 1928, for example,

committed the oil companies that made up the Turkish
Petroleum Company in Iraq – which included Anglo-Persian,
Shell, Compagnie Française des Pétroles, Standard Oil of New
Jersey, and Mobil – to a policy of not competing with each
other for concessions within the boundaries of the former
Turkish Empire. The same year, a secret agreement to carve
up the international oil market among three of the majors
sought to solve a problem of "excessive competition [that] has
resulted in the tremendous overproduction of today . . . in
which money has been poured into manufacturing [refining]
and marketing facilities so prodigally that those now available are far in excess of those required to handle efficiently the
world's consumption." Concluded at Achnacarry Castle near
Fort William, Scotland, and known as the "As-Is" Agreement,
this deal suspended international competition between Anglo-
Persian, Standard Oil of New Jersey, and Shell throughout the
world with the aim of stabilizing prices.

Although the "As-Is" Agreement was short-lived, Big Oil's
integrated production structures and "conservation" systems
afforded these firms a measure of control over international
prices for much of the first half of the twentieth century. As
the center of gravity of production slipped away from the US
and toward the Middle East, so these governance structures
came under increasing strain. An unintended consequence
of efforts by the international companies to preserve market
share in the face of growing competition was the emergence
of a new international system of proration controlled by producer states. The decision by the majors to cut posted prices
galvanized the formation of OPEC in 1960. OPEC's founders
saw in the Texas Railroad Commission a model of how price
stability could be achieved by allocating production among
producers. Like proration in the US during the interwar
years, the formation of OPEC occurred in a period of structural oil surplus and falling prices, and marked the beginning

of collective action by producer states concerned about government revenues to regulate the balance of oil supply and demand. OPEC's action to restrict oil supply in 1973 (in the context of US support for Israel in the Yom Kippur War and the decision to decouple the dollar from gold) demonstrated the capacity of nationalized oil producers to act together and, for oil-importing countries, raised the specter of supply shortages that continues to haunt contemporary discussions of energy security.[3]

Proration is fundamentally a question of who should bear the costs associated with maintaining the cushion of spare capacity. Far from being a dusty footnote to the history of oil, the issue of spare capacity is a live and contentious one. The failure of high oil prices to produce sufficient investment to restore a "normal" price regime raises the question of where new oil could come from and who should make the investments required. OPEC countries, which hold the bulk of the lowest-cost reserves, may not be willing to make these additional investments because their revenue needs can be met by higher prices. Other oil exporters – like Russia and Mexico – do not seem willing to shoulder the costs of building and maintaining spare capacity although by most calculations they have sufficient reserves to enable them to act as swing producers. Consumers also hold some responsibility for bearing the costs of ensuring a reliable supply and the capacity to buffer short-term disruptions. The "Age of Plenty" may have come and gone, but the critical issue of who bears the costs of bringing supply and demand into balance remains.

Soaking up supply: manufacturing a world fit for oil
The creation of effective demand for oil involved more than organizing its scarcity. It also required embedding oil use within the routines and patterns of daily life by building cities, highway systems and other transportation networks that

required massive and sustained inputs of gasoline, diesel, and jet fuels. In the early twentieth century, it was not a given that automobiles would be powered by oil, and the association of cars with oil took a while to take hold. In 1900, 38% of US vehicles ran on electricity, 40% on steam, and 22% on gasoline, with the electric vehicle fleet peaking in 1912. By 1930, however, electric vehicles had been fully displaced by internal combustion engines in the US and Europe. In the US in particular, the actions of corporations, planners, and architects created forms of the built environment that ensured the "American way of life" was dependent on the availability of cheap gasoline. An alliance of automobile and oil companies conspired to replace electrically driven public transportation in American cities – the street car and electric train – with diesel buses. Between 1936 and 1950, for example, the electrically driven tramcar lines in over 45 major American cities were purchased by bus companies like National City Lines and its subsidiary Pacific City Lines – formed in the early 1930s and funded by General Motors, Standard Oil of California, Phillips Petroleum, and Firestone Tire – only to be shut down, leaving oil-powered transportation in their place. By the late 1950s, 90% of US tramlines had been closed. V8 engines – initially designed for boats and mounted on aircraft – became a "must" for any decent American car after the Second World War: the largest, Cadillac's 8.2 liter displacement V8 500, averaged 8 mpg in the city. These powerful and profligate engines were largely gone by the mid-1970s following the first oil crisis and did not make a major comeback before the arrival of SUVs in the late 1980s.[4]

Broader forces were at work too. The availability of credit enabled individuals to purchase comparatively large homes on dispersed, suburban lots and the automobiles to travel between them and work, while also enabling city and federal governments to construct an infrastructure of bridges, tunnels, urban freeways, parkways, highways, and airports. In short, consumption practices were laid down in the postwar years that ensured a massive throughput of raw materials, and of oil products in particular.

New consumption norms and practices took on a geographical expression – in the spatial segregation of home and work that led to urban sprawl, the growing connectivity of urban settlements in national space via smooth rolling highways and air travel, and in the micro-geographies of the home that became structured around new products and materials – and locked in demand for oil. The reworking of urban space around the automobile has been widely studied: in extreme cases like Los Angeles, as much as two-thirds of urban space is given over to the car. Such patterns were key parts of the postwar consumption landscape in oil's major markets. Automobile ownership and suburbanization created conditions of mass consumption for oil and its products, not only in North America but also in Europe and increasingly in Latin America and Asia via a model of "development as modernization," in which transportation, personal mobility, and consumption feature strongly. These globalized practices and the landscapes they produced could soak up the abundance of production that exploration and oil field development was bringing to the market in the 1950s and 1960s. A powerful alliance between automobile manufacturers, oil companies, construction firms, and the state was created in many countries, which lobbied to produce new consumption landscapes that, in turn, reproduced their social power.

In mature markets, many of the conditions under which oil first established its dominance as a fuel no longer hold. Oil prices are higher, alternatives to oil (such as gas for heating and power generation) are more widely available and increasingly cost-competitive, and many governments have raised the level of taxation on fuels considerably. Further, consideration of the environmental, health, and development impacts of oil has begun to appear in decisions about oil consumption in a way that it never did in the mid-twentieth century. As a result of price trends, efficiency gains, and government policies on climate and energy security, demand for oil has already peaked in the OECD. In many of these economies, oil has exited the power sector altogether, replaced by the expansion of coal, gas, nuclear, and renewables while its role as a domestic and industrial heating fuel has also been squeezed by gas and electricity. In practice, "demand destruction" takes the form of retooling urban landscapes, transportation systems, and industrial machinery to disembed oil from its current incumbent position. The transportation sector, in particular, has underpinned growth in oil demand for the last 30 years and is currently the primary driver of demand in Asia. Given this tight connection between demand growth and transport, improvements to the efficiency of transportation combined with investment in alternatives to car and air travel will be particularly significant for reducing aggregate demand. The IEA has identified the potential for a worldwide demand side peak in the (unlikely) event that governments commit to maintain carbon dioxide levels at below 450ppm.[5]

Squeezing crude: new products from oil
Owners of crude oil sought to expand markets for oil by developing new products from the remarkable raw material at their disposal. In effect, this involved squeezing crude oil harder – via more sophisticated refineries and cracking techniques – so as to extract from crude a greater range of products and services. The progressive development of thermal cracking techniques in the early twentieth century allowed refineries to break down long hydrocarbon chains of low value into more volatile (i.e. short chain) products that could be sold at higher prices. The subsequent development of catalytic cracking allowed production of higher quality and more specialized

products, such as high-octane gasoline, which enabled oil products to reach further still into industrial, military, and domestic applications.

In the first half of the twentieth century, oil and petrochemicals largely replaced coal tar as the foundation of chemical engineering. The nascent plastics industry – which had its roots in organic materials (e.g. cellulose) and coal tar from the 1850s onward – became firmly affixed to oil and petrochemicals by the mid-twentieth century, particularly via the polymer technologies and thermoplastics to which they gave rise. In the 1950s and 1960s, and following crash programs for the development of synthetic rubber in the US, the petrochemical industry began seeking new markets by manufacturing substitutes for natural products. Plastics began to replace traditional materials in a range of applications – including metals, wood, and glass. Low-density polyethylene (LDPE), for example, developed commercially by Monsanto in 1945, enabled products like the "Sqezy bottle" and the replacement of glass containers for liquids such as shampoo. Both Tupperware and Lycra were introduced in 1949, the former made from low-density polyethylene and the latter from polyurethane. The plastics and chemical industries, seeking new markets for products developed for military applications in the Second World War, began marketing a suite of new products that included pesticides, fabrics, and household utensils, tying oil and oil products ever more tightly to daily life. The search for new products and markets continues, but the petrochemical sector has been confronted with a range of environmental and health challenges since the 1960s. Plastics, in particular, have acquired a bad reputation due to their environmental persistence and potential health impacts. Bisphenol A, for example – which is used to make polycarbonate plastics – is now banned from some products in Canada and the European Union, while several countries and municipalities now either ban or tax plastic bags. Environmental and health concerns have seen oil products replaced by other materials in some applications (e.g. packaging), constraining demand growth in some markets.[6]

The end of abundance?
The long-term trend has been for oil supply to grow in pace with the expansion of demand, with only relatively short-term interruptions. Since 2002, however, an enduring "supply gap" has emerged. Rapid growth in Asian economies has meant market fundamentals have pushed prices higher, yet higher prices have failed to bring forth sufficient new supply from conventional sources to rebalance the market. Some analysts interpret this "demand overhang" as evidence of the "peaking" of conventional oil production and that, from here on, the volume of oil pulled from the ground each year can only decline. Others see market tightening as evidence of insufficient investment by IOCs and NOCs rather than a fundamental geological constraint. There is agreement, however, that high and volatile oil prices since 2002 are not a temporary phenomenon but mark "the end of cheap oil" and a significant shift in the nature of the resource base. Increasingly, the gap between supply and demand is being made up by unconventional sources, which have production costs that are three to four times as high as conventional oil. The volatility of prices and their departure from historic norms of around US$20 a barrel provide a daily indication that established mechanisms for regulating the availability and affordability of oil no longer seem to be working.

Oil markets and shifts in pricing power

For much of the twentieth century, the mechanism for allocating oil among consumers and distributing it along the production network was quite unlike a market. Oil prices were set by oil producers until the mid-1980s, first by a small number of vertically integrated companies that controlled the bulk of world production until the late 1950s, and then by the governments of key oil-exporting states which linked their prices to the benchmark Arabian Light Crude. It has only been since the 1980s that a large, functioning market for oil has developed in which prices are "discovered" through the interaction of buyers and sellers rather than being set by producers. Technologies of electronic trading rapidly expanded this "spot market" (with contracts for delivery within days), which became an important source of liquidity in the oil market as well as the reference point for oil sold through long-term contracts. As the amount of oil passing through spot markets has fallen over time, so the financial futures markets have eclipsed the spot market and now have a leading role in establishing oil prices. Prices are now set by a "paper" market in which trading behavior is closely linked to other financial markets and only weakly tied to physical supplies of oil.

Producer pricing and the emergence of a consumer counterweight
For the first half of the "Age of Plenty," the price of oil (outside the Soviet Union and China) was effectively set by the integrated majors. The majors' control of upstream operations provided a means to regulate the flow of oil onto the market, while rapidly growing demand provided a context that contained inter-firm competition. Trade in oil in this period was dominated by "horizontal" exchanges among the majors (for which prices were never disclosed) and by "vertical" trades between the subsidiaries of an individual firm, the latter often using transfer pricing techniques to reduce overall tax liabilities. In short, oil markets were very thinly developed and the bulk of the world's international oil movements took place within the structure of the multinational oil firms that

dominated production. The concept of "posted prices" played a key role in keeping this administrative system together. These prices were set by the majors, rather than determined by open-market transactions, and were used as the basis for calculating the taxes and royalties the majors would pay to the reserve-holding states in which they held their concessions.

By the late 1950s, the percentage of oil entering world markets under the majors' control was slipping. The growing role of Soviet oil exports and the increased role of independents (such as Occidental in Libya and the five independents that were part of a US-led consortium to reactivate Iran's oil industry after the coup in 1953) meant that a market for oil emerged outside the structure of the majors. Competition among suppliers for market share led the majors to sell oil to refiners at a discount, creating a growing gap between posted prices for crude and the actual prices for which oil sold. When the majors moved to cut posted prices in 1959, reserve-holding states reacted by forming OPEC. The initial decision of reserve-holding states to defend posted prices evolved over time into a strategy of equity participation (i.e. nationalization), which gave governments control over a proportion of oil output. This further undermined the major's control over upstream production, and transformed governments from landlords into hawkers of equity oil. It marked a decisive shift in control over the world market from the major international companies to oil-exporting states.[7]

With the formation of OPEC, the power to set prices remained with producers but shifted from European and American companies to the governments of oil-exporting countries. Like the system of posted prices operated by the majors, the OPEC system was an administered one. Individual oil-exporting states set an official selling price for their crudes, with these prices linked to the "reference price" of Saudi Arabia's Arabian Light. The tightness of this linkage would be tested over time – and particularly in the period of falling prices in the early 1980s – but the basic idea replicated the majors' model of producer collaboration with the goal of containing the threat of potentially ruinous competition for market share. OPEC members demonstrated their power to withhold supply and drive changes in price (both up and down) during the 1970s.

In an effort to wrest some control over price and supply security back from producers, the major oil-consuming countries set up the International Energy Agency (IEA) in 1974 as a counterweight to OPEC. Created on the initiative of US Secretary of State Henry Kissinger within the structures of the OECD, the IEA directed its members to cooperate in order to address "their vulnerability to the new economic power of the oil-producer countries." The IEA's brief has broadened over time, but its core function remains as an oil-importers' club that faces OPEC across the oil market: however, although membership has expanded, the IEA does not include the countries experiencing fastest growth in demand (such as China or India) and its proportion of global oil consumption has fallen over time (from 62% in 1971 to 54% in 2007; it is expected to be 42% by 2030). The principal mechanisms at the IEA's disposal are a system of emergency petroleum reserves covering 90 days of imports, an agreement to share these among members in an emergency, and advocacy of governance structures for oil that rely on market allocation and which promote investment in new supply.[8]

Market prices and the search for price stability
The current system for determining the price of oil is market based. Its origins lie in the tension between OPEC and the IEA over the power to control price, and it stepped from the margins of the oil trade in the 1980s with the collapse of the OPEC-administered system of pricing. Between 1986 and 1988, with

its market position heavily eroded by competitive discounting by other OPEC members, Saudi Arabia – the anchor point of OPEC reference prices – moved to a market-based system of price determination, with other producers following suit. The essence of the current system is that oil prices are not set administratively by producers but emerge out of the interactions among buyers and sellers. These interactions take place either via the spot market or, increasingly, via the market in oil futures, with prices fluctuating over the course of single day rather than being set for relatively long periods of time (up to a year or more under an administrative system).

In practice, the "market-based" process of price discovery is a much less pure process than it sounds. First, only a comparatively small (and declining) proportion of trade in oil actually passes through the spot market: in 2010, trades for immediate oil deliveries on the spot market accounted for only around 3.5 percent of global crude production. Far more oil changes hand via long-term (1–2 year) contracts, although those contracts are typically based on a formula that references the spot market price. Second, market pricing revolves around a handful of "benchmark crudes" that make up the spot market. The prices of these benchmark crudes – such as West-Texas Intermediate, Dubai-Oman, or Brent/Forties/Oseberg/Ekofisk (BFOE) – serve as reference points against which the prices of other crudes are determined by the application of a differential. Benchmark crudes are also important because they are used as a price reference point in contracts for a whole series of non-oil transactions (such as the sale of oil derivatives and tax payments to governments). Third, the "price of oil" quoted on the nightly news is not an actual price revealed through trade but an "assessment" made by a price reporting agency such as Platts. This is because buyers and sellers in the spot market sell their oil "over the counter" in direct deals and do not disclose their prices (unlike the futures market where prices are visible). Price-reporting agencies use a combination of market knowledge and information about specific deals to "identify" prices and, as a result, these agencies play an important (and contested) role in the operation of the spot market.[9]

The "thinness" of spot markets and their limited liquidity mean oil prices have instead become increasingly linked to the trade in oil futures. The volume of trades and the number of market actors are much greater in these "paper" markets for oil. Initially a way of hedging against price swings in the physical oil trade – and regarded by conventional economic theory as a source of market stability – paper markets for oil have become progressively disconnected from the trade in physical oil, and are now a relatively autonomous force with significant influence on the price of oil and on the investment strategies of oil firms. The first oil futures contract – for heating oil – was offered on the New York Mercantile Exchange (NYMEX) in 1978, followed by the introduction of a futures contract for West Texas Intermediate in 1983. An extensive market in oil futures, options, and sundry other oil-related derivatives has since emerged, centered on the NYMEX and the InterContinental Exchange (ICE) in London. The scale of this market has grown rapidly since the late 1990s: the number of open futures contracts on the NYMEX and ICE rose from 149,000 in 1994 (daily average) to just above a million in 2009 – contracts equivalent to over a billion barrels of oil. Similarly striking is a parallel growth in so-called "over the counter" trades which occur off-exchange: as much as 90 percent of swaps and options trading in oil can occur this way. The volume of over-the-counter trades for all commodities is estimated to have increased 18-fold between 1998 and 2007. Not only has the size of these "dry barrel" markets increased, but the volumes of oil that change hands each day through futures and derivatives contracts can be many times larger than the number of "wet barrels" brought to the surface and circulated through the oil production network: by 2009, the annual trading volume of crude oil futures was nearly eight-and-a-half times world oil production.[10]

A shared goal of oil importers and exporters within this market system has been price stability and the prevention of "price shocks." These are experienced by consumers as sharp spikes in the price of oil that erode value; and by oil exporters as sudden changes in revenue flows (both up and down) that can have disruptive effects on economic development. Furthermore, sustained high prices – and/or a high degree of price volatility – can also undermine the market for oil as consumers switch to alternative fuels or invest in improvements in efficiency that reduce demand. This interest in perpetuating markets for oil attenuates the urge of oil producers to raise prices, and underlies cooperation between OPEC and consuming countries. A manifestation of this shared interest in price stability was the introduction in 2000 of an OPEC price band of US$20–28 per barrel: if prices fell outside this band, OPEC would take action to expand or rein in production. Significantly, this band was deemed "unrealistic" by OPEC in 2005 and suspended when oil had been trading at over US$40 per barrel for a year or so. The continued growth in prices and the apparent inability of either OPEC or the IEA to restore equilibrium indicate how pricing power has slipped out of the hands of both oil producers and consumers, and the growing influence of financial traders in oil markets.

Volatility, speculation, and the limits of the market
Crude prices rose from US$18 per barrel at the start of 2002 to US$147 in July 2008 and then fell to US$34 in December that year. The causes of this volatility have been widely debated. While high prices are linked to "market fundamentals" and a structural imbalance between supply and demand that has emerged since 2002, the recent volatility in oil appears

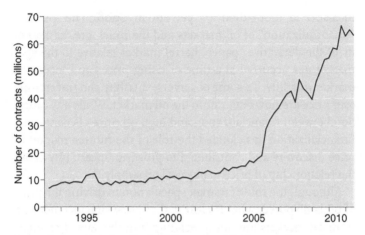

Source: Authors, based on Bank of International Settlements Quarterly
Review data.

Figure 3.2 Futures and options contracts for oil and other
commodities (1993–2010)

to be linked to the increased influence of financial activity in the markets for oil futures and derivatives (see Figure
3.2). Structural conditions of growing demand, limited spare
production capacity, and political instability in oil-exporting
regions create ample opportunities for financial speculation,
and a range of non-oil-related actors have entered the futures
markets for oil to take them up. These so-called "noncommercial traders" do not enter the futures market to hedge against
price risk as they neither produce oil nor consume it. Attracted
to oil as an asset class, noncommercial traders enter the
futures market to make a financial bet on oil: they speculate
on oil price movements and oil derivatives as an alternative to
real estate or stocks and bonds. The volume and significance
of "noncommercial" traders in oil markets increased sharply
after 2004: the volume of open contracts on NYMEX attributable to noncommercial traders grew from less than 20 percent

in 2000 to more than 40 percent in 2008. The growing "financialization" of oil markets and the much greater liquidity of the derivative "paper" barrel market relative to the spot market has occurred at a time of rising prices and increased market volatility. To some observers, volatility and uncertainty over price are now endemic to the oil market. While any causation between financialization and high oil prices is contested, financialization has clouded the role of the futures market in price discovery and contributed to growing uncertainty about the relationship of price to physical oil supply.[11]

Although the role of market speculation in driving the price of oil is disputed, what is clear is that price signals emerging from oil markets are not translating into the sort of changes one might expect with regards to oil demand and supply. Substantial rises in the price of oil since 2002 have neither caused aggregate demand to slacken nor have they generated significant growth in supply. Strong growth of Asian demand has outstripped recessionary effects in OECD markets so that demand for oil has continued to rise even while prices have risen sharply. On the supply side, the financial strategies adopted by many oil companies have prioritized shareholder dividends and buybacks over investment in production. It is widely recognized, for example, that high oil prices since 2004 have not translated into proportional increases in investment expenditure by major oil firms.

The "failure" of the normal market response mechanism to dampen demand and increase supply at a time of high prices raises questions about who now controls the oil market and illustrates the limitations of the market-based model of oil allocation that has dominated consuming countries since the 1980s. Some analysts suggest we may be on the cusp of a new price regime in which the price of oil is no longer set by the marginal costs of production (the cost of the last barrel necessary to meet demand). With its availability constrained, prices

Box 3.1 Compartmentalizing the market – China's loans-for-oil

Along with its "go out" policy of foreign direct investment by state-owned firms (see chapter 2), China has concluded a series of bilateral loans-for-oil deals. The essence of these deals is balanced two-way trade, in which China receives oil and gas in exchange for industrial machinery, infrastructure development, and other goods, including arms. They are typically long-term commitments lasting 20 or more years. A deal between China and Iran in 2004 is credited with introducing a "new energy mercantilism" into the oil market that "changes the international oil and gas game." Worth between US$200 and US$400 billion over 25 years, this oil and gas deal was anchored by an agreement to export gas from Iran to China in exchange for financing, infrastructure, and the development of a tanker fleet. In 2009, China concluded deals with Brazil, Kazakhstan, and Russia worth US$50 billion. These include a 20-year deal with the Russian state-owned companies Rosneft and Transneft that will give China access to 300,000 barrels a day via the Eastern Siberia–Pacific Ocean pipeline. All together, the three deals in 2009 provide access to 1.2 mmbd within the next 10 years. The effect of these bilateral deals is "to compartmentalize the international oil trade, receiving volumes from selected buyers and withholding oil and gas from open market trading." Critics also point out how bilateral deals undermine efforts to secure multilateral agreements to stabilize prices and, by preventing price transparency, can also facilitate corruption.[12]

become separated from the costs of production and it is the value to end consumers (rather than the marginal costs of production) that determine price. In the language of economists, oil ceases to be a commodity and becomes a strategic good. The growth of bilateral deals in the international oil market – such as China's use of loans-for-oil as a complement to its equity oil positions (Box 3.1) – suggests that this may already be happening as consumers seek nonmarket mechanisms to "lock-in" supplies. These deals effectively segment the international crude oil market and mean that "purchasing power is no longer enough of a guarantee for access to all oil flows."[13]

Conclusion

This chapter has shown how the centrality of oil to modern life is not a natural state of affairs but has been assiduously produced through creative enterprise during the twentieth century. A vast range of markets for oil products developed as producers struggled with the problem of overproduction. For much of this period, oil supply was led by growth in demand and, in the face of surplus, producers devised various mechanisms to retain control over price. The inherent conflict between oil producers and consumers over the distribution of value takes the form of a struggle over price. The shift from high oil prices in the 1970s to low prices in the 1990s reflected a loss of pricing power by OPEC. Since 2002, prices have risen dramatically and price volatility has increased, raising the question of where in the production network pricing power now lies. High prices are clearly to the advantage of oil producers yet, critically, pricing no longer seems to be within their control. While producers are able to restrict supply, they appear unable (in the medium term, at least) to expand it to meet growing demand.

The result is that demand for oil appears no longer to be driving supply, marking an end to the historic pattern that has governed the flow of oil to markets during the twentieth century. Some argue this state of affairs is the result of geological constraints and evidence of "peak oil." Others see it as a function of underinvestment by oil companies and reserve-holding states. While we side with the latter as an analysis of current constraints on supply, we do not regard expansion of production capacity as the most desirable solution. Rather, we see in emerging evidence of "demand destruction" in OECD economies an alternative response to high oil prices and a different way to balance demand and supply. Although they are currently too small and too slow to be effective, moves in this direction are promising because they seek to undo demand by disembedding oil from urban and transportation infrastructures.

CHAPTER FOUR

Securing Oil

In 1980, US National Security Adviser Zbigniew Brzezinski convinced President Jimmy Carter to declare that: "an attempt by any outside force to gain control of the Persian Gulf region will be regarded as an assault on the vital interests of the United States of America, and such an assault will be repelled by any means necessary, including military force." What became known as the Carter Doctrine responded to the recent overthrow of the Shah in Iran, the Soviet invasion of Afghanistan, and an attack on Mecca's Grand Mosque by a fringe Saudi Islamist group. Framed by the US defeat in Vietnam and the impact of the OPEC oil embargo, the doctrine revealed deep US anxieties over oil supplies and consolidated a common understanding of oil security centered on the Persian Gulf and driven by military means. Three major wars later – and after the occupation of Iraq by American troops for nearly a decade – the Persian Gulf remains the epicenter of energy geopolitics and among the most tense and militarized areas of the world.[1]

Oil markets and importing states have reacted not only to major tensions and conflagrations in the Persian Gulf but also to armed militancy in the Niger Delta, piracy in the Gulf of Aden, and insurrections in Russia's periphery. Geopolitical scenarios of international disputes, and even "oil wars," are played out in many locations where oil reserves overlap disputed territories, as in the Gulf of Guinea, the Arctic, the China Seas, and more recently the Mediterranean (see Table

4.1). Despite incidents, such as Suriname's navy forcibly halting oil exploration in waters disputed with Guyana in 2000 or skirmishes between China and its neighbors, most of these disputes are solved through negotiations or international arbitration toward a sharing agreement or boundary definition. The Law of the Sea tribunal and the International Court of Justice (ICJ) often intervene but so do regional power brokers such as Nigeria. Resolution at state level occasionally leads local populations to resist, for instance, the failed secession attempt by Bakassi Peninsula's Nigerian population following an ICJ decision and UN-brokered bilateral agreement attributing the area to Cameroon in 2006.

Geopolitics looms large in all approaches to oil security, but conventional, state-centered perspectives on geopolitics provide only a partial understanding of what it means to "secure" oil. Governing the risks associated with oil dependence is at the core of securing oil, for oil producers and oil consumers, as well as those who witness the production network but are not integrated within it. For producers, it is about a form of governance that secures the greatest benefits from oil and that reduces internal tensions associated with frustrated development and perceptions of corruption, mismanagement, or foreign interference. For consumers, it is about reducing the volatility and uncertainty of supply, including those associated with political tensions and economic upheavals in oil-producing countries. In this way, the new oil security agenda links reducing volatility and uncertainty in oil markets to the broad development of oil-producing societies (as discussed in chapter 5), rather than a narrowly conceived regime stability paradigm that seeks simply to uphold contracts and oil deliveries. Part of this new security agenda is, therefore, also concerned with addressing the environmental and social costs of oil and seeking energy alternatives.

Table 4.1   Main internationally disputed oil areas

Area	Countries	Status
Arctic Ocean	Russia, Canada, US, Norway, Denmark	Prospective fields – arbitration, negotiations, militarization
Barents Sea	Norway, Russia	Proven fields – agreement 2010
Baltic Sea	Lithuania, Latvia	Prospective fields – negotiations
Mediterranean Sea	Israel, Lebanon, Turkey, Greece	Proven fields – negotiations, militarization
Persian Gulf (Abu Musa and Tunb Islands)	Iran, UAE	Proven fields – militarization
Caspian Sea	Azerbaijan, Turkmenistan, Iran	Prospective fields – negotiations
East China Sea (Senkaku/Diaoyutai Islands)	Japan, China, Taiwan	Prospective fields – negotiations and militarization
South China Sea (Spratly and Paracel Islands)	China, Vietnam, Philippines, Malaysia, Taiwan, Brunei	Prospective fields – agreement 2011 and militarization
Celebes Sea	Malaysia, Indonesia	Producing fields – negotiations
Timor Sea	East Timor, Australia	Producing fields – agreement 2002
Gulf of Guinea	Cameroon, Nigeria, Ghana, Ivory Coast	Producing and proven fields – arbitration, negotiations
Mid-Atlantic	Guyana, Suriname	Proven fields – arbitration
South Atlantic (Falkland/Malvinas Islands)	UK, Argentina	Proven fields – Argentina withdrew from 1995 agreement in 2007, militarization
Abyei	South Sudan, Sudan	Producing fields – militarization, negotiations
Lake Albert	Uganda, DRC	Proven fields – agreement 2007

Energy security

The "security" of energy normally refers to the maintenance of a reliable supply at prices that are affordable to consumers, yet profitable enough for producers to justify investments in future production. Intuitively appealing it may be, but a host of complications lies behind this simple definition. First, energy security and oil security are not the same thing. Oil is only one potential source of energy, and national and regional strategies to secure oil can work against broader goals of energy security. On its own, the desire of governments to secure oil supplies can distract attention (and divert resources) from strategies that seek to diversify the energy mix and enhance resilience to oil "shocks." Fixed infrastructure can create a false sense of supply security and leave an importing country at the mercy of a political reversal, such as a sudden regime change in a long-allied, major oil supplier, or of a natural disaster like an earthquake that results in multiple pipeline ruptures. Second, oil security does not mean the same thing for consumers, oil companies, or for oil-producing countries. Cheaper oil may increase a sense of security for consumers, but it lowers investments by energy companies and revenues for energy-producing countries. A lack of investment leads to falling production volumes, increasing energy insecurity in the long term. Reduced production, if not offset by rising prices, can lessen revenues for producing countries and thus increase the risks of political instability. For governments of oil-producing countries, energy security means an ability to satisfy domestic energy consumption *and* the export markets vital to their economy.

Third, (in)security can arise out of the way the oil network is organized. State-driven models of organization raise concerns about political interference in access to reserves, distorted investment incentives, or restrictions on trade. Market-driven models, on the other hand, have left some governments anxious about supply as the oil market tightens. The vitality and adaptability of markets so valued by their proponents can also be a source of vulnerability. In 2012, for example, the largest independent refining company, PetroPlus, filed for insolvency, creating anxiety about the loss of gasoline, jet fuel, and other petroleum products from some of its refineries including Coryton, one of the largest refineries in the UK. The participation of sovereign wealth funds in the equity of now fully privatized "national" oil companies, such as the French company Total, has also raised concern about the degree of control and intentions of the foreign governments controlling these funds.

Fourth, (in)security arises from the way vulnerabilities and benefits are distributed along the production network. Global energy markets tend to spread risks among a large number of players, attenuating the impacts on individuals. The release of strategic oil stocks by wealthy industrialized countries, for example, can help all oil importers by decreasing global prices. Yet the transmission mechanism of a global market also means localized events can trigger broad chain reactions: a pipeline sabotage or unexpected refinery shutdown can send tremors throughout world oil markets. Fifth, efforts to "secure oil" by one set of actors can create various forms of insecurity (including violence) for others, most notably for those who live alongside and around the infrastructure of oil extraction, transportation, and refining (not to mention gas station staff exposed to fumes and violent crime). Abuses by security forces are common, especially when local populations resist displacement or challenge pollution and the social disruption arising from oil development. Energy projects can leave local populations more energy insecure by destroying traditional energy sources, while refineries, pipelines, and electricity transmission systems often fail to serve their immediate communities:

despite their proximity to tremendous wealth, those who live in oil's extractive zones are often among the most fuel poor. The consequences of energy security choices extend beyond energy to other sectors of the economy. Subsidies and diversion of farmland for biofuel production, for example, were partly driven by US security concerns over the country's reliance on oil from the Middle East, but can compromise food security for farmers and urban consumers. More broadly, the concerns raised by oil-related GHG emissions are particularly acute for the populations most vulnerable to climate change (and least responsible for it).

Finally, conventional definitions of oil security adopt a national scale of reference, but attention to alternative geographical scales – municipalities frustrated by lack of action on greenhouse gas emissions, households anxious over fuel bills, agricultural communities facing declining yields from oil-induced climate change – reveal the trade-offs that "securing oil" entails, and how security has a *relational* character: thus (in)security and vulnerability are a function of position within the oil production network (and energy networks more broadly). Our goals in this chapter are to explore these multiple and contested dimensions of oil security, and to show how "securing" oil requires addressing four criteria: oil's availability, accessibility, acceptability, and affordability.

Comparing energy sources
As a first cut, we provide a "snapshot" comparison of how four key criteria – availability, accessibility, affordability, and acceptability – play out across the five main primary sources of energy at the world scale: oil, coal, gas, hydro, and nuclear (see Table 4.2). Such comparisons are implicit within contemporary debates about energy transition and a move away from fossil fuels toward more secure, affordable, and lower-carbon energy systems.

Table 4.2	Energy security criteria by resource type				
Resources	Oil	Coal	Natural Gas	Hydro	Nuclear
Availability	Medium↘	Very high ↗	High ↗	Low ↘	Medium ↗
Accessibility	High↘	High ↗	Medium ↗	High ↗	Low ↗
Acceptability	Medium↘	Medium ↘	High ↘	Medium ↗	Low ↘
Affordability	Medium↘	High ↗	Medium ↗	High ↘	Medium ↘

Note: ↗ means "and rising", ↘ "and declining"

Oil is still the dominant source of primary energy supply in the world, but its 33 percent share is on the decline. Large reserves of unconventional oil exist in the form of bituminous sands and "shale oil," but these provide a lower energy return on the energy invested in their extraction (EROEI) and have higher environmental impacts, thus reducing their affordability and acceptability. The accessibility of oil to IOCs has declined, due to greater competition from NOCs and the politics of resource nationalism among some producer countries. On the other hand, technological innovation and higher prices have increased the commercial viability of unconventional resources (and conventional resources in unconventional locations – e.g. Arctic, deepwater) and extended the resource frontier. The accessibility of oil via open international markets is likely to decline as oil equity stakes increase (notably through Asian NOCs) and exporting countries consume a larger share of their production. Oil's acceptability is also declining as evidence grows of its connections to climate change, soil and water contamination, human rights abuses, and links with political violence and military interventions. Affordability is widely perceived as declining over the long term, contrary to previous oil price cycles where downturns and overproduction could generate very affordable prices – such as US$10 per barrel in late 1998.

Coal, by contrast, is more widely available, easily accessible, and cheaper to produce, characteristics that make it the fastest-growing fuel. Yet its uses are more limited, and it is not easily transformed into a liquid fuel for transportation. Although coal is often deemed less acceptable than oil, this judgment hinges in large part on the efficient capture of carbon dioxide emissions which is both more feasible and advanced for point-sources like coal-fired electricity generating plants than the diffuse emissions associated with oil combustion. Some rapidly growing economies – such as China, India, and South Africa – rely heavily on coal for electricity generation, an energy policy legitimated in part by the historic coal-powered industrialization of many OECD economies and which sets the national need to address energy poverty via expanding electrification against the international climate change agenda. Like coal, hydroelectricity and nuclear power supposedly provide "cheap" energy when socio-environmental costs are ignored. Hydro and nuclear options are further limited by suitable location criteria, massive capital costs, and nuclear proliferation concerns. China is revisiting its hydropower policy after acknowledging the costs and risks of the Three Gorges dam, while Germany and Switzerland have decided to phase out nuclear generation in the wake of the 2011 tsunami-related Fukushima nuclear plant disaster in Japan.

In contrast to these energy sources, natural gas reserves and production are growing rapidly and in a way that, to its proponents, makes gas a "transition fuel" and "energy bridge" to a lower-carbon future. To its critics, however, any dash for gas comes at the expense of investment in renewables and effectively "locks in" a new era of carbon-intensive energy. Increased production of liquefied natural gas (LNG), combined with marine shipping with cryogenic vessels and a larger distribution network of standard gas pipelines, has greatly increased the accessibility of gas for consumers. Increased recovery and processing of natural gas liquids (NGL) also adds to the supply of unconventional liquid fuel for transportation markets. The sharp increase in the availability of natural gas – in the North American market in particular – stems from the rapid development of unconventional "shale gas" deposits, a process that involves hydraulic fracturing, a practice widely deemed unacceptable due to underground water pollution and methane release risks.[2]

Oil matters because of its energy density and transportability, making it difficult and costly to substitute given existing needs and infrastructures. Some substitution occurred in the late 1970s and early 1980s when natural gas, coal, and nuclear or hydropower replaced heating oil throughout most industrialized countries, and fuel efficiency in transport was significantly improved. Oil is not easily substituted in crucial economic sectors such as transportation, although with the right policies or price incentives car transport could shift to electrification and natural gas. But oil insecurity has also been *made* to matter: it is not simply a function of oil's superior energy density, geological limits, or China's rapid growth. Insecurity also derives historically from the wastage and shortsightedness of an "Age of Plenty" that considered oil the lubricant of infinite growth.[3]

Availability

The traditional focus of oil geopolitics is the strategic actions of firms and states to secure advantage from the balance of oil supply and demand. This balance rests on geological and economic foundations, with political action selectively opening up or closing down the flow of oil. The availability of oil at a planetary scale is central to debates over the significance of "peak oil." Optimists point out that conventional oil reserves are at an all-time high, the number of oil-producing countries is increasing, vast unconventional reserves are available, and natural gas could to some extent replace oil as transportation fuel. By contrast, pessimists highlight the exhaustible character of oil as a resource, a significant drop-off in the rate at which giant oil fields are discovered, the technical limits and environmental impacts of unconventional sources, and fast-rising demand from Asia. As discussed in chapter 2, the state of reserves remains debated, but there is a growing consensus that it will be difficult to increase conventional oil production. The number of oil-producing countries has increased as high oil prices promote investments in new regions (in Africa, for example, Ghana and Uganda are joining the ranks of oil producers), but many of these recent discoveries are marginal in terms of the volume they add to global supply and the bulk of conventional oil production within the next two decades is still expected to come from the largest estimated reserves, especially those around the Persian Gulf.

In 2004, the International Energy Agency and US Energy Information Agency forecast a global demand of 120 mmbd by 2030. Many analysts, including some employed by these organizations, now think this will be impossible to meet. Oil companies have been at pains to produce 85 mmbd for most of the last decade. Reaching 100 mmbd will require about US$6 trillion in investment which would be a major feat, although not one celebrated by environmentalists.

There are multiple strategies for securing availability. The US has long followed a military option, deploying its own military in strategic locations, consolidating its local allies, and intervening militarily when the conditions are seen as imperative (as in the 1991 liberation of Kuwait) or opportune (as in the 2003 invasion of Iraq). The latest such measures include the creation of the US African Command (AFRICOM) that critics see as focused on protecting oil flows from the Gulf of Guinea region, and further naval deployment in the Persian

Gulf to deter (or prepare for) a confrontation with Iran. Yet the setbacks in Iraq have demonstrated the limits and horrendous costs of such militarization. Other governments have chosen alternative strategies but may not stick to them. The European Union currently bases its energy security policy on greater market interdependence through the Energy Charter Treaty, strategic partnering (e.g. the EU–Russia Energy Dialogue), and facilitating improvements to governance within oil-producing states. Yet European Union member countries have frequently "hardened" their oil security strategy. The UK has a long history of military interventions in the Persian Gulf and remains a key ally for the US. France has also militarily propped up allied oil regimes, including in Gabon and more recently Chad, and – along with the US and UK – used military force to help bring down oil-funded regimes, such as that of Gaddafi in 2011. China is cautious not to signal any external military aggressiveness, but it is building up its navy, suggesting that it also retains military options.

Tensions over oil regions and so-called "oil wars" should not be understood as simply driven by resource competition, but rather as the political interplay of major oil-importing countries, oil companies, oil-funded states, and local populations. Oil revenues provide petro-states with the ability to pursue their ambitions through military means, while often creating a sense of vulnerability resulting from a history of foreign interference and contemporary dependence on oil exports. This context has often given rise to (populist) "revolutionary" petro-states, whose leaders have been more inclined to conduct wars of conquest and preemptive aggression, while motivating international powers or neighboring countries to take countermeasures, including economic sanctions and military interventions. International powers, such as the UK and US have been eager to undermine regional powers that could challenge their political or military dominance and economic interests. One result has been the arms race and multiple armed conflicts that have marked the Persian Gulf over the past hundred years.[4]

Accessibility

Only 35 countries are currently net oil exporters, a number likely to decline within two decades as small producers exhaust their fields and domestic oil consumption increases in producing countries. Accessing this shrinking resource base is a major conundrum for oil companies and consumers alike. For companies, it means chasing opportunities to develop new fields and/or grow reserves, securing financing for exploration and production, and creating the infrastructure to get oil to markets. Competition among IOCs and NOCs has long been part of the "Great Game" to secure access (and exclude others) but increasingly this competition over resource and market access has to take into account the acceptability of conditions of exploitation, transit, and emissions (see p. 119).

For consumers, a diminishing supply of conventional oil is likely to mean average prices will rise, although the impacts of this will vary, as not all consumers are the same. High-income importing countries (such as Japan) worry mostly about *supply risk* or the disruption of supplies, while for low-income countries (such as Mali), *market risk*, or the unaffordability of oil, is the main preoccupation (see p. 111). Although distinct, supply and market risks are often tied together as disruptions increase prices.

Supply risks
The reliability of supply is affected by the risks associated with a high dependence on oil imports, limited geographical diversification of imports, and instability in oil-supplying countries.

These factors can be compounded where a country is exposed to international sanctions that make oil imports difficult, or where there are few import route options or an absence of refining capacity and/or emergency stocks. Exposure to weather events (that drive spikes in demand or disrupt distribution) and to strikes and social unrest (that prevent the distribution of oil products) can often pose a more significant supply risk to individual consumers than international events.

Countries treat supply risk as a strategic concern. Such concerns were clearly at work with respect to the two world wars: preparing for war, the British and German governments sought to control oil sources as they had converted their navies from coal to oil in the 1910s. Hitler's failed *Fall Blau* military campaign in 1942 first aimed to capture and later to destroy oil fields in the Caucasus. Japan's preemptive strike on Pearl Harbor responded in part to the threat of an oil embargo by the US as Japan attempted to consolidate its power in Southeast Asia to secure access to natural resources, including oil from the Dutch East Indies. Western powers did not hesitate to intervene militarily when Saddam Hussein seized Kuwaiti oil fields. Oil security concerns have further risen during the past decade, especially supply risks concerns as a result of the post-9/11 "war on terror," terrorism and piracy in the Gulf of Aden, and popular uprisings in the Middle East and North Africa (MENA). Saudi military intervention to protect the Sunni minority government in Bahrain during the uprising of an aggrieved Shi'ite majority exposed the increasing vulnerability of autocratic (often pro-western) governments in the region, while uncertainty remains as to the outcome of the Arab Spring in 2011 for oil supplies and access by foreign oil companies.

At the moment, the most common geopolitical threats to oil security include a sustained interruption of commerce through key shipping lanes, such as the Strait of Hormuz in

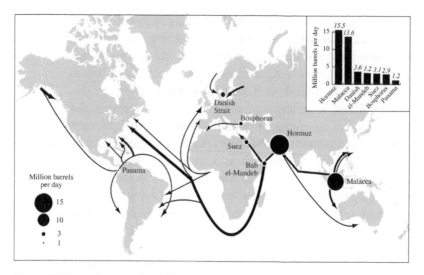

Source: US General Accounting Office, 2007.

Figure 4.1 Maritime choke points

a conflict with Iran or rising tensions between the US and China; civil war in large oil-exporting countries, and especially Saudi Arabia, as demonstrated in Libya in 2011; embargoes on oil imports, as in the case of Haiti and Serbia during the 1990s; and, more tenuously, a military conquest to consolidate oil reserves as was feared in the case of the Iraqi takeover of Kuwait in 1990. The geography of supply risk is classically defined by "choke points" or bottlenecks, with vulnerable parts of the oil transportation network protected by military bases (along key pipelines) and navy patrols shadowing maritime oil flows (see Figure 4.1). Some of the most severe if brief disruptions, however, result from domestic unrest and fuel protests targeting refining and distribution. Blockades by angry truckers, farmers, or fishermen seeking to maintain fuel tax rebates, as seen in France and the UK in 2000, have blocked refineries, tanker off-loading sites, and gas stations, turning these infrastructures into strategic sites of political mobilization and police intervention.

Prices are also an indirect concern for supply security. Low oil prices push marginal producers out of business and over the long run concentrate supply around the cheapest producers which are also often the largest, thus reducing supply diversity. Low price trends in the mid-1990s and indications of depletion among many smaller producers (such as the UK) have raised medium- to long-term supply security concerns among major oil importers. Concerns have also been raised over the growing shift of refining capacity outside the OECD, with most new refinery investment in Asia.

Supply risks are also affected by the foreign policy concerns of producing countries. Bolstered by vast foreign currency reserves and long-term forecasts of high prices, many exporting countries invest heavily to extend their influence. Nigeria and Angola have become dominant players in regional security within the Gulf of Guinea, seeking to rival western powers. As discussed in chapter 6, some GCC (Gulf Cooperation Council) countries such as Qatar have taken very proactive foreign policy stands. Yet, embargoes *by* producing countries have tended to be brief and ineffective, thanks to alternative supplies and producer reliance on oil export revenues, while embargoes *on* producing countries have been more common and sustained (see Box 4.1). Their economic impact can be massive, however, especially when markets overreact and consumers panic, as seen with the 1973 oil embargo by Arab OPEC members against the US and the Netherlands. More widespread is political unrest in producing countries that tighten supplies, as demonstrated by the impact of oil unrest in the Niger Delta that chronically brought down production in 2008, or the civil war in Libya, which took about 1 mmbd of high-quality crude off the market in 2011.

Box 4.1 Revisiting the "oil weapon"

Oil embargoes can put acute pressure on importing countries. Used by the US against US-oil dependent Japan in 1941, the "oil weapon" came to fame in October 1973 when Arab members of OPEC took measures against countries supporting Israel during the Yom Kippur War. These included a 70 percent increase on the posted price of Arabian Light, gradual restrictions on production, and country-specific measures, including an embargo on oil deliveries to the US, Netherlands, Portugal, South Africa, and Rhodesia. Taking place over a five-month period, these measures proved very blunt, as they affected most countries rather than only supporters of Israel, and largely ineffective, as targeted countries obtained oil indirectly or from other sources. A side effect, much appreciated by oil companies and exporting countries alike, was a massive increase in oil revenues. Over the medium term, however, this "oil shock" accelerated the diversification of oil supply away from OPEC countries. Geopolitically, the oil crisis nevertheless proved momentous by revealing the rising vulnerability and decreasing power of western countries, especially that of the US. By then, the US had lost the war in Vietnam, devalued its dollar by pulling out of the Gold Exchange Standard, and its stock market had crashed, while US oil companies lost ground to producing states.

The "oil weapon" has since scarcely been used by producing countries. During the 1991 Gulf War, the Iraqi government set fire to about 500 Kuwaiti oil wellheads and dumped up to 3 million barrels of oil into the Persian Gulf – among the largest oil spills in history. This was more out of anger for losing the war and to punish Kuwait, another oil producer, than to affect oil importers, with prices only briefly spiking in January 1991. In April 2002, Saddam Hussein declared a one-month suspension of oil exports to protest Israeli actions in Palestine and unsuccessfully called for Arab producers to cut output by 50 percent and cease exports to Israel and the US. In 2008, Libya suspended crude oil deliveries to Switzerland after one of President Gaddafi's sons was arrested in Geneva. Despite relying for 15 percent of its imports on Libyan crude, Switzerland did not suffer major disruptions, thanks to alternative supplies. NATO's intervention and UN sanctions on Libyan oil companies during the 2011 Arab Spring, in contrast, put major strains on the market by taking about 1 mmbd off the market. If attacked, Iran is the most likely country to use the oil weapon through selectively cutting its oil production and disrupting oil traffic out of the Persian Gulf through the Strait of Hormuz. Both would have a major effect on oil prices. A barrel of Brent crude reached US$147.27 on July 11, 2008, following Iranian missile launch exercises. Iran, however, heavily relies on oil exports and such a move would be very costly and bring major military response from the US. In fact the "oil weapon" is more frequently used *on* oil exporters. The US imposed sanctions on about half a dozen oil exporters, mostly unilaterally but also through the UN Security Council as in the case of Iraq, while it is now joined by the EU and Japan to put pressure on Iran.

Ensuring reliable oil supplies

Supply reliability is traditionally pursued through geographical diversification, dependable infrastructures, commercial incentives, and military force. Diversifying supplies is relatively easy for oil, given its transportability and relatively low cost of transportation. It is common for countries to import oil from a dozen producing countries, although the calibration of refineries to specific crudes limits this flexibility. Supply diversification was at the core of the 2001 US energy strategy defined by Vice-President (and former Halliburton CEO) Dick Cheney. It was also a policy that suited oil corporations struggling to maintain their booked reserves and weary of energy conservation and climate change mitigation measures. Iraq, with the world's largest undeveloped and most profitable conventional oil reserves, became a chief target of this policy post-9/11.

Access to oil is an important component of China's energy policy, and to a lesser extent that of India, with massive investments in Africa but also the Middle East and Central Asia. By 2030, the OECD plus China and India are expected to account for 70 percent of world consumption but only 15 percent of production. Oil pipelines to China are being rapidly developed, with links established with Kazakhstan (Atyrau–Dushanzi pipeline) and Russia (Eastern Siberia–Pacific Ocean–ESPO pipeline), and with plans for pipelines to Burma (Sittwe–Kunming), Pakistan (Gwadar–Kashgar), and an additional link between Canadian tar sands and the Pacific (Edmonton–Kitimat). Between 2006 and 2010, Chinese companies laid more pipelines within and into China than in the previous four decades, and they plan to double that amount by 2015. China is also ramping up its emergency reserves at a rate of 50 million barrels a year to meet IEA standards of 90 days of supplies by 2020. India lags behind, but completed its first major strategic reserve in 2011 to cover two weeks of demand.

Military force is also deployed to ensure reliable supplies, especially along transportation corridors but also at production sites and refineries. The British maintained a military force along the Suez Canal after conceding formal independence to Egypt in 1922 (before being expelled as a result of the Suez Crisis in 1956). The US relinquished control over the Panama Canal only in 1999, withdrawing troops as a Chinese company took over the canal's management lease, but maintaining its Guantanamo naval base in Cuba. By far the largest oil-related military expense is that of the US in the Persian Gulf, with estimates in the range US$30–250 billion per year since the mid-1970s. The US navy first entered the Gulf during World War II to protect US oil installations in Saudi Arabia and Bahrain from Italian bombers, and replaced the British as the dominant western force from the 1960s onward. US forces played a leading role in protecting oil flows from Kuwait during the Iran–Iraq war of 1980–88, liberating Kuwait in 1991 and invading Iraq in 2003. Oil-related military expenditure by China is rising as the country relies on tanker traffic going through the Malacca Strait for 80 percent of its oil imports. Rather than explicitly pursuing the mega-military base model of the US, China is improving its operational conditions to ensure "safe sea-lanes" throughout the Indian Ocean by helping to build or modernize "civilian" ports in Bangladesh, Burma, Pakistan, and Sri Lanka and progressively securing docking and defense agreements. Nevertheless, China launched its first aircraft carrier in 2011 and aims to have at least four carriers by 2020.

More broadly, importing countries see regime stability in producing countries as a major asset to maintain supplies and contractual arrangements. Oil tends to reinforce regime durability, especially for dictatorships, through populist programs, stronger patronage networks, well-funded security apparatus, and foreign military assistance. Several rulers have seen their tenure shortened by *coups d'état*, suspicious accidents, and outright invasion, however. One important paradox is that efforts to create oil security for some – rulers, oil companies, and consumers – often actively produces insecurity, violence, and dispossession for others, which in turn can undermine oil supply security. As discussed further in chapter 7, solving this security paradox requires a shift from a conventional geopolitical perspective on oil security to one that addresses the social and environmental impacts of oil and the improvement of governance in oil-rich countries.[5]

Affordability

Affordability is *the* major criteria for consumers fearing "pain at the pump" and governments worrying about the economic impacts and social backlash of price hikes. More importantly, affordability is a key element of energy security for billions of people living in relative poverty. About 2.5 billion people still rely on biomass for household energy uses; at least 1.5 billion have no access to electricity; and many cannot afford motorized transportation and agricultural tools. The question of fuel prices (and subsidies) is thus crucial for the poor, especially in countries with large rural populations relying on diesel generators for electricity, motorized transport to access distant markets, and basic mechanized tools, such as water pumps, for their livelihoods. This is perhaps most striking in supposedly "oil-rich" countries such as Iran, Yemen, and Nigeria. Fuel subsidies negatively affect the national balance of payments, disproportionally benefit the richest and largest oil consumers, and divert funds from alternative energy and, notably, electrification infrastructure. Yet, eliminating fuel subsidies without a compensatory social welfare mechanism can remove a crucial safety net for the poor.

Affordability is achieved first and foremost by high

incomes, infrastructure availability, and improved energy efficiency. Low energy taxation also helps in the short term, but is counterproductive in the long term as a sense of entitlement builds up, along with higher volume consumption, leaving consumers vulnerable to future price hikes. Affordability influences demand, but oil prices are relatively inelastic: higher prices will not immediately and proportionally cut down consumption. US households, for example, will first cut savings, then food, before vehicles and fuel. Still, oil consumption peaked on a per capita basis in several OECD countries around the time of the second oil crisis in 1979, mostly as a result of a shift away from oil for heating. Affordability – along with contribution to urban air quality – is an important design objective for new more fuel-efficient cars being developed for the flourishing Chinese and Indian markets.[6]

The *market risks* defining affordability not only relate to the capacity to pay for oil, but also to the oil intensity of an economy. Countries that are cash-strapped with heavily oil-dependent economic sectors – such as heavy manufacturing or a tourist sector reliant on cheap flights – face a higher degree of market risk than others. Affordability also varies within a given country with, for example, fuel costs varying in the US between 3 percent of average household income in California to 10 percent in Maine, as a result of local climate, driving patterns, and heating infrastructure. Income inequalities, residential areas, and housing play a major role. The most vulnerable populations include low-wage long-distance commuters relying on fuel-inefficient cars and living in houses lacking effective insulation while often still using oil furnaces for heating.

High and volatile prices are now seen as a major energy security issue, with efforts being made to regulate oil markets and to ensure a better flow of information to them to reduce uncertainty – such as through the Joint Organizations Data Initiative (JODI). Still, energy poverty ranks low on the international energy agenda compared to supply risks and environmental impacts. Mobility probably should rank below education and food, but rural transportation can be a major factor in poverty alleviation, while oil is used for multiple purposes in poor countries, including for electricity generation. Affordable oil is therefore a critical issue for many low-income, oil-importing countries that often spend more on their oil bills than on health and education. There is thus an equity issue attached to "wasteful" patterns of oil consumption in affluent economies that drive prices up for essential services in poor countries. Energy poverty is also particularly striking among some of the communities living in and around oil fields. Despite much recent progress, about 30 percent of gas production in Nigeria was still flared by 2011, while 50 percent of the population – in a country that produces around 2.4 mmbd and is the world's twelfth largest oil producer – has no access to electricity. More broadly, the question of oil price subsidies in producing countries is politically sensitive: low or "at cost" prices reduce energy poverty in producing countries but they also reduce revenues for local authorities that could be allocated to the poor while encouraging wasteful consumption by those who are better off.[7]

Some oil-producing countries have played on this notion of affordability. Internationally, former Libyan ruler Gaddafi exported oil at cut-rate prices to allied governments in the region, such as the Central African Republic. Venezuelan President Hugo Chavez also sent "cheaper oil" to a dozen countries, including Cuba, as a foreign policy tool. Since 2005, Venezuela has provided heating oil to poor communities in the US, calling it a "humanitarian gift" after US Congress cut similar subsidies and US oil companies refused to help the "energy poor." It is domestically, however, that the largest effects are felt through low taxation and oil price subsidies.

The high consumption–low taxation trap
Heavily taxing oil may seem like an odd idea to increase energy security. Low fuel taxes do reduce a family's energy bill over the short term, but increase consumption over the long term and increase vulnerability to future price hikes. Low taxation also increases a sense of entitlement and thus resistance to higher fuel taxes. The end result is a high consumption–low taxation trap, for which the US is the first culprit and victim. By 2006, 60 percent of Americans recognized the need for a shift in energy policy, but 85 percent resisted higher fuel taxes. In the past two decades, taxes were only raised twice in the US: the Clinton administration battled Congress to obtain a four cents' increase in 1993, and Obama got a seven cents' increase in 2009, a far cry from the doubling or tripling of taxes necessary to motivate changes in consumption. Not only are fuel taxes in the US among the lowest in the world, but much fuel tax revenue is earmarked for highway expenditures, thus reinforcing road transport.

European governments, in contrast, have long imposed high fuel taxes to reduce energy dependence, improve energy efficiency, reduce trade deficits, and finance social programs. Even Norway, a major oil producer with a dispersed population, imposes one of the highest fuel tax rates in the world (see Table 4.3). By 2006, gasoline tax in Europe averaged 60 percent of the final price, compared to 20 percent in the US, the lowest among OECD countries. The US is not the only country caught in the trap. Many oil exporters sell gasoline at cost or even subsidize it, including Venezuela, Saudi Arabia, and Iran. With a gasoline price of 3 cents per liter, Venezuela in effect loses US$8 billion per year to make oil more affordable to its population. Until 2007, Iraq had maintained cheap

Table 4.3   Gasoline taxes or subsidies for selected countries

Countries	Norway	Europe	Japan	India	Russia	China	US	Saudi Arabia	Iran	Venezuela
US cents per liter	127¢	80¢	56¢	48¢	24¢	16¢	10¢	−37¢	−44¢	−50¢
Tax rate	70%	60%	51%	48%	31%	23%	16%	−70%	−83%	−94%

Source: Calculated from international theoretical price of 53 US cents per liter (incl. refining and distribution) and domestic price at the pump for 2006. Negative numbers express subsidies relative to theoretical price. GTZ International Fuel Prices Report, 2010.

gasoline prices, despite a lack of refining capacity following years of embargo and military attacks, with the government having to import and subsidize fuel at a cost of US$7 billion per year. Price hikes and subsidies removal frequently result in "fuel riots" feeding larger protest movements, as in Nigeria in 2012.[8]

Raising fuel taxes in the US remains paradoxically the most important factor in improving oil security in that country in the longer term. While price elasticity is low for oil, consumers respond more to an increase in fuel tax than to a market price hike. Had the US imposed high fuel taxes early enough – to reduce a sense of entitlement to "cheap oil" and thereby influence the choice of cars and lifestyles – the US could be now consuming half as much as it does. This would not only have saved the US about the equivalent of its trade deficit with China, but fuel taxes would have brought much needed revenues for its now near bankrupt authorities – a bankruptcy itself aggravated at the federal level by oil-related military interventions in the Persian Gulf. The politics of fuel prices and taxation are very sensitive, however, and often considered a political taboo. As long as the US was a major oil producer, low taxes on oil products were effectively a subsidy for its economy. Industrial goods could be more cheaply produced and shipped. Cheap gasoline also boosted car manufacturing, which in turn became a major economic driver. The US became a net oil importer in 1948, but oil remained cheap and no serious measures were taken until the 1970s' oil crises when fuel-efficiency standards and consumer concerns increased the average fuel economy of residential vehicles from 12.2 miles per gallon in 1977 to 21.3 in 1987. Fuel-efficiency regulations were later relaxed as oil prices deflated, leaving the US exposed to sharp price hikes in the new millennium. Even the price dip that followed the 2008–9 economic recession did not give US consumers much respite, as China largely avoided the downturn and sustained oil demand. China in the meantime is trying to prevent a US scenario, increasing taxation and pushing for low-consumption vehicles that further increase the risk of wiping out US carmakers who do not adapt. With oil prices expected to remain high and domestic production continuing to decline, the US needs to take major steps to curtail consumption, including getting out of the high consumption–low taxation trap that so few politicians seriously challenge.[9]

China's growing oil insecurity
China is the world's fifth largest oil producer, yet the growth of its oil sector dates back only to the 1960s and, unlike the US, the country has never been a major oil exporter. Domestic oil production did help the country's rapid development since the mid-1980s but the country returned to a net importer status in 1993 (see Figure 4.2). No immediate shock ensued as oil prices remained low until 2003, while China may have become even more competitive as oil price increases affected its competitors more deeply. This situation may not last, however, with consumption rising at 7 percent per year while its

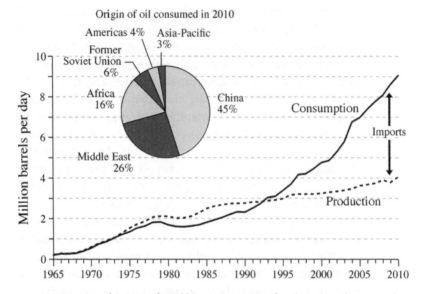

Sources: BP Statistical Review of World Energy June 2011 for Chinese production and consumption, EIA for origin of oil.

Figure 4.2 Chinese oil production and consumption (1965–2010)

domestic production is expected to reach a plateau within less than a decade. By 2010, China had become the world's second oil consumer and oil importer after the US.

Chinese companies are actively securing oil supplies through new pipelines, offshore exploration, long-term supply contracts, and overseas oil ventures. Government assistance includes preferential loans to companies, as well as diplomatic, financial, and military support for host countries. Most controversial, but not unprecedented, is the "blocking" of UN sanctions against oil-exporting governments accused of grave human rights abuses, as in the case of Sudan. Chinese companies also benefit from cheap and qualified staff, which is particularly valuable for labor-intensive projects such as pipeline construction. Chinese companies, including CNPC ("PetroChina"), were able to increase equity oil from 140 thousand barrels in 2000 to 1.4 mmbd in 2010, with plans to reach 5 mmbd by 2020, roughly a third of China's expected demand. The Chinese government's active and largely successful *oil diplomacy* is in part motivated by its own survival. The government is most attentive to energy supplies as its legitimacy rests on the assumption of rapid economic growth improving the lives of its citizens. Yet it is also well aware of the risk of overemphasizing oil supply and the commercial success of its oil companies. Energy efficiency and slowing down oil demand growth are also key priorities.

The rise in passenger vehicles presents the Chinese government with its strongest challenge. Only 80,000 cars circulated in China in 1991, but 14 million cars were sold in China in 2010 alone, and there could be 200 million cars on Chinese roads by 2020, raising demand above the government's target of a peak oil demand of 12 mmbd. China paid over US$130 billion for oil imports in 2010, not far from its foreign trade surplus of US$181 billion. Many measures are being taken by Chinese authorities to curb car-related consumption, including strict vehicle fuel efficiency regulations, higher taxation on fuel, a car licensing quota, and restricted vehicular access to business districts. China is already 10 miles per gallon (mpg) ahead of the US in terms of car-fuel efficiency and pushing for 42.2 mpg in 2015, compared to Obama's plan for 35.5 mpg by 2016. However, effective restraints on demand for cars (and miles traveled, more generally) will prove challenging in the face of rising consumerism.[10]

Acceptability

By the end of 2001, acceptability had become a prominent criterion for oil security. Climate change was high on the international agenda, the Kyoto Protocol had been signed in 1997 while record sales of SUVs exacerbated critiques of selfish consumerism. The rise of civil society organizations reaching broader audiences through the internet also helped raise awareness of social acceptability: about half of the world's oil production comes from countries listed among the bottom third performers for human rights protection. The 9/11 attacks caused much anger among US citizens against supposed oil-rich "sponsors of terrorism" in the Middle East, while millions of people opposed the US-led invasion of Iraq shouting "no blood for oil." By 2011, however, high oil prices, an economic crisis, and energy security concerns had somewhat trumped climate change and human rights.

The oil sector has responded to claims about its social and environmental performance. The case for oil's acceptability now often rests on cutting GHG emissions through carbon capture and sequestration, improving the governance and human rights records of producing countries, and claims that alternative energies represent "unrealistic" options. There is some truth to these positions and claims but also serious limits (as further discussed in chapter 7). The oil sector can live with social concerns about scarcity and peak oil: after all, it is up to the industry to demonstrate it can deliver *more* oil. Climate change, human rights abuses, and governance are much more tricky issues for the oil sector to address. They require changing practices so as to deliver *better* oil, as well as embracing a systematic reduction in demand for their products.

Making oil acceptable
Securing acceptability is a concern for oil companies seeking to expand markets, ease staff recruitment, or avoid consumer boycotts and divestment campaigns. Even national oil companies face such issues, for example when seeking to raise funds

on western financial markets, as in CNPC's attempted US$10 billion initial public offering on the New York Stock Exchange in 1999. Oil still remains a mostly anonymous commodity branded by retailers. No gas pump informs consumers where the oil is coming from and what its environmental and social impacts are. Consumer perceptions of oil are largely based on popular conceptions of geopolitics, corporate advertisement, and targeted advocacy campaigns. But even selecting a retail brand does not ensure that oil will come from that company: most oil comes from the nearest oil refinery and tanker truck filling racks.

To alter these perceptions and "secure acceptability" for their practices and products, oil companies – mostly IOCs – invest massively to improve their safety record, reduce emissions, and address governance issues. Oil majors also routinely spend hundreds of millions of dollars in the US alone to polish their image and promote gas sales. Damage control can push public relations departments into overdrive, as with BP spending about US$93 million in advertising in the four months following its 2010 *Deepwater Horizon* oil rig spill. Companies will also invest in technological innovation and investments to reduce environmental impacts and especially emissions within the industry, while some are investing in renewable energy development. Acceptability is also a concern for producing states. Equatorial Guinea spent millions of dollars on Washington, DC lobbyists to avoid its regime being portrayed as one of world's worst dictatorships. The Canadian government has invested billions of dollars into carbon-capture technologies, advertisement, and lobbying to get rid of the tar sands and "dirty oil" image that sticks to its bitumen-based synthetic crude and threatens its access to the US market. Following 9/11, favorable US public opinion toward Saudi Arabia dropped from 47 percent to 27 percent, a perception that renewed calls to shift oil imports away from the Middle East and increase energy self-sufficiency in the US. The Saudi government replied with campaigns denying its support for terrorism.

The social acceptance of oil projects by host communities in producing countries and the related reputational risks in consuming markets have become a major concern for many companies. Protests, blockades, and sabotage can undermine production, and repression by local authorities – such as the outrageous hanging of Ogoni activist Ken Saro-Wiwa by the Nigerian dictatorship in 1995 – can result in both consumer boycotts and an escalation of hostilities in production areas. Many recent campaigns seek to persuade people that oil companies care deeply about society and the environment. Corporate social responsibility (CSR) can involve significant changes in practice, although it is ultimately conditioned by corporate objectives and often cannot address broader governance and macroeconomic issues. Some oil companies have supported new standards, such as the Voluntary Principles on Security and Human Rights, to prevent abuses relating to company operations. To address more structural factors, many companies are also participating in governance reforms such as the Extractive Industries Transparency Initiative (EITI).

Acceptability will remain an important factor for some countries and consumers, especially given trends that push oil development into more challenging social and ecological contexts. Major issues include the exploitation of conventional oil in high biodiversity areas and the Arctic, and the high energy and environmental demands of extracting and upgrading unconventional oil sources like Alberta's bitumen. More broadly, the criterion of acceptability questions the role for oil (and other fossil fuels) in an energy future that must square social demands for affordable, reliable, and lower-carbon means of providing energy services.[11]

Conclusion

Securing oil, from a conventional perspective, is about ensuring supply. In this chapter, we have shown that a broader understanding is necessary to grasp the challenges ahead. Tight markets over the past decade have reinforced a supply-driven security paradigm but its singular focus occludes other dimensions of security. The changing resource base and the increasing role of higher-cost, "hard-to-reach" conventional crude and oil from "dirty" unconventional sources in global supply is diversifying the geography of oil availability (away from the Middle East) and changing established geopolitical calculations. At the same time, the extension of oil's extractive frontier has placed the acceptability of oil center stage – via concerns about human rights, water pollution, biodiversity conservation, and climate change – and challenged many oil companies' claims about their contribution to social welfare, development, and environmental sustainability. For some, supply security and concerns about affordability dictate the rapid growth of unconventional production. For others, the environmental implications of pursuing unconventional sources justify a more rapid transition out of hydrocarbons. Emerging regulation of carbon-heavy fuels (e.g. synthetic crudes from bituminous sands) by some importing markets, such as California and the European Union, is likely to lead to bifurcated markets characterized by price differentials between "clean" and "dirty" fuels. Countries producing "dirtier" fuels may seek to access and/or develop alternative markets (most likely found in countries with lax acceptability criteria and/or limited supply options) while opposing the internationalization of tighter regulation. The battle to "secure" markets for oil from Canada's tar sands is a case in point and demonstrates what is at stake as oil producers, oil consumers, and other witnesses to extraction contest the availability, accessibility, affordability, and acceptability of oil.

A second significant geopolitical shift is the relocation of demand growth away from most OECD countries to China, India, and so-called "emerging economies." Investments by these fast-growing economies to secure supply should increase the global availability of oil. At the same time, however, equity oil arrangements and upstream competition make it less accessible to OECD economies and to the traditional IOCs, while demand growth outside the OECD may also reduce oil's affordability. Higher oil prices raise the question of fair access to energy and augur growing tensions between producing and consuming countries, as well as among major oil importers. Higher prices also raise issues of macroeconomic impact (for both importers and exporters): for importing states, a significant paradox is the (so far) very limited impact of higher oil prices on China's economic growth, in contrast to the negative effects observed on already weak growth in most western countries. A third dimension is greater awareness of the need to ensure broad-based development in oil-producing countries (further discussed in chapter 5). Gains here are also likely to have positive effects on the accessibility of oil although, over the longer term, economic growth and social development will entail growing domestic consumption and thus reduced oil exports.

The geopolitics of oil, then, is rather more complex than "oil wars" scenarios suggest. We have interpreted "securing oil" not as a zero-sum game over a fixed and scarce resource, but as a broader struggle to define the role that oil will play in an energy future. We have sought to show how oil security means different things to different people: while there are some synergies among the four criteria of availability, accessibility, affordability, and acceptability, it is also clear that there are significant trade-offs. Much of the new geopolitics of oil is about defining its role with respect to bringing about more affordable energy at lower environmental costs and improving the contribution oil makes to development in producing countries. As discussed in the following chapters, reaching these seemingly contradictory objectives is a difficult, but not an impossible, task.

CHAPTER FIVE

Developing through Oil

Oil seduces those who would control it, feeding dreams of instant wealth and economic transformation. The Polish journalist Ryszard Kapuscinski once remarked how "oil creates the illusion of a completely changed life, life without work, life for free. Oil is a resource that anesthetizes thought, blurs vision, corrupts . . ." Developing through oil is an aspiration for many oil-producing countries but the reality of everyday life for many in Angola, Iraq, Iran, Libya, Kazakhstan, Nigeria, Congo, and Saudi Arabia falls far short of this goal. Turning oil wealth into broadly based social development is a massive challenge for producing countries. Oil-field development draws in very large capital investment but creates relatively few direct jobs; the revenues it generates can be vast but also highly volatile; and the wealth and opportunities it creates fall disproportionately to ruling elites and foreign corporations, despite oil being "public property." These challenges require sound long-term policies, robust and accountable governance institutions, and a diversified economy able to withstand the effects of oil wealth. Yet oil wealth can work against these requirements. It fuels short-term populist policies or unrealistic long-term plans, weakens institutions through corruption, bloated bureaucracies, and lack of accountability, and concentrates (rather than diversifies) economic activity through overvalued currency and labor-market distortions. Furthermore, most of the new oil producers are poor countries where capacities for meeting these requirements and sustainably absorbing oil wealth are limited. When oil begins to flow, it quickly dominates and distorts the economy.

The expectations associated with oil and its potential for socioeconomic and material transformation is key to understanding the politics of oil and development. Cheap oil fuels hope and desire for greater mobility, material abundance, fast economic growth, and modernization. For those who control its flow, oil provides a concentrated revenue stream without equal and a source of enormous social power. Economic development in the twentieth century owes much to the cheap and flexible energy that an expanding flow of oil has provided. But this development has come at a high price, especially for the people and environments in and around sites of extraction and refining. In many oil-producing countries, oil's promise of modernization is honored in the breach. In this chapter, we show how oil's role in development is complex and multifaceted. We try to account for the role of oil in development, who wins and who loses, and why oil-based development often proves so difficult. We then consider the development consequences of the end of the "Age of Plenty."

Accounting for oil in development

Oil's high energy density, relative abundance, and easy portability have made it a powerful enabler of economic development. From the 1920s onward, oil became widely adopted across a range of uses and economic sectors, from heating and power to transportation and plastics. Oil transformed agricultural production in a way that coal never did: in the US, for example, gasoline tractors replaced horses and manual labor, growing from barely a thousand in 1910 to over a million in 1932. Oil and gas underpinned the rollout of high-yielding, input-intensive arable crops from the 1960s onward (the "Green Revolution"), via the use of pesticides, fertilizers,

Box 5.1 The oil we eat: petroleum in the geopolitics of food production

About two billion people spend only a few hours per week to get food. Only 2 percent of the active population in the US, the world's largest net food exporter, is directly involved in food production, and US households spend around 10 percent of their income on food – among the lowest in the world. Oil and gas inputs makes food production cheap, while trucks and cars make "food gathering" easy. Such rich diets would require three weeks of production by a subsistence manual farmer for a single day of consumption, and a single food calorie requires ten calories from oil and gas. Not everyone is benefiting, however. Billions of people still spend much of their time producing food but are often outcompeted by the rich world' s dumping of agro-products subsidized in part by lower fuel taxes.

Without oil and gas, the current industrial food system is unsustainable. Replacing oil by biofuels, such as corn ethanol, mostly compounds the problem by allocating farmland to fuel rather than food production, while most biofuels have a low energy return on energy invested (EROEI) and still require high natural gas inputs.[1]

pumped irrigation, and climate-controlled storage and transportation. Freeing up people from backbreaking agricultural work, lowering food prices, and generating economic surpluses, the massive energy surpluses provided by oil have allowed both economic growth and diversification (see Box 5.1). More generally, cheap oil has enabled economies to outrun local resource depletion and achieve huge economies of scale in production and transportation (via, for example, the application of more powerful engines and motors, or cool-chain technology).

Easily transportable, petroleum products fuel generators in many poor or remote parts of the world, providing vital electricity for health care, basic infrastructures, and access to education and mass media. Oil's rich chemistry has made it the basic material of the "Plastic Age." The ease with which it can be transformed into myriad products – from lipstick and clothing to car parts and containers – has facilitated rapid increases in rates of material consumption in industrial economies since the 1950s. The global draw on oil is immense: it is equivalent to 150,000 cars filling their tanks every minute, a rate of flow two and a half times that of the River Thames. Propelling over a billion vehicles – from mopeds to jets and cargo ships – oil continues to be central to economic growth and the geographical mobility so characteristic of the modernization and globalization of economies in the twentieth century.

Low-income countries caught in colonial relationships were largely bypassed by the economic growth and broad social gains achieved in western economies through an increased dependence on oil. For many, the fruits of their independence turned bitter during the successive oil crises and recessions of the 1970s and early 1980s. Lower oil prices after 1985 were advantageous to oil-importing countries, although high levels of debt and dependency on primary commodity exports often overwhelmed potential gains for poor countries. In India and China, however, oil-fueled agricultural modernization and growing international trade have contributed to lifting hundreds of millions of people out of poverty. These periods of growth have been several times more oil intensive per unit of GDP than in already industrialized countries where economies have shifted toward services. After growing rapidly in the 1970s, the oil intensity of GDP in China has been steadily declining and is now about twice that of the US and EU. India's oil intensity peaked in the late 1990s but remains high. In absolute terms, however, oil consumption and its impacts have risen considerably as surging GDP outstripped this general decline in oil intensity.

Accounting for environmental and social costs

Oil may facilitate the lives of many (and provide extreme wealth for a few) but the production network for this versatile resource also distributes a series of social and environmental costs. Media coverage of dramatic events makes some of these costs highly visible, such as the 1.6 million barrels spilled following the wreckage of the *Amoco Cadiz* in Brittany in 1978, the 1989 *Exxon Valdez* tanker spill in Alaska, or the *Deepwater Horizon* fire and Macondo blowout in the Gulf of Mexico in 2010. So does environmental campaigning against "dirty oil" from the Alberta tar sands or "marginal oil" from Arctic drilling. But beyond these iconic cases of the "deeper, dirtier, and riskier" pursuit of oil, many of oil's social and environmental costs are hidden from view. Worker injuries, traffic accidents, respiratory infections, pesticide accumulation, plastic trash, and leaking pipelines are a chronic corollary of oil's global production network. Often occurring on a small scale, these events when aggregated together build up into large-scale consequences affecting millions.

Environmental costs
At a global scale, oil is among the largest sources of pollution. From highways and plastic bags to oil spills and carbon dioxide, the life cycle of oil products – from exploration to extraction, transportation, refining, consumption, and disposal – endangers ecosystems all over the planet. Over 3,500 rotary oil rigs are drilling for oil, and 5 million oil wells tap 30 billion barrels of oil each year from 40,000 oil fields around the world. Crude oil is then sent through 540,000 kilometers of oil pipelines and 4,500 oil tankers to about 650 refineries. These provide fuel through 600,000 gas stations to a billion motor vehicles parked or circulating on a vast extent of man-made hard surfaces. A chief source of air pollutants (such as particulates, benzene, and nitrogen oxides), oil also accounted for about 20 percent of anthropogenic CO_2 emissions in 2009.

The exploration and extraction phases of oil production

can produce seismic disruptions and large amounts of solid and liquid waste, some of which have high concentrations of toxins. Worldwide, drilling wastes may amount to 300 million barrels, while oil extraction generates about 90 billion barrels of so-called *produced water*, the saline water in the mixture of oil and water lifted from reservoirs. Nearly all produced water is reinjected into oil reservoirs, but some ends up in waste pits. Leaks from pits into streams have been a core health complaint of oil-field communities in Ecuador. Vast amounts of water are injected into reservoirs to enhance oil recovery, between 1.4 and 4.6 barrels to every barrel of oil produced in Saudi Arabia, while the extraction and upgrading of bitumen from the tar sands requires about 4 barrels of water for every barrel of synthetic crude oil. Accidental spills during drilling or lifting oil to the surface can have massive consequences, especially at offshore sites where well plugging and relief well drilling are complicated. The explosion of Pemex's exploratory well *Ixtoc I* in June 1979 spilled 3.3 million barrels into the Gulf of Mexico. Two decades later, the explosion on BP's *Deepwater Horizon* platform, also in the Gulf of Mexico, resulted in the deaths of 11 workers and a spill estimated at 5 million barrels between April and July 2010. Intentional spills from Kuwaiti oil terminals and tankers by Iraqi forces during the 1991 Gulf War provoked the largest oil spill in history with estimates ranging from 4 to 11 million barrels. Iraqi forces also set approximately 600 oil wells on fire as the Allied air offensive began. Around 5 million barrels of oil burned each day at the height of the crisis (8 per cent of world production at the time). The last oil well on fire was capped on November 1991, nine months after being set on fire by Iraqi troops.

Transport-related impacts affect mostly coastal and riparian communities along tanker and pipeline routes. The Persian Gulf is the geographical area most affected by major tanker accidents, two-thirds of which were the result of Iraq–Iran hostilities. The second most affected area is the Atlantic coast of Europe and especially the entrance to the English Channel with major spills in Brittany and Cornwall since 1967 (the *Torrey Canyon*, the world's first supertanker accident). There is mounting concern over the potential impacts from accidents in the north Pacific and Arctic sea-lanes for moving oil to East Asia. Coastal ecosystems and communities are the most affected, with fishing and tourism-based communities waiting years, if not decades, to be often inadequately compensated. Exxon declared having spent US$4.3 billion as a result of the 1989 *Exxon Valdez* spill in Alaska, which included about US$2.1 billion in clean-up costs and US$900 million in a civil settlement, but appealed some compensatory and punitive damages for nearly two decades. Tanker and production accidents make headline news but they account for only a fifth of the total volume of spills, the rest coming in part from illegal bilge and operational discharges. Other marine pollution includes plastics – which constitute about 90 percent of all rubbish adrift on oceans, contributing to "dead zones" such as in the massive Pacific Gyre – and noise pollution associated with seismic exploration.

Land-based pollution results from pipeline ruptures and spills. About 2.5 million barrels spilled from 5,000 pipeline incidents in the US between 1991 and 2010. Extensive networks of aging pipelines linking small and widely scattered fields to oil terminals are particularly prone to spills, and chronic occurrences can build into very significant volumes over the years. An average of 800 spills per year was reported in Nigeria between 2006 and 2009, and up to 13 million barrels of oil may have been spilled in the Niger Delta since oil exploitation started in 1958. There is much controversy over the relative importance of causes, including pipeline corrosion, poor maintenance, and operational mistakes versus oil theft and sabotage. The oil pollution of creeks and acid rain from gas flaring have had devastating impacts on the health and livelihoods of local communities.

Pipelines are often routed through low-income communities that have limited access to economic and political power, especially in urban settings such as Los Angeles. Construction itself is frequently marred by criticisms of inadequate compensation of land users, heavy-handed evictions, and, in some cases, human rights abuses. Construction of the Chad–Cameroon pipeline sought to set a new standard with the most sophisticated efforts to date to avoid such problems in low-income countries (see chapter 7), but dissatisfaction has remained among many affected communities while broader concern for human rights abuses in Chad persists.

The environmental risks associated with upstream activities are increasing. Environmental regulation and scientific knowledge and monitoring are greater than ever, but oil companies are increasingly seeking to develop reserves in locations that are technologically complex and environmentally challenging. Many of the remaining significant reserves of conventional oil lie in the ultra-deep water offshore and in the Arctic, while accessing the substantial known reserves of unconventional oil – such as in Canada or Venezuela – requires wholesale landscape transformation through open mining or vast amounts of energy to liquefy and extract bitumen or ultra-heavy crude in situ. Likewise, alternative liquid fuels – such as biodiesel and ethanol production – are associated with deforestation and the development of biomass plantations.[2]

The last two stages of the oil life cycle also distribute environmental and health impacts in ways that are highly uneven. Refineries mostly affect the health of local communities, again often low-income marginalized populations, with higher reported rates of leukemia and cancer, as well as psychosocial reactions to perceived or actual emissions. Oil consumption results in localized air and water pollution, as well as the emission and accumulation of greenhouse gases, while car travel demands massive infrastructure and can negatively affect the health of users and bystanders. In the US, 6.3 million kilometers of paved roads, which along with car parks for about 215 million cars cover around 16 million hectares, compete with other land uses including agriculture – itself increasingly directed at biofuel production. Cars themselves consume vast amounts of raw materials, the production and disposal of which have environmental impacts. Air and water pollution mostly concentrate in areas of use, with many urban areas – particularly in rapidly growing cities of the global South – turning into cesspools of toxic chemicals. GHG emissions have a global reach, although their effects on local and regional climates are highly differentiated. Whereas the benefits of oil consumption (car ownership, low-cost travel) accrue mainly to the richest fifth of the world's population, it is the poorest who are expected to experience the most serious consequences of climate change, including urban poor and rural populations in drought-prone regions.

Social costs
The people most directly exposed to the oil production network are oil workers and the local communities that host oil infrastructure. A dozen major accidents have occurred with oil platforms since 1980, taking the lives of 623 people. Oil refinery workers show higher levels of occupational cancer hazard. The most exposed communities are those in poorly regulated production areas. Oil exploration often involves accessing ecosystems in remote locations, resulting in disproportionate impacts on indigenous communities, with at least seventy indigenous groups currently affected around the world. Environmental and social impacts resulting from oil sector activities include deforestation, road building, and

Box 5.2 Swapping "oil for nature" in Ecuador

The Yasuni–ITT initiative in Ecuador seeks to forgo the development and production of oil in part of the Ecuadorian Amazon in exchange for international funding equivalent to about half their value. The estimated reserve of 900 million barrels of heavy crude oil amounts to about 20 percent of Ecuadorian proven oil reserves, and ten days of world consumption. Proposed in 2007 by Ecuadorian President Correa as a larger policy shift away from oil export dependence, the initiative received some support from several European governments, and may interest carbon offset markets. This is one of the first attempts by a so-called "petro-state" to become an "eco-state" through carbon emission reduction financing that associates biodiversity conservation with indigenous rights.

the arrival of migrant oil workers. Impacts extend beyond the oil sector itself as, for example, road construction can facilitate land colonization by settlers. Although "opening" land for development can help reduce poverty and is often promoted by national authorities, colonization can have strong negative impacts on indigenous communities. Communities located near transportation and refining infrastructures are also disproportionally affected, many of these being low-income minority populations.[3]

Oil usage also creates risks within the more familiar, everyday environments of industrial economies. About 1.3 million people die in traffic accidents every year while up to 50 million more are injured, mostly pedestrians and cyclists run over by cars in developing countries. The World Health Organization (WHO) reports that traffic accidents are now the world's leading cause of death among youth between 5 and 29 years of age, while a 2005 WHO study suggested that more premature deaths could result from car exhaust than traffic accidents in Europe. Kerosene lamps provide another example of the large social costs of oil-fueled technologies. A source of light for more than a billion people, kerosene lamps are also polluting, dangerous, and inefficient, causing burn injuries and respiratory diseases affecting millions and demonstrating the importance of moving up the "energy ladder" toward safer (and more affordable) fuels. Indirectly, oil-fueled mechanized warfare since the First World War has made armed conflicts more devastating, especially through civilian deaths by aerial bombing and the far-flung deployment of armed forces. Arguably, many lives are also saved thanks to rapid transportation to hospital and the medical progress and equipment that oil has made possible, not to mention increased food production. Yet deaths, injuries, and disease are part and parcel of the worlds made through oil and should not be ignored. They highlight the central role oil plays in the development of livelihoods and how, in ways not often imagined, oil now sets the conditions for the possibility of life. As such, they point the way to an alternative perspective on the "true costs" of oil and a politics of oil that addresses both the "goods" and "bads" that oil can create.[4]

Oil revenues: who gets what?

Every year, between three and five trillion US dollars change hands along the oil "value chain." About two-thirds of this money ends up with governments in oil-exporting and importing countries in the form of taxes, while much of the rest goes to some of the world's largest companies as profits. Oil is one of the largest revenue transfer schemes in the world: revenue is transferred from consumers' pockets to governments and corporations, and from consuming countries to oil-exporting countries. The question "who gets what?" matters because oil's production network generates striking inequalities, both between and within countries. On the consumption side, the US accounts for only 4.5 percent of the world's population, but consumes about a quarter of world oil supplies and a third of road transportation fuel, and while consumers complain of high prices at the pump, these prices do not (yet) reflect the full social and environmental costs of oil. On the production side, whereas oil enriches some of the world's wealthiest people, it is often extracted from under the feet of the poorest. The wealth of Nigerian elites and the misery of Niger Delta populations exemplify this pattern, but it is repeated to various degrees across the world. In Angola, China, Ecuador, Iran, Iraq, and Saudi Arabia, oil is pumped in areas inhabited by often underprivileged minority populations. Very little of the oil industry's profits have so far been spent mitigating the negative impacts of oil and helping to transition from an oil economy. Instead, they have been plowed backed into the industry or dispersed to shareholders.

Distribution of oil revenues
Every day, consumers worldwide spend about US$11 billion on oil products. Oil provides many different services, but for many consumers the gas station is where the politics of revenue distribution come alive. Because gas stations are on the frontline of oil price awareness, a few display information showing that they make only a few cents of profit on every dollar in sales. Such seemingly petty earnings contrast with news headlines of massive profits among oil companies, with Exxon Mobil earning US$45.2 billion in 2008 – the biggest annual corporate profit in US history. Such profits, in turn, pale in comparison with the earnings of governments in the main producing countries, such as the $262 billion collected that year by the Saudi central government on oil exports. Oil-producer governments capture on average 70% of the net revenues from oil production, varying from 40% in the US to 95% in Iran. Many governments in importing countries, and especially in Europe, also heavily tax oil products. Governments in the European Union get about 10% of their national tax income from fuel taxes, or about US$252 billion in 2009. French drivers often compare their car to a cash cow:

Table 5.1	Distribution of cash flow from oil sector			
	Percentage	US$ per barrel	US$ per gallon	US$ per liter
Finding costs	5%	11	0.26	0.07
Lifting costs	2%	5	0.12	0.03
Production taxation	33%	70	1.67	0.44
Production company profits	7%	14	0.33	0.09
Transportation costs	1%	3	0.07	0.02
Refining costs	7%	14	0.33	0.09
Retailing costs	3%	6	0.14	0.04
Consumption taxation	40%	84	2.00	0.53
Refining and retailing company profits	2%	4	0.10	0.03
Total	100%	211	5.02	1.33

Sources: EIA and IEA, based on US$100 per barrel and global average gasoline price; field development capital expenditures included in finding costs.

taxes can account for as much as 80% of the retail price of petrol when oil crude prices are low.[5]

To answer "who gets what" from oil revenues, we break down the oil value chain into its different components (see Table 5.1). Oil production and refining costs are relatively fixed, amounting to about a dollar per gallon of gasoline. The remainder consists of government taxes and corporate profits, which vary considerably. Using a crude oil price of US$100 per barrel and average world price of gasoline of US$5.02 per gallon, costs amount to 20% of the final value, producer governments earn 33%, consumer governments 40%, and companies 7%. This distribution of revenues from end-product sales reflects the relative power of governments, oil companies, and consumers. Producer governments justify their claim through resource ownership of a depleting nonrenewable asset, as well as compensation for damages in the case of local landowners and communities. Consumer

governments point to the costs of road infrastructure, traffic accidents, and pollution. Oil companies see themselves
as the rightful producers of the resource. Finally, consumers
supposedly decide if oil is to be extracted, but most are price
takers, in the sense that they have a limited capacity for influencing the price of oil, hooked on lifestyles and locked into
infrastructures that demand a strong will and some sacrifices
to opt out of.

This assessment provides only a general snapshot, and
there is considerable variation among producing and consuming countries, different oil companies, and types of oil. The
oil industry also benefits from large subsidies and tax exemp-
tions, amounting to about US$4 billion in the US. Overall,
consumer governments control the largest share of oil revenues, but in effect they simply channel consumer spending
through public budgets, rather than create new wealth. It is
producer governments that gain the most from the oil sector,
a "petrodollar" wealth from which development is supposed
to flow (see Box 5.3).[6]

Wealthy producers?
Volume and price are not the only determinants of "who
gets what" among oil producers. Contractual arrangements,
as discussed in chapter 2, matter a great deal to determine
the share of operational revenues obtained by producer governments. This percentage of tax revenue relative to total
revenue – the rent or "government take" – reflects in part
the geological potential, costs of production, and risks taken
by oil companies. As a consequence, "government take" is
not easily comparable between countries or even between
contracts. Yet some governments (and their populations) do
better than others, with Norway, for example, capturing 75
percent of total revenue compared to 30 percent for the UK
(see Table 5.2).

Box 5.3 Petrodollars

Producer governments have long received oil revenues, but until the late 1960s this income was relatively small, due to the dominance of western companies in revenue distribution. Petrodollars were ironically born out of the context of US dollar devaluations in 1971 and 1973 that led OPEC to attempt a shift to a basket of currencies; but the 1973 oil embargo unintentionally reinforced dollar-denominated oil trading. Reacting to the huge new flow of dollars collected by oil-producing governments, US Secretary of State Kissinger vowed "to return extorted funds to our economy." To do so, the US government and lending agencies pushed petro-states to buy US-dollar denominated assets and invest in US services and infrastructures. This set a development model geared toward modernization dependent on US technologies and financial products, and ultimately on the value of the dollar itself.

Petrodollars were also recycled through US banks to low-income countries in the form of loans, tied in part as well to the provision of (overinflated and often inadequate) US goods and services – with loan pushers, or "economic hit men" as popularized in John Perkins's non-fiction book, being active in both oil-exporting and low-income countries.[7] This model of development resulted in some social benefits, but it frequently yielded massive debt overhangs and a growing gap between an oil-related elite and the rest of society.

The current oil boom is also seeing much financial recycling, although the US now channels only about a quarter of that wealth compared to three-quarters in the 1970s. Iran already trades oil in euros, and Saudi Arabia is the only OPEC member staunchly defending the status quo of dollar-based oil trading over a basket of currencies, even if most countries also hold much of their reserves in dollars. Standing as an exception, Iraq was forced into a major petrodollar recycling scheme under US occupation through largely wasteful "reconstruction" schemes.[8]

Politics, ideology, and negotiation skills also affect revenue distribution between companies and governments. Foreign governments and oil companies have toppled regimes undermining their oil interests, as in Iran, while producing governments have nationalized foreign oil ventures. Some governments are able to grow their participation and capture of revenues from the sector for long-term benefits, while others negotiate bad deals, occasionally for corrupt purposes. Short-term horizons, such as the reimbursement of massive debts or the payment of civil servants' salary arrears, can

Table 5.2	Government "take" from oil revenues		
Country	Government take (%)	Country and US reserve type	Government take (%)
Iran	93–96	Azerbaijan	68–72
Venezuela	89–91	Angola	66–71
Libya	73–89	US Onshore	51–53
Nigeria	78–83	US Shallow offshore	48–51
Norway	73–76	US Deep offshore	37–41
Russia	69–72	UK	30–32

Sources: US Government Accountability Office, "Oil and Gas Royalties," May 2007; Daniel Johnston "Higher Prices, Lower Government Take?" *Petroleum Accounting and Financial Management Journal* (2004).

motivate large up-front "signature bonuses" to be paid at the time a contract is awarded at the expense of future revenue flows. Government take tends to be higher in producing countries with a strong national oil industry, such as Iran and Venezuela. Yet such high shares can be deceptive, hiding inefficiencies and declining production, as well as cross-subsidies such as domestic oil consumption.

Government revenues should not be confused with the flow of benefits to citizens. As wryly noted by Human Rights Watch's Arvind Ganesan, "The government's 'take' is not necessarily the public's 'take'. It may *just* be the government's take." Oil revenues can reach people through public goods and tax rebates, but also through direct cash payments and pension funds. Very few governments directly distribute oil revenues to its citizens, a pioneer being Alaska which has handed annual payments averaging about US$1,500 to every resident since 1982. If implemented across all mineral-producing countries, cash transfers could halve the number of people living on incomes of less than US$1 per day. Yet most countries prefer to use other means of distributing oil revenues. Many authorities such as Alberta's provincial government prefer to slash taxes, a popular policy that has helped keep the same party in power for 40 years, even if low taxes and lack of oil savings has put the government in debt during oil downturns. Aware that oil is running out and seeking intergenerational equity, Norway directs its oil revenues to a national pension fund, while maintaining heavy taxes and generous public services. Norway now stands as a model for escaping the "oil curse," though it benefited from favorable initial institutional and economic conditions compared to most other oil-producing countries.

The "oil curse"

"The US should take our oil, yes take it all, and then leave us alone. We'll be better without it."
Baghdad resident, *Iraq in Fragments*, 2006

One of the tragic paradoxes of oil wealth is recurring misery. Many oil-rich countries face large economic shocks and distortions, remain under authoritarian governance, and suffer from armed conflicts. As a result, social indicators and economic performances in oil-producing countries are often below those expected from their level of income and resource endowment. Many oil-producing countries rank well below their GDP per capita ranking in terms of the Human Development Index (HDI), the worst case being Equatorial Guinea with a rank of fiftieth for GDP per capita compared to 117th for HDI in 2010. That Equatorial Guinea only became an oil producer in the mid-1990s could explain such a discrepancy, but many other factors are at work to explain what political scientist Terry Karl calls the "paradox of plenty."[9]

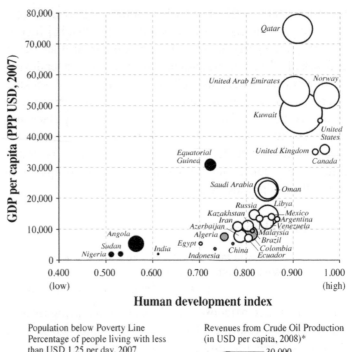

Source: Revue internationale de politique de développement, data from BP, UNDP, and WB.

Figure 5.1 GDP, HDI, and poverty levels among oil producers

Debt overhang and Dutch disease

Two of the most important economic problems facing oil-producing countries are oil-revenue volatility and impediments to economic diversification. Price volatility and fluctuations in production result in massive budgetary problems for governments and shocks to the economy. The risk is high of overspending during boom times, with governments turning to loans during bust times in the hope of better days. Most oil-producing governments ended up heavily indebted after the fall of oil prices in the mid-1980s. Some producing countries are now more cautious despite widespread belief that prices will stay high, if volatile, over the next couple of decades.

Oil revenues also tend to result in massive economic distortions that can increase oil dependence over time. Whereas oil windfalls provide capital to help accelerate industrialization, modernize agriculture, and diversify the economy, large oil revenues tend to undermine other productive economic sectors through local currency appreciation and cheap imports. This "Dutch disease" was named after the negative impact of North Sea natural gas development on the Netherlands' industrial and agricultural sectors in the 1970s. The impact on the structure of the economy is compounded by lower opportunities for participation of women in the labor market. Oil windfalls should also help relieve poverty, but in the worst cases both poverty and inequalities rise over the long term. For example, although oil revenues increased from the 1980s to the 1990s, the percentage of Nigerians living on less than a dollar a day increased from less than a third to 70 percent over the same time period. Poverty results, in part, from the "crowding-out effect," as the oil sector encroaches on other sectors that would employ many more people than oil, and encourages economically inefficient investments (such as uncompetitive industries, prestige spending, and "white elephants"). Greater poverty and inequalities also result from the concentration of oil revenue flows into a few hands, essentially politicians' pockets and corporate coffers. That these revenues are generated from a handful of state or foreign companies, rather than via taxation of the general population and a diversity of business sectors, facilitates secrecy and discretionary spending while reducing government accountability.

Governance, grievances, and corruption

Oil wealth can have a number of negative impacts on the quality of governance in oil-producing countries. The first is its potential for enabling authoritarian forms of governance and foreign interference. Simply put, oil wealth provides rulers greater autonomy from civil society and exacerbates foreign commercial and strategic interests. A population may be better off materially under authoritarian rule and with foreign oil companies, compared to a dysfunctional democracy or mismanaged national oil company. Yet, without transparency and accountability around oil revenues and budgetary expenditures, the risk is high that authoritarian rulers and foreign companies will abuse their position. Popular revolutions or oil industry nationalizations are rarely effective solutions: popular uprisings have often given way to renewed authoritarianism (Iran), sometimes aggravated by recurring *coup d'états* as armed forces take on a greater governing role (Nigeria). Nationalizations have also been followed by punishing treatment from foreign oil companies and their powerful home governments, including the use of oil export embargoes (Mexico), or military interference (Iran). Some national oil companies have also lacked technical expertise to run efficiently, or become so close to a corrupt government as to become slush fund providers.

Price volatility also exacerbates governance problems. Domestically, low prices increase general grievances among the population, while during periods of high prices populations may voice demands for the state to take a greater control and/or share of oil revenues. Regionally, low prices may entice producer-country governments to divert public attention from falling revenues through war or seek resources through military conquest, while high prices may result in a combination of increased military capacity and a greater appetite for military interventionism. Internationally, low prices create few incentives among importing countries to maintain stability in oil-producing countries for the sake of affordable oil, while high prices may result in oil consumers opposing political and military support for wealthy regimes. In turn, political instability and hostilities taking place in oil-producing countries, especially major exporters, influence price movements.

The oil boom of the 1970s brought massive increases in fiscal earnings for producing countries through nationalizations, contract renegotiations, and rising oil prices. Greater financial strength and autonomy, however, created many challenges as fast-growing, overstretched, and sometimes fledgling bureaucracies faced new or increased expectations from the population and ruling elites. With the collapse of oil prices in the 1980s, states became doubly weakened. Financially, petro-states faced massive indebtedness – a "debt overhang" that resulted in part from the overoptimism and fast growth of the boom period. Bureaucratically, petro-states faced new challenges of underfunding and accompanying structural adjustments.

The mismanagement of the boom and bust cycle of the 1970s–1990s had major geopolitical dimensions and consequences. It contributed to the collapse of the Soviet Union as a drastic fall in oil revenues after the mid-1980s precipitated the need for reforms and undermined their implementation. It drove Iraq to first invade Iran in 1980 when wealthy, and then Kuwait in 1990 when broke. And it contributed to a growth collapse and deepening cycle of corruption, resistance, and repression in countries such as Algeria and Nigeria. As the oil price went down to an all-time low of US$9 per barrel in December 1998, anxiety built up that cash-starved oil exporters facing restive populations would descend into civil war if the glut in the oil markets continued. Eurasian and some of the Persian Gulf countries were the most at risk.[10]

Saudi Arabia raised the most concern, as unemployment

grew and dissent became more vocal, notably among the Shi'ite minority residing in the Eastern Province, the richest oil area of the country. By 2000, even Saudi Arabia had accumulated a national debt of US$36 billion, while its GDP per capita plummeted from US$35,000 in 1980 to stagnate at around US$20,000 since the mid-1980s. In common with other oil-dependent countries, low oil revenues exacerbated domestic grievances and tensions, particularly against national governments perceived to be unable to harness oil wealth for the benefit of people. When Saudi dissidents struck at the World Trade Center in September 2001, much of Saudi Arabia's population had been experiencing economic decline. As in other countries, oil revenues incited radical opposition and divisive identity politics even amongst the elite. Chief among these was Osama bin Laden, who in 1995 publicly blamed Saudi King Fahd and his "elite circle" for their "wastefulness" in building palaces and the poor state of the economy. Bin Laden also denounced King Fahd's financial backing of former ally Saddam Hussein, the lowering of oil prices "to harm Iran during the war with Saddam" and to serve western interests, useless and corrupt spending on inadequate military equipment and the payment of the coalition's bill for the Gulf War, and the "lack of serious action to find other sources for income." He denounced the US–Saudi agreement on low oil prices during the 1990s as "the greatest theft in history", estimating an annual loss of US$1,200 for every Muslim in oil-exporting Islamic countries. Oil prices fell by US$13 dollars in the days following bin Laden's execution by a US commando in Pakistan in 2011.

Corruption is a major problem in many oil-producing countries, generally resulting from the volume and concentration of revenues, the discretionary power of authoritarian elites, the relative absence of businesses and civil society organizations financially independent from oil rents, and the collusion

of some international banks. Corruption and misguided policies in Nigeria mean that more than half the population lives
on less than US$1.25 per day, despite oil government revenues
of about US$500 billion since the end of the Biafran War in
1970. The late Nigerian President Abacha and his family and
collaborators embezzled between US$2.3 and 5 billion over a
four-year rule, with the assistance of at least 23 banks, many
from Switzerland and the UK; about US$1.2 billion was later
recovered by the Nigerian government.

Corruption and its redistribution through political patronage is sometimes perceived to "keep the peace" through
handouts to vocal opposition groups. There is often a tension,
however, between local political and corporate elites capturing
the share of oil revenues and local communities who see few
benefits, especially in production areas where the gap between
commitments by authorities to reward and compensate local
populations and what they actually receive is wide – as docu-
mented for the Niger Delta, the Angolan enclave of Cabinda,
or Western Siberia. More broadly, tensions frequently run
high between the central government and communities in
oil-producing regions who perceive themselves as the rightful
owners of the oil, leading in turn to the rest of the population
resenting unequal treatment.

The risk is that high and volatile prices will exacerbate
tensions both within countries over the redistribution of oil
revenues, and internationally between importing and exporting countries. Higher prices should nevertheless benefit
poor countries that experience protracted periods of conflict, such as Angola and Sudan, through both economic
recovery and greater political stability. Much will depend,
however, on the quality of domestic governance and the
legitimacy that governments gain through wealth redistribution. Efforts to improve governance and thus reduce the risk
of corruption have so far focused on revenue transparency

Box 5.4 Oil revenue transparency

Calls for greater transparency in oil revenues emerged in the late 1990s as part of an anticorruption advocacy campaign launched by British NGO Global Witness and international financier George Soros demanding that oil companies "publish what they pay" to governments. Motivated notably by BP's stakes in Angola and the Caspian, British Prime Minister Tony Blair launched in 2002 the Extractive Industries Transparency Initiative (EITI), a voluntary process whereby governments agree to minimal criteria of revenue transparency in order to participate and gain compliance status. The criteria require extractive companies (including state companies) to publish their payments to governments, governments to publish what they receive in revenue from companies, and an independent audit reconciling the payments and revenues to note any discrepancies. In addition, the initiative requires the active participation of civil society in the design, monitoring, and evaluation of the audits. By March 2011, the EITI had validated eleven countries, and 24 other countries were working toward compliance validation. Several countries long targeted by the initiative, including Angola (which motivated Global Witness to launch transparency initiatives in the first place), are still not participating in the initiative but new mandatory legislations are also pushing the transparency agenda, such as the US Dodd–Frank Wall Street Reform and Consumer Protection Act which mandates the US Securities and Exchange Commission to require disclosure of payments to governments by publicly listed oil companies. More broadly, there is also growing momentum to require *contract* transparency, which will assist civil society and parliamentarians to assess whether a country is getting a "fair deal" and check if payments match agreed terms.

and accountability, including the Extractive Industries Transparency Initiative (see Box 5.4), and the more rigorous application of legislation such as the US Foreign Corrupt Practices Act (see chapter 7).

Although many oil-producing countries suffer from poor governance, including corruption, it is important to note that many governments (and individual officials) are attentive to reducing extreme poverty in order to avoid grievances and conflicts. They are less attentive to the inequalities which can be rife but frequently "invisible" because of an absence of official statistics (as for many Persian Gulf countries), or hard to detect by usual survey methods due to the extreme concentration of wealth. Governments may seek to prevent local

Table 5.3	Secessionist conflicts in oil-producing countries
Country	*Region and duration*
Angola	Cabinda (1975–2002)
China	Xinjiang (1991–ongoing)
Indonesia	Aceh (1975–2005)
Iran	Kurdistan (1966–ongoing), Arabistan (1979–80)
Iraq	Kurdistan (1961–2003)
Nigeria	Biafra/Niger Delta (1967–1970, 2004–ongoing)
Sudan	South Sudan (1983–2005)
Yemen	South Yemen (1994)

grievances and preempt a secessionist struggle by granting local populations some autonomy and revenue compensation. Nonetheless, many countries have experienced secessionist struggles in oil-rich regions (see Table 5.3), while high debts, declining oil prices, and demands for democratization have set the context for civil wars, as in the case of the Republic of Congo in the mid-1990s.[11]

Conclusion

The growing availability of cheap oil since the beginning of the twentieth century boosted economic growth for those economies that could command it. In the United States, oil first revolutionized the conditions of agricultural and industrial production in the early decades of the century, and then transformed the conditions of consumption in the immediate post-Second World War years. Cheap oil was at the heart, therefore, of a modernizing economic development model. If oil has been replaced by gas and electricity in some heating and power applications, its role in transportation and manufacturing remains central to the contemporary consumerist, trade-based model of development. For both oil-exporting and importing countries, the price of oil continues to be a critical influence on rates of economic growth.

Oil poses major development challenges for oil producers, both economically and politically. As discussed in greater detail in chapter 6, sound policies and robust institutions can help alleviate these problems. Norway has avoided some of these problems by investing oil revenues into a public pension, worth half a trillion dollars in 2010, knowing that its population was aging and that oil windfalls would distort its advanced but relatively small economy. But many poor countries cannot afford to follow this "savings" approach, given the dire needs of their population. Governments must be attentive to buffering economic shocks but also invest wisely to reduce poverty, promote long-term growth, and ensure the sustained affordability of public expenditures. The catch is that oil dependence tends to foster and sustain authoritarian regimes relying on a mix of populist welfare policies, repression, and foreign support. These problems are generally exacerbated in low-income countries with high oil dependence but relatively low oil abundance generating small per capita oil revenues. Low-income oil-importing countries also face oil-related development issues resulting from high oil prices and petrodollar recycling.

The strategies mentioned above are for the short term only, given that tighter oil supplies and rising prices will change the political economic landscape significantly within the next few decades. Two major issues arise in such a context. First is the short-term issue of oil's affordability and growing price volatility. Much of the domestic and international politics of oil revolves around the way energy markets and the geopolitical strategies of oil-exporting countries can exacerbate economic crises. "Oil shocks" are often blamed for these crises, though their origins often do not lie in the policies of oil-exporting countries but in the unsustainable fiscal and trade deficits of major importers. The 1973 oil crisis, for example, can be traced back to the end of the convertibility of the dollar to gold in 1971, itself the result of US inflationary deficit spending partly associated with the Vietnam War. The rise in oil prices from US$20 to over US$140 per barrel between 2000 and 2008 underpinned the fundamentals of tighter supplies in the face of fast-growing demand. But it was also linked to mounting US debt, US dollar devaluation, and the wars in Afghanistan and Iraq. Betting on sustained Chinese growth and seeking shelter from a depreciating US dollar, financial markets invested massively into primary commodities, including oil, thereby further increasing prices and volatility. Oil exporters saw major revenue windfalls resulting from these two crises. However, history indicates that the ability to turn such windfalls into longer-term development gains is mixed.

The second issue relates to the longer-term prospects of oil availability. As further discussed in chapter 6, oil may need to be reserved for economic sectors where it is hard to substitute by placing, for example, a much higher value on the chemical diversity of hydrocarbons than on their combustible properties: burning the essential building blocks of chemical engineering may one day seem as short-sighted as clearing tropical forests rather than harnessing their biodiversity. Pricing can help address such sector prioritization, and the ethical issues surrounding the allocation of oil, by moderating the tendency for consumption (and CO_2 emissions) to rise as a result of low prices. Governing oil for development is also about increasing the affordability of fuel where it can play a critical role in poverty alleviation, such as poor populations in rural areas.

Oil-fueled development now faces the dual challenge of rising oil prices and climate change, both of which call for an alternative to hydrocarbon-fueled growth. The underperformance of many oil-exporting countries in the wake of the 1970s' oil boom also points to the challenge of securing development from this extractive sector. The picture of rising oil prices, climate change, and the "oil curse" need not lead to fatalism, however. The oil intensity of growth is decreasing in many economies, there is growing awareness about climate change, and international policies are finally seeking to address the "resource curse" on a more systematic level. For optimists, oil helped build the modern economies from which smart energy alternatives are beginning to emerge. For pessimists, the end of oil will force industrial countries to restructure their economies and require emerging countries to blaze alternative developmental paths that respond to new energy constraints. As we discuss in the following two chapters, a number of institutions and initiatives can help ease this transition and ensure that developing beyond oil does not sharpen inequalities and aggravate environmental impacts.

CHAPTER SIX

Governing Oil

Oil is still a fuel without equal, yet its dominance is assailed from every quarter. More oil is being produced, refined, and sold than ever before but the rules of the game are changing. First, growth in conventional oil production has stalled, and the iconic firms of Big Oil have steadied their reserves only by moving heavily into either gas and/or nonconventional oil. New production is coming increasingly from lower-quality reserves, in more technically demanding environments, and from settings which present complex social and political dynamics. In the face of rising energy demand and competition within the sector, both companies and governments are now more concerned about security of supply. Second, high prices and record industry profits have made the fuel unpopular, even if changes in price also in part reflect rising production costs. Third, the performance of the oil industry on broad social grounds is increasingly scrutinized as concerns are raised about working conditions, corruption, speculation, and the contribution of extraction to development, democracy, and social justice. The oil sector, then, is feeling the pressure, as it responds to a growing diversity of demands and stakeholders. Many consumers loathe the idea of their gas money ending up in the coffers of corrupt and oppressive oil-funded regimes, or paying for troops to either support or bring down these regimes. Local populations and advocacy organizations, meanwhile, are increasingly demanding change and calling the industry to account. Finally, the oil sector has become increasingly implicated in climate change. Oil companies have been called upon to account for the GHG emissions associated with producing, refining, and transporting oil for some time: more recently, some NGOs have begun to argue that companies also bear responsibility for the "ultimate downstream" or backstream – the fate of the carbon dioxide and other pollutants produced by fuel combustion.

The implications of this pressure, however, are unclear. There is no consensus on whether oil's primacy will be lost, at what speed this might happen, what the consequences may be for producing and consuming countries as well as, more broadly, for geopolitics and the global economy. In the most cataclysmic accounts, major consuming countries will fight over the last reserves while experiencing domestic economic upheaval and social unrest. Meanwhile, exporting countries facing depletion may experience the decline (if not collapse) of their economies, while the few remaining major producers will seek to assert their autonomy in the face of mounting foreign interference. Under less cataclysmic scenarios, demand reduction and fuel switching will draw oil's "Age of Plenty" to a close. The most environmental and socially contentious oil projects will be dropped, a new post-carbon economy will renew prosperity, and the geopolitical significance of oil-rich regions such as the Persian Gulf will slowly decline and potentially remove a major source of international tension. Business-as-usual scenarios predict that technological progress and commercial incentives will sustain a long undulating plateau of relatively constant oil production until the end of the twenty-first century, with unconventional sources of oil taking a larger role. In the context of uncertainty over the future of oil, this chapter sets out to explain how oil can be governed.

At the moment, the governance of oil – by which we mean the set of rules and organizations that guide how decisions over oil are made and the inclusion (or exclusion) of different stakeholders in those processes – is fragmented and incoherent, consisting mostly of a patchwork of organizations with mandates focusing on the vested interests of their members. Furthermore, the prevailing institutions and mechanisms for governing oil are ill matched to the new challenges at hand. Some hoary challenges of governance endure – such as matching oil supply and demand (the focus of both OPEC and the IEA) – but such concerns are now surrounded by a host of others that define the "new geopolitics" of oil (as we discuss in chapter 7). The goal of governance now should be to shape the future of oil in ways that reduce price volatility, improve oil's contribution to development in producing countries, and ensure transition to a more diverse and less harmful energy system.

Most governments consider oil to be a strategic commodity, one that links economic development and national security like no other – even if oil is paradoxically one of the most abundant and freely traded resources. Many governments are highly dependent on oil revenues, whether through export revenues or fuel taxes, and wary of popular reactions to oil price volatility. With some of the largest corporations in the world, the three trillion-dollar oil industry can influence both oil-fueled dictatorial regimes and money-driven electoral democracies. Consumers have a sense of entitlement about oil, and see little way out of their "addiction." So how to govern oil rather than be governed by it?

Addressing the oil governance deficit

Oil governance institutions are thinly developed at the international level, particularly so given the size of oil trade and the diversity, importance, and rapid evolution of issues associated with the oil sector. We argue here that the current

Table 6.1	Main positions on oil governance
Categories	*Main perspectives and policy positions*
Interventionists	Access to oil is strategic and requires unilateral interventions, including support for local regimes (even if authoritarian as long as allied) and hardened supply security infrastructure
Isolationists	Dependence on foreign oil is costly and can only be resolved through energy independence (even at the cost of greater environmental impacts)
Liberals	There is no oil curse and market mechanisms can address oil shortages and climate change
Reformers	Cooperative institutions can help resolve complex challenges and international tensions over oil

Source: Adapted from M. E. S. Said, "Global Civil Society: Oil and Activism," in H. K. Anheier et al. (eds), *Global Civil Society 2004/5* (Sage, 2004, pp. 76–93).

institutions are not up to the job as both the oil production network and expectations about how it should perform (for whom, over what time scale) are changing in significant and enduring ways. The absence of a proactive governance regime can be attributed to four factors, all of which are evolving. The first one is ideological, and concerns the divide between those who believe energy investment, prices, and demand should be left to the virtues of the market, and others – by far the largest group historically – who believe that national sovereignty and government action are key to energy security (see Table 6.1). The views of economic liberals came to dominate during the 1980s and 1990s, when low prices and resource plenty pushed the energy privatization and liberalization paradigm. The 2008 financial crisis demonstrated that markets could lead oil prices to reach unaffordable levels for many people, and then collapse to such low levels that many oil development projects were suspended for at least a year, resulting in pro-cyclical effects that exacerbated price volatility and supply uncertainty. As prices rose and supply security concerns have increased in the past decade, the arguments of interventionists (e.g. US "stabilization forces" in the Gulf) and isolationists (e.g. "drill, baby, drill" of the 2008 Republican campaign) seeking to maintain oil governance within a unilateral or sovereign sphere have made a comeback. Yet neither market forces, isolationism, nor unilateral policies alone will succeed in achieving the goals of securing environmentally and socially sustainable energy. Cooperative international strategies are required and the views of reformers need to gain further ground.

Many governments, however, remain wary of the implications of international agreements limiting their sovereign control of energy policy – whether these deal with subsidies, access to resources, or the protection of a domestic energy industry. The mid-twentieth century tradition of state monopolies on energy delivery, itself largely the result of the "natural monopoly" created by the huge capital costs of utility infrastructures, is increasingly giving way to private operators. The rules of the World Trade Organization (WTO) do not specifically deal with the energy sector, despite its significance in global trade, and although basic WTO rules should apply to the energy sector, it is rarely the case. Several key oil and gas producers, including Iran, Iraq, Libya, and (South) Sudan, are only observers and not (yet) members – a situation that may change (for the last three) given recent shifts in political regime. Negotiations over energy services began in 2000 and exclude resource ownership issues. There is a consensus around the importance of a WTO Framework Agreement on Energy that would help coordinate a shift toward clean energies, without countries fearing trade sanctions. Such an agreement would not only aim at reducing CO_2 emissions, including by reducing consumption subsidies, but also at making clean energy more affordable. Critics fear a further privatization and liberalization that would undermine sovereign control over energy issues and increase disparities in energy access.[1]

A second reason for the lack of proactive governance is the temporal (and also spatial) disjuncture between consumers, politicians, and the corporate sector. While oil markets are global and oil supply is shaped over decades by the rate and pattern of investment, politicians and consumers operate under local considerations and over short time spans. Constrained by electoral cycles and populist policies, some politicians seek to win votes by cutting taxes, and regard gas prices at the pump as a barometer of popularity and confidence in the economy. Proactive intervention to reshape consumers' habits (or gas prices) is subject to political disincentives that have not, to date, been surmountable in most countries.

The third factor is geopolitical. The global oil economy is frequently perceived as a zero-sum game – a "battle for barrels" as Duncan Clarke puts it – whereby producers and consumers compete for a larger share of the oil pie. This perspective is driving countries such as China to increase its "equity oil" from overseas fields, underpinning an agenda of "oil independence" in the US, and OPEC countries to maximize revenues rather than optimize a long-term production/ consumption balance. As we have shown in previous chapters, the geopolitics of oil are complex and interdependent. There is still too little international cooperation to bring about meaningful reductions in oil consumption and more sustainable models of development. In the absence of a global and cooperative approach, market prices and unilateral state interventions (including through the use of "equity oil" as supply insurance, consumption subsidies as instruments of regime survival, and oil embargoes as foreign policy tools) will continue to create tensions and anxieties.

The fourth reason why governance institutions are poorly

developed is economic. The sheer size of oil companies makes them quasi-autonomous players. Even national oil companies are often considered as "a state within a state," with their own budget, hierarchy, and even their own security. This insulation often makes them "self-serving," with employees enjoying benefits of which other civil servants may only dream and actions that do not always serve the public interest. Oil companies also seek autonomy through political influence. Reflecting profit motives, such influence is pursued through hundreds of millions of dollars spent by these industries on political lobbying and electoral campaign funding, and more indirectly through values shaped by the US$40 billion spent annually on advertising by the car industry to promote vehicle sales and use. Such influence affects regulatory processes and values, both domestically and internationally. This was the case with lobbying in the US against emissions reductions to mitigate climate change impacts. Most recently, it has been in evidence around international accounting standards, with the industry successfully capturing regulatory process to ensure that new regulations on financial disclosure that would help pinpoint tax evasion and corruption merely codify existing industry practice. Corporate altruism is a rarity, and this is why governance institutions – ranging from mandatory regulations to market incentives and consumer values – have such a key role to play in reshaping the oil production network and improving its impacts. The debate over corporate social responsibility (CSR) is informative, here, with many oil companies at the forefront of accusations of environmental and human rights abuses. While CSR has evolved from a tool deployed to compensate and "pacify" local communities in production areas, it is now scaling up to governance issues in host countries and global environmental and financial responsibilities. The playing field among oil companies is far from level, given their diverse sizes, relative influence, and exposure to reputational risks, while the effectiveness of accountability processes in producing and consuming countries remains generally weak. Beyond the reinforcement of "voluntary" norms and the capacity of civil society to hold companies to account, this requires broad mandatory instruments backed by stringent enforcement.[2]

Oil governance actors and institutions

The future of oil will emerge from the interaction of three broad groups of actors: the oil companies that control investment and production decisions, the governments of exporting and importing states, and civil society organizations (CSOs) who increasingly are demanding change and holding both corporations and governments to account. For most of the twentieth century, oil companies and governments dominated oil governance processes. There were primarily three issues that defined governance in this period: market share and prices in conditions of oversupply; security of supply in the face of market failures as a result of adverse geopolitical and natural disaster events; and access to sovereign resources. For the most part, governments and companies engaged international oil governance as a zero-sum game in which access to oil (and oil markets) underpinned economic growth, political clout, and military power. Oil security may be a global affair that no country can single-handedly address, yet nationalist agendas and commercial competition have dominated public policy and markets. Most governments have treated energy policy as a sovereign matter, cooperating only in their self-interest and generally along the lines of core producer or consumer groups. The formation of OPEC in 1960 – and its actions a decade later – demonstrated the potential of cooperation among states to transform the international political economy of oil. The formation of the International

Energy Agency (IEA) in 1974 likewise showed how states – in this case, OECD countries – could work together on a common agenda around oil. Yet, OPEC and IEA also sharply demonstrate the limits to that cooperation. Each represents a different end of the oil production network, and they operate as restricted-access producer and consumer clubs that, for the most part, look after the interests of their members. Given the international governance vacuum, the IEA has gone beyond its initial mandate of protection against supply shock to serve as a major information provider and forum on a broad range of energy issues, including efficiency and sustainability – yet there is a need to broaden its membership (to include China, India, and Brazil) and mandate to make it more effective.

Multilateral approaches to energy governance have not been taken forward at the United Nations and resource access agreements have been largely concluded through bilateral investment treaties rather than multilateral agreements such as the EU-initiated Energy Charter Treaty (1994) and the North American Free Trade Agreement (1993) seeking to facilitate capital flow and investment. With the end of the Cold War, the European Council launched the Energy Charter Treaty (ECT) to engage former communist countries and focus on energy efficiency and environmental aspects of energy security. In force since 1998 and frequently beset by conflicts over Russian gas flows to Central and Western Europe, the ECT remains a Eurasian club whose signatories agree to rules on investment, trading, and transit issues. Bernard Mommer, Venezuela's one-time representative to OPEC and a critic of these recent multilateral deals, describes them with irony as part of "a grandiose framework of international trade and investment treaties, an attempt to create one global economy united by free trade and free investment (in which) mineral resources would be subject to the global sovereign: consumers."[3]

The international oil governance landscape has been recently transformed through the development of a broader "energy" agenda and the emergence of several new international organizations (see Table 6.2). The International Energy Forum (IEF) serves as the broadest oil governance initiative by organizing the world's largest gathering of energy ministers, while a new International Renewable Energy Agency (IRENA) is charged with promoting a rapid transition to renewable energies. For some, that these two international energy institutions – IEF and IRENA – are hosted and chiefly sponsored by oil and gas producers (Saudi Arabia and the United Arab Emirates) is a source of concern. The two institutions are also outside the UN which, for some, also raises questions of representation and legitimacy.

With its secretariat in Saudi Arabia's capital city Riyadh and both the IEA and OPEC Secretariats on its executive board, the IEF acts as the (still informal) conduit for negotiations between oil and gas exporting, importing, and transit countries. Its 87 member countries account for 90 percent of the global oil and gas market, and include IEA and OPEC countries as well as key energy players such as Brazil, China, India, Mexico, Russia, and South Africa. The IEF also involves major energy companies through its International Energy Business Forum (IEBF). In contrast, participation and representation of low-income countries and civil society organizations remains limited. Given its links with the IEA and especially OPEC, the IEF is mostly a "fossil fuel" organization. The IEF's recent concerns have been oil price volatility and its economic and social consequences, and the "bad press" that both the financial and energy sectors have received. Concrete policy outcomes remain essentially limited to the application of the "transparency" and "reliability" principles on oil data through the Joint Organizations Data Initiative. Still, the IEF also deals with a broad range of issues, including IOC/NOC cooperation,

Table 6.2 Oil and energy-related international initiatives and organizations

Organizations	Creation	Mandate	Members
WPC	1933	Dialogue among stakeholders, especially intra-industry exchanges	60 countries and numerous professionals
IPC	1944	Foster an international agreement for the "orderly development of the international petroleum trade"	US and UK, but failed
OPEC	1960	Price control through oil-production quotas	12 producing countries
IEA	1974	Supply security among OECD members	28 countries
GCC	1989	Prevent actions seeking to reduce GHG emissions	Mostly US oil and auto industry
IEF	1991	Meeting of Energy Ministers from producing, consuming, and transit states	87 countries
ECT	1994	Facilitate energy cooperation among Eurasian states	51 member countries, 24 observer countries
UNFCCC	1994	Climate change mitigation and adaptation (including via Kyoto Protocol, 1997)	195 member countries or parties
US–UK Voluntary Principles	2000	Reduce risk of human rights abuses by security forces protecting production sites	6 countries, 18 companies, and 8 NGOs
GGFR	2002	Reduce gas flaring from oil production	22 countries, 19 companies, 5 IGOs
EITI	2003	Revenue transparency	28 producing countries
UN–Energy	2004	Promotion of energy access, renewable energy, and energy efficiency	World Bank and UN agencies
IRENA	2009	Adoption of renewable energies	148 countries

Note: Acronyms not listed in this chapter include WPC: World Petroleum Congress, IPC: International Petroleum Council, GCC: Global Climate Coalition, GGFR: Global Gas Flaring Reduction initiative.

Sources: Websites of organizations by mid-2011.

energy poverty reduction, and climate change mitigation. Backed by the G20, and collaborating with the other agencies in their respective domains, the IEF could become the core institution of international cooperation on oil governance and energy more broadly, but it remains for now a "soft institution" promoting informal dialogue rather than negotiation or arbitration. Forced to resign in 2010, IRENA's first director-general argued that a number of countries, including the US, Japan, Australia, and to a lesser extent the UK, do not want to see an effective renewable energy agency emerge or prefer the IEA to retain that authority.[4]

Widening the circle: civil society organizations take on oil
By the early 1990s, civil society organizations increasingly brought environmental and social issues to the forefront of the oil governance agenda, though more often in the form of event-focused protests, boycotts, or advocacy campaigns than a systematic drive to change policy. Several prominent actions by local communities in the early 1990s put corporate social responsibility and indigenous rights on the agenda, such as the struggles of the Ogoni people in the Niger Delta in the mid-1990s and U'Wa in Colombia. An international campaign initiated in the late 1990s against the construction of the Baku–Tbilisi–Ceyhan (BTC) pipeline denounced both the geo-political motives of this energy supply infrastructure (seeking to bypass Russia and Iran) and its human rights and environmental impacts. This groundwork, along with mounting evidence of the many problems associated with oil, broadened the international oil governance agenda, which now includes a wide range of issues, including climate change, corruption, and human rights. Prominent among these are the Publish What You Pay campaign for greater transparency in extractive industries, and environmental campaigns against the exploitation of oil in the Arctic and tar sands in Alberta.

Some companies have responded to these campaigns, with European oil corporations often the first to do so. Shell agreed on the need to prepare for a transition to renewables in 1995. BP's CEO acknowledged the growing scientific consensus on climate change in 1997, and in 2000 BP rebranded itself as (going) "Beyond Petroleum." In contrast, companies such as Exxon continued to lobby against GHG emission reduction measures, most notably through the Global Climate Coalition (GCC) – a US-dominated industry lobby set up in 1989 – and despite contrary evidence from their own scientists. Deactivated in 2002, some of the lobbying activities of the GCC against emission cuts are now pursued by the American Petroleum Institute, the lead US industry association. The industry as a whole has focused on better managing emissions from upstream and midstream operations to lower its polluter profile, developing alternative fuels and energy sources to diversify its portfolio and help legitimize any "green" credentials and, in some cases, facilitating consumers in offsetting their emissions. Yet, as demonstrated in the case of the Keystone XL pipeline – planned to link the tar sands in Alberta to the US Gulf Coast refining and shipping complex – old lobbying habits die hard, with the pipeline company spending over US$1.3 million in Washington DC in 2011, only to see Obama refuse to accelerate the permitting process following massive public opposition. Groups lobbying for the industry have also not hesitated in misrepresenting issues, vilifying opponents, and using the cover of dubious "grass-root organizations" for their public relations ventures seeking to promote carbon-intensive fuels.[5]

Faced with growing accusations of complicity in human rights abuses, oil and mining companies worked in the early 2000s with human rights NGOs and the US and UK governments to curb the risk of abuses by security forces protecting extractive ventures by defining good practices through the Voluntary Principles on Security and Human Rights. The World Summit on Sustainable Development (WSSD) in 2002 provided the context to launch several initiatives, including the Global Gas Flaring Reduction (GGFR) partnership between governments, oil companies, and the World Bank. On that occasion, British Prime Minister Tony Blair also called for greater transparency in oil revenue flows, leading to the creation of the Extractive Industries Transparency Initiative (see chapter 5).

The results of voluntary schemes have been mixed, however, with critics pointing to the lack of enforcement mechanisms, the limited participation of worst offending parties, and the "insurance" role against reputational risks that such schemes offer to oil companies in return for little accountability. The UN–Energy mechanism was set up in 2004 to help implement energy-relevant recommendations of the WSSD and UN Commission on Sustainable Development. Acting as an inter-UN agency coordination body with the collaboration of the World Bank, it seeks to foster greater energy access for the poor, renewable energy, and energy efficiency. Its main potential is in defending the interests of low-income countries that are poorly represented in other institutions, although direct representation would be preferable – rather than via UN specialized agencies and the World Bank. Preexisting international oil-related organizations have also broadened their mandate, with (for example) the International Energy Agency integrating climate change issues following the 1997 Kyoto Protocol, and being mandated in 2005 by G8 leaders to provide advice on energy policy issues linked to climate change. OPEC took an even more guarded approach to resist emission reductions that, from its perspective, would put an "inequitable" burden on its members, stating in 2009 that reductions need to account for "the historical responsibilities of developed countries, the principles of equity and of common but differentiated responsibilities, and fully taking into account the overriding priority of economic and social development and the eradication of poverty." Outside the adoption of the UNFCCC by its members, OPEC's first concrete move was the creation in 2007 of a US$750 million research fund for carbon capture and sequestration.[6] OPEC is most worried about discriminatory tax policies negatively affecting oil markets and would only accept climate change-related taxation that would be imposed "on all forms of energy – not just oil – according to their carbon content," a position that would look at life-cycle carbon content, even for renewables.[7]

The (real) politics of oil governance

In their efforts to maximize profits, oil companies have to account for the respective (and often conflicting) interests of their home government and host authorities. Reciprocally, home governments are often eager to facilitate lucrative ventures by their domestic oil companies which, especially if these are state-owned, can improve energy security and foster other foreign policy goals. Resource diplomacy is thus a major element of foreign policy. Host authorities, in turn, have to ensure that oil companies maximize fiscal returns and do not "sit on their concession." As mentioned above, this tripartite game is complicated by international and domestic civil society groups eager to put human and environmental rights before profits. This combination of profit motive, political sovereignties, and rights concerns has given rise to a governance model that seeks constructive engagement, for example, through the Extractive Industries Transparency Initiative (see Box 5.4).

If international cooperation is crucial to improving energy security and socio-environmental outcomes, many oil policies remain within the domain of domestic governance. There, too, major forces are at work. Chief among these is the influence that oil companies and national authorities can bring to bear on each other. Three areas are of particular concern: the influence of oil companies on foreign policy, the protection of corporate interests by domestic governments, and the impact of host governments on oil companies.

Oil and foreign policy

Oil contracts are signed by companies with host governments and typically last for two to three decades, if not more. This means that oil is highly politicized and enters into bilateral agreements over extended periods, where it faces the vagaries of political changes and economic cycles. Oil companies generally assume that whoever is in power will need the revenues; but "expropriations" have frequently occurred, and sometimes become a matter influencing foreign policy. If IOCs, and especially NOCs, can generally count on the support of their home government to win and keep contracts, they do not always share the same foreign policy interests. IOCs have the greatest challenges (there are also opportunities) with interventionist governments such as that of the US – the imposition of economic sanctions being a main point of contention. US companies have lobbied hard to prevent or lift embargoes barring them for extended periods from Iran, Sudan, and Libya – to cite only the main ones. They have mostly done so through USA*Engage, a lobbying group formed in 1997 by the National Foreign Trade Council to facilitate trade and corporate investments in countries under sanction, dictatorship, or with a dismal human rights record. US company Gulf Oil (now part of Chevron) was eager to keep pumping oil from Angola, even after a socialist government took power after independence in 1974. The US government opposed this and froze tax revenues owed by Gulf to the new government for two years. In the end, however, it rescinded its ban in the face of growing international recognition of the new regime in Luanda and turned to financing armed opposition through the CIA.

Oil companies can push for their home governments to assist in opening up access to oil fields and winning contracts. There is a long tradition of "resource diplomacy" among the home governments of oil companies. Initially pursued through "gunboat diplomacy" and the enthronement of local potentates (so-called "puppet governments"), support for oil companies has mostly given way to a mix of strategies ranging from military and diplomatic support, to bilateral aid and active policy of "noninterference," in effect supporting local regimes against both domestic and external threats. The US, France, and Britain have a long tradition of interventionism, including through military force, as discussed in chapter 4. The US administration liberalized all sectors of the Iraqi economy during its occupation, with the exception of the oil industry. While IOCs were extremely keen to access Iraqi's giant oil fields, there was simply too much legal uncertainty in granting contracts during the formal US occupation and too much Iraqi political opposition to privatizing the two Iraqi NOCs. Even attempts to impose production sharing agreements (PSAs) met with stiff and successful opposition by Iraqi unions and parliamentarians after these were rightly understood as privatization in disguise. Oil companies ended up having to bid for service contracts earning them comparatively low fees – between 1.3 and 7.5 dollars per barrel – like in most other Persian Gulf countries. Conditions for IOCs under Saddam Hussein had been better – but at that time US and UK oil majors had no access. After US and UK taxpayers spent respectively a total of US$806 billion and US$15 billion for the war in Iraq between 2003 and 2011, the two largest contracts went to Exxon-Mobil (West Qurna Phase I, 2.3 mmbd) and BP (Rumaila, 2.85 mmdb). Most recently, western governments successfully pushed to open up oil and gas reserves in Algeria, following a decade-long civil war, and cozied up to Gaddafi's regime in Libya in a mutually – if relatively brief – profitable agreement over financial compensation for the 1988 Lockerbie bombing, anti-terrorism collaboration, and access to oil fields.[8]

Finally, contractual stability is key for oil companies making huge investments in decades-long ventures. But, as prices rise, host authorities may hope for a larger share of revenues than set by initial contracts. The recent price hikes have generated such demands in many countries, most often in the form of a windfall tax. Oil companies have also sought the support of their home government to ensure stability and to cancel (or compensate for) expropriation by host authorities. International political risk insurance, including that provided by national export credit agencies, offers some limited coverage. Home governments can also seek to leverage their military presence and bilateral aid, the latter being statistically proven to reduce the risk of expropriation.[9] Home governments called upon by oil companies may find the price of intervening on their behalf too high, however, or simply be unable to exert effective leverage. In the context of rising international tension with Nazi Germany, Roosevelt did not want to take the risk of alienating the Mexican government, despite its nationalization of US oil companies in 1938. Following the nationalization of Exxon's assets in Peru in 1968, the US government refrained from taking a hard line with the Peruvian government after being lobbied by hundreds of other US businesses present in Peru and wary of a potential backlash. Most recently, home governments have been frequently called by oil companies to pass bilateral investment treaties that help stabilize their contracts, especially with regard to expropriation in the form of tax increases or asset nationalization. Such treaties facilitate the seizure of overseas assets belonging to host authorities (or their national oil companies). Furthermore, while most contracts include international arbitration clauses in case of conflict, home governments are often called in by oil companies to advise and, where possible, to put pressure on host authorities.

Oil and domestic politics

Oil constrains domestic politics on energy transition in oil-importing states. The degree to which oil is structurally embedded in national, urban, and personal economies means that large proportions of the electorate are exposed to changes in oil prices. This takes a number of forms, but it is around fuel prices for transportation that this exposure becomes clearest. Actions that increase prices risk a strong rebuke from the electorate. The decision to exclude transportation from Phase 1 of the European Emissions Trading Scheme in 2005 reflects this political sensitivity. In many countries, policy choices over fuel taxes, transport infrastructure, and land use planning have been influenced by the supremacy of cars as a tool and object of economic development. As persuasively argued by political scientist Matthew Paterson drawing on the US experience, states generally promoted the car over its competitors because "of the state's structural role in promoting accumulation, . . . of the consequences of interstate competition, the importance of a car industry for development, and in some instances the car industry's connection to a state's war-making capacities." The lobby of oil, car, and construction companies has been very successful in persuading policy makers, notably in the UK where its proposed plans were readily adopted by the government after the Second World War. In the US, freeways recycle fuel taxes and keep them away from financing competitors, in contrast to France where road transport competes with the national railroad and most highways are toll roads.[10]

Ironically, it was bicycles that paved the way to the dominance of automobiles: in the UK, cycling lobbyists obtained the improvement of roads, while the decision of activist judges in the US to deny the right of cities to regulate the use of bicycles set a precedent that would later enshrine the freedom of the automobile. Cyclists have fought their way back into the city since the late 1970s in Europe and more recently in the US. City councillors and planners have pushed back against cars, promoting walking and cycling as more socially and environmentally friendly alternatives and constraining the spaces and speeds allotted to cars. Again, higher-density land use planning, mixed development, car-free city centers, cycling lanes, hefty car registration fees, and high fuel taxes subsidizing alternative transportation have allowed European countries, and to a lesser extent Canada, to push much further than most US municipalities in challenging the dominance of the car.

Transportation and land use policies are two significant areas where oil's economic and political power constrains the scope for political action. Others include the regulation of oil production and refining, and the growth of energy markets. The limits of regulation were dramatically exposed by BP's *Deepwater Horizon* blowout and oil spill in the Gulf of Mexico in the spring of 2010. The incident has its roots in reforms for offshore oil leasing first undertaken in 1982 during the Reagan years. The reform resulted in a tenfold decline in fees collected by the federal government and a centralization of regulation and fee collection into a single bureau – the Minerals Management Service (MMS). In 1995, in response to low prices and the squeezed margins of oil producers, Congress passed the Outer Continental Shelf Deep Water Royalty Relief Act that suspended all royalty payments for five years at depths greater than 800 meters. Designed to spur domestic production, this rewarded companies that drilled in deeper water within the five-year window. The result was to lower government take, increase risk-taking behavior on the part of oil companies, and assign regulation of the industry to the branch of government charged with generating revenue by selling leases. Errors in the MMS-approved BP Oil Spills Response Plan suggest the MMS failed in its due diligence, while shortcuts were apparently taken during drilling to save time and money. The blowout that killed 11 crew members and became the largest oil spill in US history was not simply a technical failure, but a result of corporate practices focused narrowly on short-term cost management combined with pro-development government regulations carried out by a federal agency facing conflicts of interest (e.g. tax collection) and regulatory capture (e.g. its own scientists being reportedly asked to alter assessments unfavorable to project development). So why has the political process failed to deliver better oil? The apparent political infeasibility of raising fuel taxes, for example, touches upon several cherished ideologies, such as that of "small government," "freedom to roam" (by car), and "market prices." Many critics have also pointed at the political influence potentially exerted by the oil industry through lobbying and political campaign funding. According to the Center for Responsive Politics, the oil and gas sector spent a billion US dollars on lobbying between 1998 and 2010. The oil and gas industry also has a clear political skew when it comes to supporting presidential and Congressional electoral campaigns, with 75 percent of total sector contributions going to Republican candidates. Despite the industry not being the prime political contributor, ranking only twelfth, critics of Big Oil and former US President G. W. Bush, such as Antonia Juhasz in her book *The Tyranny of Oil*, like to argue that the "oil industry got what it paid for: an administration that has arguably gone further than just about any other in American history to serve Big Oil's interests through deregulation, lax enforcement, new access to America's public lands and oceans, subsidies, tax breaks, and even war." Even with a Democratic majority in Congress after 2006, a bill attempting to eliminate US$16 billion in oil tax breaks to fund renewables ultimately died. A study of political donations by the Center for American Progress found that members of Congress who had voted against the bill had received four times more campaign contributions from the industry than those who voted in favor.[11]

But times may be changing for the oil industry. In the US, three successive Acts since 1991 have sought to rebalance transportation modes. More federal funds are being plowed into transportation alternatives, including walking and cycling, which increased from US$5 million a year in 1990 to about a billion dollars by 2009 (including stimulus funds). After more than two decades of relative deregulation – the result, in part, of intense lobbying to cut costs in order to

Box 6.1 Deregulation and oil price speculation

The ability to speculate on oil prices increased with the deregulation of energy derivatives. In 1992, Enron and eight other energy and financial companies lobbied the US Commodities Futures Trading Commission Chairwoman Wendy Gramm, who successfully pushed to allow energy contracts to be traded outside of regulated markets and be exempt from anti-fraud provisions of the Commodity Exchange Act. Wendy Gramm went on to sit on ENRON's board of directors five weeks after the approval of this loophole and joined the Mercatus Center, a conservative economic think tank founded by Koch Industries who had lobbied her along with Enron. Her husband, former Texas GOP Senator Phil Gramm and a recipient of ENRON campaign donations, maneuvered to pass further energy trading deregulation in December 2000, despite recommendations to the contrary by the President's Working Group on Financial Markets in 1999. The legislation facilitated the growth of an alternative US derivatives market – Intercontinental Exchange (ICE) – created seven months prior to the bill by several of the original energy companies. ICE then purchased the London-based International Petroleum Exchange in 2001 (now ICE Futures Europe) and shifted it to its electronic quotation system. By 2011, ICE Futures Europe boasted of hosting the trade of half of the world's crude and refined oil futures contracts.[12]

maintain profits during the doldrums of the 1990s and a pro-industry administration in the 2000s – regulation is back. Its return, however, may be brief as high prices are this time driving moves to open up environmentally sensitive areas to new drilling. The industry is also facing greater reputational costs and, at times, stringent application of regulations. The Foreign Corruption Practices Act, established in 1977 but long ignored, led to US$1.2 billion in settlements and fines being imposed on oil companies between 2007 and 2010.[13]

Producer influence on oil governance

With rising oil prices and depleting resources, what will be the influence of oil producers in the governing of oil? Part of the answer can be seen in the growing dominance of NOCs in oil production: producer states are eager to maintain as much control of their oil resources as possible. But this is not the case everywhere, especially in low-income countries with technologically and financially challenging oil fields. In such circumstances, producer governments have generally been more amenable to IOCs (or NOCs), opening their reserves and accepting a lower government take. Nationalizations can have various motives, sometimes overlapping, including increasing government revenues from the sector (especially if contractual terms prevent production increase during low price periods, or do not maximize government share during high prices), taking a popular policy decision to rally support from the population, or gaining political leverage over the US. Companies have responded to threats of expropriation and changes in contracts by suspending expansion of production, as Chevron did in 2002 following Kazakhstan's request to rewrite its 1993 PSA. With a few exceptions, such as Saudi Arabia, Russia, and Venezuela, producer countries have limited leverage over international policy unless spare capacity is low or producer companies cooperate.

Rising oil revenue does not automatically translate into political dominance. International political assertiveness can be forcefully confronted and lead to a pariah status, as in the case of Saddam Hussein's regime and, increasingly, Iran. Many producers are eager to develop or integrate into regional or international governance structure to assert a growing role. Qatar has pursued this strategy very successfully, gaining a degree of influence far beyond its relative size (and even its economic importance) through channeling some of its oil and gas revenues through influential media outlet Al-Jazeera, the hosting of numerous international events (including on progressive oil governance such as the EITI Global Conference), the facilitating of peace talks, and siding militarily with NATO and Libyan insurgents against Gaddafi. As mentioned above, Saudi Arabia and the United Arab Emirates are the host and main backers of three of the four most prominent energy governance institutions (OPEC, IEF, and IRENA). At a regional level, Angola is supporting and hosting the Gulf of Guinea Commission, counterbalancing its more militaristic interventions in neighboring countries such as the Republic of Congo or Côte d'Ivoire. If current reserve estimates are to be trusted, the countries with the largest reserves – many of them in the Persian Gulf – may come to further dominate the market as many smaller producers lose their net exporter status. The main question will thus be what kind of politics these better-endowed countries adopt, whether oil markets will benefit from their domestic stability, and how major importers will react to any supply disruptions. These questions are of course not new, the main new variable being the conduct of China and the deterrence that it may exercise in the type of interventionism that has affected the region for the past century.[14]

Conclusion

A series of oil governance institutions have developed over time to regulate the critical issues of the day, such as supply security, price, and market access. Until the mid-1990s, the international governance system consisted mostly of three relatively small clubs. The first and oldest is the club of International Oil Companies, the Seven Sisters or Big Oil. Although competitive, companies do collude and generally have the same "industry" interests in mind, making it the most cohesive if informal of the three clubs. The second club, OPEC, consists of "developing" oil-producing states, which is now mostly dominated by middle- to high-income Persian Gulf monarchies and dictatorships, which adopted a Third World rhetoric to break the hold of the IOC's club on their resources. Finally, there is the IEA, the club of rich oil-consuming states that seeks mostly to ensure oil supplies by breaking the hold of OPEC through coordination and holding large supply stocks but has come to take on a broader role in energy govern-ance. Although these clubs are marked by competition, both between them and within, they have on the whole cooperated to achieve energy security in a narrow sense: oil could pollute and finance dictatorships, but as long as it would flow at a rea-sonable pace and price, few club members would bother to challenge the system. These clubs have now lost part of their relevance due to relatively new and cross-cutting issues, such as sustainability, human rights, development, and climate change. The growing weight of economic players like China, India, and Brazil is also questioning the relevance of the restricted membership of these institutions.

The legacy of this system is still in place: the IEF remains an "informal" club through which energy ministers meet. Official sovereignty, and thus supposedly individual interests, are preserved, thereby allowing the most powerful states to still dominate in the absence of a formal collective and representative decision-making process. This system is showing strains, however. Some oil companies, for example, have been parting from the club on certain issues, seeking to build or mend their reputation and market share through good deeds, as seen in the case of climate change or revenue transparency.

One of the major drivers for this shift has been the effectiveness of a number of civil society movements and advocacy campaigns which, from the early 1990s, successfully moved a number of issues such as indigenous rights, environmental protection, or corruption onto the oil governance agenda. Part of that effectiveness relied on broader shifts in the processes and agenda of international governance, the end of the Cold War and institutionalization of environmental sustainability constituting an important watershed. Other factors have included the mounting scientific evidence on climate change and growing evidence of the economic and political challenges of resource dependence, as well as increasing recognition of conventional oil depletion. The governance game and players have also been changing: demand is shifting from western OECD members to Asian consumers; NOCs are internationalizing and directly competing or collaborating with IOCs on a global rather than domestic level; and different constituencies and ethical priorities are represented, including through the more frequent participation of civil society organizations in negotiations.

While the current context requires international cooperation, a rapidly changing oil sector and volatile prices mean that countries are cautious and very protective of their sovereignty over energy policy. Some key economies, such as China, are reluctant to promote and adopt broad multilateral agreements on energy based on free trade principles, such as a future WTO Framework Agreement on Energy. Countries like China do recognize the limits of bilateral agreements and are interested in adopting multilateral agreements, most notably with respect to transit. They remain tempted, however, to craft their own regional intergovernmental agreements in order to limit the extent of their commitments and the implications that such free trade agreements could have on the control of their domestic oil production and distribution sectors, as well as for bilateral agreements already passed.

On this basis, three main governance reforms are currently at play. The first is the further institutionalization of the IEF with decision-making power backed by the UN General Assembly and supported by the G20. Inclusive of civil society, grounded in clear principles and objectives for energy security and sustainability, and with a fair collective and representative decision-making process, such an organization could help bring about the cooperation needed to smooth the transition in the interests of both consuming and producing countries. This process will be slow, and in the meantime the current patchwork of organizations can work together through ad hoc projects that will foster greater trust and cooperation.

The second reform concerns market governance through international standards and coordination of market regulations and reporting standards for accounting to reduce price volatility and foster better governance of oil revenues. The third governance reform concerns the political lobbying and influence of the oil industry which needs to be adequately circumscribed, or effectively counterbalanced by those advocating alternative energy systems and modes of transportation. In the following chapter, we turn to the some of the specific policy priorities that oil producers, consumers, and governance institutions have to address.

CHAPTER SEVEN

Better and Beyond: The Future of Oil

The "end of oil" is nigh: so goes the popular theme. Yet it is much too soon to write an epitaph for oil. Right now, over one trillion barrels of oil are available underground for extraction. With unconventional oil reserves coming online, liquid hydro-carbon production looks set to "plateau" rather than peak and rapidly decline. Above ground, the extraction and combustion of oil are firmly embedded in the fabric of modern societies – via political patronage and the social power of automobile, construction, and financial corporations, in the geographies and materials of the built environment, and in cultural norms of consumption. Oil looks set to be with us for some time to come. But it is precisely because oil has a future that we need to be concerned. In this concluding chapter, we consider oil as part of a broader "global energy dilemma" – the problem of how societies that have developed around and through fossil fuels must now find ways to ensure affordable and reliable sources of energy while also reducing the emission of carbon dioxide and improving the developmental impact of oil for producing countries. We describe this as oil's "new reality," and consider the strategies by which states and other par-ties might seek to respond. We discuss how these strategies might be deployed differently in oil-producing and -consum-ing countries. In the final section, we highlight four priorities that must be addressed through better governance of the oil production network. The goal of such governance is to make oil *better* – that is, to improve the performance of oil's global production network on economic, social, and environmental criteria. In the longer term, however, the goal should be to move *beyond* oil by decoupling it from society's demand for energy.

In writing this book, our objective has been to show how wresting value from the earth's resources is not only a tricky business, but also one that is necessarily political because it brings together a complex range of different actors and interests. Firms, states, and civic society organizations may have some common objectives, yet they are frequently also in competition – over control of resources, the distribution of value from production, the availability of supply, the share of revenues from oil development, and the distribution of oil's environmental and social costs. We introduced the framework of the global production network to characterize these actors and their interrelations and account for the ways in which oil is socially organized. We also showed, by reference to oil's rich history, how the organizational structures through which oil is extracted from the earth and shuttled through economies are changing in significant ways. Some of the actors may have the same names, but today's global oil industry is not that of 1950s' Seven Sisters or 1970s' resource nationalism. Such changes are, in part, the result of a "global shift" in the center of gravity of the world economy. They also are related to changes in the resource base to which the oil sector is ultimately tethered.

Our objective has not been just to show how the global oil industry is changing. Rather, we have wanted to explore its implications, and show how many of these changes ramp up the economic, social, and environmental challenges that have been long associated with the hydrocarbon age. Among these are: the development of new and often dirtier or riskier reserves; the promotion of sustainable economies and broad-based development in oil-producing countries; the volatility of prices; a mismatch between supply and demand aggravated by the fast-rising oil consumption of "emerging" economies and exporting states; and the accumulation of carbon dioxide in the atmosphere. As evidence of these challenges mounts, the global production network for oil appears to be out of step with social demands. Oil, it can be said, has failed in significant ways and must engage this "new reality."

Oil's new reality

The main implication of the new reality is the ongoing re-organization of the oil production network as a function of geological, geo-economic and geopolitical shifts – namely the depletion of the resource base, the shift of economic weight to Asia, and a more interdependent "multipolar" world. These changes, together with an increasingly complex set of social demands, have exposed a "governance deficit" around oil. Today, the "politics of oil" are increasingly about the way states, companies, and civil society organizations negotiate a solution to this governance deficit and, in so doing, determine the future of oil.

Oil continues to be firmly embedded in current forms of economic growth, and growing demand has exposed the diminishing availability and accessibility of the so-called conventional oil that has been the bedrock of the industry for most of its 150 years. The erosion of surplus has raised prices and reduced affordability, shifted oil from a commod-ity (obtainable in the marketplace) to a strategic good (where market mechanisms alone are insufficient for procuring the resource), and, at the same time, created additional volatility through scope for speculation. Economic growth in coun-tries like China, India, Brazil, and Russia are indicative of an emergent world political order that is less defined by the eco-nomic and political power of the US, of which the emergence of state-owned, transnational oil firms – like PetroChina and Petrobras – is a particularly powerful expression.

Meanwhile, efforts to address the shortfall in supply and secure oil in an increasingly competitive market have required accessing unconventional oil (bitumen) or conventional oil in unconventional places, in part because the bulk of the world's conventional oil reserves are controlled by national oil firms (predominantly in the Middle East). The governments of these countries can therefore control the rate at which conventional oil is produced and they have been either unwilling – or unable – to increase production. New supply, therefore, is typically harder to get and of poorer quality, so that the supply gap is increasingly being filled by dirtier and more costly oil extracted in riskier operating environments. As firms push into these environments, the long-standing social and environmental challenges of extraction and development are made visible – as with BP's *Deepwater Horizon* oil spill, GHG emissions from tar sands, and oil-related conflicts in Iraq or Sudan. Increasingly, oil firms are being held to account for their performance on social development, human rights, and the protection of the environment. At the same time, growing oil demand – combined with falling energy grades, due to higher energy costs of extraction and the additional energy needed to upgrade heavy, sulfur oils to transportation fuels – means that the oil production network is responsible for a large and growing quantity of CO_2 emissions. The acceptability of oil is therefore increasingly in question.

Responding to the new reality

The new reality is complex, and past experience indicates that societies respond to such crises in a range of ways. We identify here seven potential state-level strategies in response to oil's new reality. As we go on to show, these are not mutually exclusive and they involve strategic action at different geographical scales.

- *Liberal markets*: open up national oil reserves to foreign investment and lower barriers to trade in oil and oil services through multilateral treaties on investment and trade (e.g. ECT, NAFTA).
- *Neo-mercantilist resource control*: strategic partnering between an importing state and an exporting state to lock in privileged access to oil via infrastructure and development deals and "equity oil" contracts which give the investing partner – often a national oil company from an importing state – the right to take or market oil (e.g. investments by China's state oil firms in Africa).
- *Oil welfare*: subsidized oil production and consumption through royalty and tax relief for oil producers, deregulation of working practices, removal of environmental restrictions on access, low fuel taxes, and rejection of carbon pricing (e.g. US under Bush Jr).
- *Socioeconomic adaptation*: addresses supply constraints and climate change through public policies and community initiatives that build resilience to market shocks, drive the decarbonization of energy systems, and reduce demand (e.g. UK government's Low Carbon Transition Plan; Transition Towns Movement; Cuba in early 1990s).
- *Technological innovation for energy transition*: investment in the development and application of alternative energy sources that substitute for oil in major markets, via a mix of public policies and private sector commitments (e.g. hydrogen highways).
- *Predatory militarism*: reshapes accessibility through force, using either clandestine means (e.g. Iran's 1956 *coup d'état*) or military force (e.g. Japan in 1940s; Iraqi invasion of Kuwait).

- *Totalitarian retrenchment*: authoritarian allocation of remaining oil supplies and top-down decisions over lifestyles and livelihoods (e.g. North Korea in 1990s).

This stylized spectrum of responses suggests some very different potential outcomes. Much is at stake in how collectively we respond to the new realities of oil. In practice, we can expect a mix of responses that will vary from country to country. Such geographical variation will reflect country characteristics, including the nature of its political regime and the historical experience of its population, as well as the degree of exposure to supply and price risks and to the environmental externalities of the oil production chain (for regional scenarios, see Table 7.1). Furthermore, there will also be variation within countries in how regions and municipalities choose to respond. In the US, the most likely scenario in the short term at the federal level is the current combination of a liberal markets approach (via bilateral investment and multilateral trade deals and increasing regional market integration with Canada and Mexico), and the continuation of oil welfarism (involving low taxation for consumers, continued oil production subsidies, and the opening of environmentally sensitive acreage). Recent experience suggests, however, that market integration and support for current demand norms ("the American way of life") may be supplemented with bouts of predatory militarism (in Colombia and the Persian Gulf). At the same time, there are initiatives at state and municipal level in the US around socioeconomic adaptation and federal subsidies and incentives to encourage substitution (e.g. biofuels) and technological innovation. Europe's current strategy centers on a combination of market liberalism (via the Energy Charter Treaty, and also via the EU Emissions Trading Scheme), elements of regional strategic partnering (e.g. the EU–Russia Energy Dialogue), and technological innovation and rollout –

Table 7.1	Adaptation strategies for selected regions						
	Liberalism	Neo-mercantilism	Oil welfarism	Socio-economic adaptation	Technological innovation	Militarism	Totalitarianism
North America	√√	√	√		√	√	
Latin America		√		√√			
Europe	√			√	√√	√	
Eurasia		√	√	√			√
East Asia		√√		√	√	√	
South Asia	√	√		√√	√		
Southeast Asia	√			√√			
Middle-East North Africa		√	√√		√	√	√
Sub-Saharan Africa	√	√		√		√	

√ √: very likely, √: likely. A more detailed assessment would require country-by-country analysis.

Sources: Based on J. Friedrichs, "Global Energy Crunch: How Different Parts of the World Would React to a Peak Oil Scenario," *Energy Policy* 38(8) (2010): 4562–9.

particularly around alternative fuels and engine technologies in the transport sector. There are also national-scale efforts at socioeconomic adaptation (e.g. national energy transition policies in Holland and the UK) as well as city-based and corporate initiatives for adapting to climate change and improving oil resilience (e.g. the Peak Oil Task Force in the UK). Europe is also engaged in limited predatory militarism (in Libya and the Persian Gulf, for example). East Asia is likely to see a combination of technological innovation (such as electric vehicles), liberalism, and limited socioeconomic adaptation and some possible predatory militarism in the China Seas, with China continuing to opt for neo-mercantilism through bilateral treaties for supply access and multilateral ones for transit. Most low-income countries are likely to turn to socioeconomic adaptation, with some risk of militarism.

The new reality of oil creates particular challenges for oil producers and exporters which face a different set of challenges around price, security, and development via oil. They need to balance export and domestic demands, particularly where domestic economic growth absorbs export capacity (e.g. Indonesia, and increasingly Iran, as well as Saudi Arabia which will be a net importer by 2037 given current trends). Such choices between domestic and export demand may be constrained by trade agreements. Oil-exporting states have recently begun to question the security of demand. Uncertainty over demand arises from fluctuations in economic growth and technological and policy shifts in the transport sector and, over the longer term, from the prospect of an expansion of carbon legislation beyond Europe. The impacts on oil demand could be considerable: OPEC models indicate a difference of around 14 million barrels per day between high- and low-growth scenarios out to 2030. Beyond investing in enhanced oil recovery to get more oil from aging reservoirs, oil exporters are likely to open up new fields, increase strategic partnerships with consumer countries (e.g. downstream deals between Saudi Aramco and PetroChina), and make efforts to grow the non-oil sector and diversify the economy "beyond oil." Producers with strong national oil companies are most likely to pursue neo-mercantilist strategies, protecting access to domestic reserves and limiting foreign investment to oil services. Producers with low-capacity NOCs – such as Kazakhstan and Azerbaijan – are likely to pursue liberal market strategies that continue to see them open to investment in the upstream and downstream sectors. Oil exporters also face distinctive challenges on climate change, via its potential for demand destruction and the question of whether those who extract oil from the ground should bear some responsibility for the "custody" of carbon down the full length of the production network, including the "backstream" phase that currently sees carbon dioxide accumulate in the atmosphere. OPEC's position here is clear: carbon emissions are the historical responsibility of developed economies, and it affirms the distinction drawn in the UN Framework Convention on Climate Change between the responsibilities of developed Annex I countries and those of non-Annex I countries. Other oil producers may voluntarily decide to limit extraction and forswear oil – as with the Yasuni–ITT proposal in Ecuador (see Box 5.2) – particularly if they are able to generate alternative revenue streams by leaving "the oil in the soil." There will, then, be a diversity of responses to the new reality as some states seek to maintain commitments to oil while others look for security and economic opportunity by reducing their dependence. Collectively, these different adaptation strategies will reconfigure the geographies of uneven development associated with oil's global production network.

Four priorities

The new reality of oil sets four main priorities for oil governance: reducing price volatility, matching oil supply and demand, transitioning to low-carbon energy sources, and addressing the "oil curse." The order of these priorities and their potential impacts will vary for different countries and social groups, and over time. High-priority measures should not only include those tasks that can be rapidly achieved, but also those that have longer-term effects. Chief among these is the stock of vehicles: low-mileage gas guzzlers purchased today will exacerbate relative demand growth for 10 to 15 years. Prioritization also needs to consider equity dimensions: similar efforts cannot be demanded from poor countries as from rich ones. Reducing rural poverty remains a priority for many countries, with hydrocarbon-based rural transportation having an important role to play.

Reducing price volatility
Oil prices are volatile, yet price variations can be tempered. For much of the 1990s, OPEC largely succeeded in maintaining prices within the range of US$22–28 per barrel. Yet such policies can only work if there is spare capacity to meet supply disruptions or rapid demand growth, if the US dollar holds its value, and if speculators do not dominate financial markets. This proved not to be the case after 2003. OPEC tightened supplies while few non-OPEC fields were put on line, Asian demand boomed, the US dollar declined against gold and the euro, and by 2008 speculators held half of oil futures positions compared to 20 percent prior to 2002. Price volatility flared most acutely during 2008–9 when prices reached US$147 in July 2008, before plunging to US$37 within six months, and rebounding to US$113 by March 2011. Fear of future turbulence – and its economic and political consequences – is now a feature of oil markets.

These conditions have led many governments to look into preventive measures. In 2008, an emergency meeting brought together the OPEC, IEA, and IEF Secretariats and energy ministers to address the price crisis. The "Jeddah Meeting," however, resulted in familiar calls for investment in production, closer cooperation among oil companies, and greater market transparency, but few concrete outcomes; the host, Saudi Arabia, increasing production by only 200,000 barrels per day as a goodwill gesture was interpreted by some as evidence that the "Central Bank of Oil" had already reached maximum capacity. Heads of state at the G20 summit in 2009 committed to improving transparency in energy markets, to reinforcing producer–consumer consultation, and to strengthening market supervision. Mandated by the G20, the Task Force on Commodity Futures Markets of the International Organization of Securities Commission is working toward a central registry of trades for the financial oil market. In the US, the Dodd–Frank Wall Street Reform and Consumer Protection Act (2010) had a similar goal: to increase transparency and reduce volatility risks by requiring public disclosure and trading through clearinghouses. This would prevent traders in over-the-counter (OTC) markets from taking large speculative positions without the knowledge of other traders. Implementation of these measures faces much opposition, reflecting a long history of efforts at deregulation on the part of financial and energy companies (see Box 6.1). Other potential initiatives include stricter regulation of oil markets; improving the accuracy, immediacy, and frequency of statistics on oil stocks, flows, and investments (e.g. JODI); harmonizing oil taxation; and controlling demand. Reducing price volatility is also of interest to producers. Price volatility is very damaging to their economies' growth, posing major problems for public budgets and investment planning in the both the public and private sectors. Although most analysts agree that high oil prices are likely to be sustained over the medium term, prices remain volatile and vulnerable to a major economic crisis, as demonstrated in 2009. Savings funds can buffer price shocks, with excess revenue over price benchmark being earmarked for such funds. Yet many governments have found it difficult to resist spending windfalls, later exposing themselves to large deficits when prices collapse and foreign direct investments decline. Governments, like companies, can also hedge prices through long-term contracts. The goal of reducing price volatility, however, will also be enhanced by better matching demand to supply.[1]

Matching oil demand with supply
Supply constraints around conventional oil, the rapid growth of new oil consumers, and the environmental risks associated with unconventional sources mean new thinking is required if supply and demand are to be brought into balance. Continuing the twentieth-century practice of expanding supply to meet demand not only presents very significant economic and political obstacles, but is also now carbon-constrained. A slow-down in demand growth is possible, whether via prolonged economic recession, high market prices, increased fuel taxes, or the use of consumption quotas. Demand destruction is already happening in Japan and many European countries, and more recently in the US; the major challenge is the pace of demand growth in China, India, and major Middle East oil exporters.

To keep pace with demand, an estimated $1.2 trillion dollars of investment are needed every year. Mobilizing this financing is difficult, not only because of its sheer size and the relative uncertainty of exploration and oil prices, but also because of the pattern of reserve control and opposition to unconventional oil production. First, most reserves are under the control of national governments eager to increase revenues through price rather than volume. Second, NOCs dominate the supply market and as a result of public listing, government support, and higher oil prices are facing easier conditions of access to capital (a former advantage of IOCs). This can be addressed through fostering greater NOC–IOC collaboration, and facilitating NOCs' access to capital markets. As discussed below (see p. 194), a set of constraints and incentives could also help redirect some of these investments to reducing demand and shifting to alternative fuels. Given the unwillingness of many oil producers to move in that direction, a strong measure likely to face much resistance from the oil industry is to increase the taxation of oil companies while capping prices. Another, if more painful, approach is to increase fuel taxes at the consumer level and redirect revenues toward the reduction of demand. Production increases also face environmental and other regulatory constraints on access which have come under criticism from all but progressive reformers – especially in the US. Opening up many of these remaining reserves would have only a marginal impact on oil availability and affordability while entailing major social and environmental costs.

To reduce demand, higher fuel efficiency and fuel taxes are needed. Shifting to 42 mpg cars in the US could save 3mmbd. Fuel efficiency can be improved on conventional vehicles through more efficient engines and power-trains (e.g. turbocharged gasoline, diesel, hybrid electric-gasoline), better transmissions (e.g. continuously variable transmissions), improved aerodynamics and rolling resistance, lower weight, and smaller size. Halving fuel consumption by new vehicles in the US from 21 mpg to 42 mpg by 2035 is feasible, while maintaining similar performances and without jeopardizing safety; additional costs of 20 percent would be recouped within less than five years through fuel savings at current prices. Greater fuel efficiency may motivate additional travel, but increased mileage through this "rebound effect" is less than 10 percent. Fuel efficiency alone, however, will only buy limited time as the number of vehicle users increases. Greater efficiency can also result from a shift to more efficient modes of transportation such as mass transit. Each additional mile of public transport use can save three to seven passenger miles in a car, due to more direct travel routes (think bus lanes), trip chaining, ownership of fewer cars per household, and an increased preference for higher-density residential areas.

Fuel efficiency works in synergy with prices: higher fuel prices reduce fuel demand, especially over the long term. This "price elasticity" means that higher taxes can reduce oil consumption and carbon emissions, but they work best over the long term. Price increases can result from changes in both the market and taxation. But markets send mixed signals, as people hope for a return to "low prices." Increased taxation offers the advantage of a longer time horizon, especially if rising tax rates are instituted over time. Europe would possibly be consuming twice as much oil if it had followed the US approach of low fuel taxes since the 1960s. With oil prices expected to remain high and domestic production continuing to decline, the US needs to take a major step to curtail consumption, and a gasoline tax remains the single most effective solution. The irony is that US consumers ultimately pay a high price (because of poor fuel economy standards and limited investment in mass transit) but that these dollars end up with producer countries and oil companies rather than their government and public services. China in the meantime is seeking to avoid the US pathway to oil dependence by progressively increasing fuel taxes, mandating stricter fuel efficiency, and promoting electric vehicles. Higher fuel prices need not hurt households: fuel tax revenues can be redirected to low-income families, while Iran set up an innovative system with a monthly (household) allocation of 132 liters at a subsidized price and additional consumption at full market price plus hefty taxes. By contrast, western consumers swipe air miles cards rather than fuel ration cards, their purchases rewarded with a flight's worth of free jet fuel. Such commercial logic flies in the face of current concerns. Even with major efficiency gains, sustainable transportation practices imply travel restraint and a departure from the trends that have seen annual distance traveled per capita increase tremendously over the past five decades.

Oil addiction and car obsession are already widely recognized, and the time of selective prohibition may be approaching. Will the fate of the car industry follow the path of tobacco, with restrictions on advertisement and limited access to public space? By the early 1970s, cigarettes ads had been banned from TV and radio in the US. Three decades later, tobacco advertising is internationally prohibited through the World Health Organization's Framework Convention on Tobacco Control. The global auto industry spends about US$40 billion per year on advertising to push its products, a third of which is spent on television. Advertisements focusing on car speed are prohibited in the UK. Cars are banned from some school zones to entice children to walk more, but also to reduce accidents and improve air quality. Several cities, such as London, Stuttgart, and Paris, have a congestion charge or low emission zoning regulations that limit car access to downtown areas. In 2011, the European Transport Commissioner unveiled a plan to ban conventionally fueled cars from cities by 2050; a plan that spurred comments of "insanity" and "greenwash grandstanding" by carmakers and driver associations. A long-term priority is to shift away from fossil fuels and reduce transportation needs through improved urban planning, cultural change, and a re-localization of some production processes.[2]

Decarbonizing transportation fuels
If oil-related governance in the "Age of Plenty" was mostly about controlling oil prices and supplies, it is now also about decarbonizing oil and moving to alternative energies. Decarbonizing oil is a major challenge. The industry is already reducing some of the emissions associated with oil production, including the use of carbon capture and sequestration techniques developed as part of enhanced oil recovery that involve injecting carbon dioxide into oil reservoirs. Much

more can be done to capture emissions from refining using conventional technologies. However, about 80 percent of the emissions from the fuel cycle come from final combustion. Post-combustion emissions can be reduced through more efficient and cleaner combustion, but carbon dioxide remains a necessary end product of the reaction. Current carbon capture technologies cannot be applied to mobile sources and so decarbonizing vehicle emissions requires new technologies that are still in their infancy.

Fuel alternatives to oil include natural gas, biofuels, and hydrogen, as well as electricity. Of the three liquid fuels, only hydrogen has the potential to move beyond fossil fuels if generated through a renewable energy source. Natural gas can substitute for gasoline and is already available in many countries as a transportation fuel and to upgrade unconventional oil, such as Alberta's bitumen. Biofuels are often presented as an environmentally friendly alternative to fossil fuels. Yet current modes of production are fossil fuel-intensive and, when cultivated on cleared land, often release much more GHG than they save compared to gasoline. Furthermore, first-generation biofuels, such as ethanol from corn, place major pressures on water resources, farmland, and food production. Second-generation biofuels, including crop residues and wood by-products, offer a more viable option but remain difficult to process and their allocation to fuel transportation undermines their contribution to soil quality.[3] Hydrogen is by far the cleanest liquid fuel, as it only emits water vapor, but like electricity it is only an *energy carrier* that requires primary energy inputs. Hydrogen vehicles are also less efficient than electric vehicles.[4]

Clean forms of energy with a flow rate equivalent to 85 mmbd are hard to come by. Hydrocarbons could provide a clean energy source under conditions where concentrated production facilitates carbon capture and where a non-emitting energy carrier – hydrogen or electric battery – is used at the point of consumption. Energy produced in excess of demand (surplus energy) is limited but includes, for example, idle electricity during off-peak periods. Global hydropower output represents only about 10 mmbd, nuclear power half that, while wind and solar are currently negligible. Geothermal energy could provide a long-term option due to continuous base-load power, minimal visual impacts, and a small environmental footprint. Current geothermal systems, however, release GHG gases sequestered in underground reservoirs. Tax reforms that shift profits from fossil fuels to the development and rollout of cleaner fuels are needed to accelerate this transition.[5]

Moving beyond petroleum remains a lofty goal, even for advanced economies with a strong public policy tradition such as the Scandinavian countries. In 2005, the Swedish government appointed a commission to reduce the country's dependence on fossil fuels by 2020. The government motivated its initiative by arguing that "the price of oil affects Sweden's growth and employment, ... [while] the extensive burning of fossil fuels threatens the living conditions of future generations." The commission recommended phasing out heating oil, reducing oil-based transportation fuels by half and industrial uses by up to 40 percent. Forest products, low-energy housing, and information technology would also contribute to reducing oil dependence. The incoming government did not take on these recommendations. With the world's highest fuel tax and low-cost hydroelectricity, Norway already has strong incentives in place to shift to electric vehicles. Authorities added free parking, access to bus lanes, and no congestion charges. Although usage is increasing, it remains very low. Vehicle acquisition cost, around US$30,000 for a small car, is the main obstacle – even if running costs are only a tenth of those for a gasoline car. Norway's homegrown electric vehicles company – THINK – filed for bankruptcy in 2011; yet, over the longer term, greater competition and larger production volumes are expected to bring costs down. By mid-2012, two major Japanese companies were already successfully putting all-electric vehicles on the market, with Nissan selling about 20,000 of its 99 "mpg equivalent" LEAF electric car within a year of its launch and planning to operate three factories worldwide producing 250,000 vehicles per year.

One of the main obstacles to shifting beyond petroleum is that many people are stuck with existing infrastructures, including a lack of public transportation, widely spread suburban housing, and "nonresidential" downtown areas. Several alternative models exist in North America, such as New York and Vancouver. As an old North American city, New York grew up before the automobile industry reshaped America and only one in two households currently has a car. As a very new city, Vancouver learned from the mistakes made elsewhere. The West Coast city planners banned city highways, densified the population through laneway houses in suburbs and residential high-rises in the downtown core, intensified public transport, and privileged cycling lanes over car traffic in key locations such as bridges. It is now the only Canadian city where the car ownership rate and average automobile commuting distance are falling. Unsurprisingly, Vancouver is also rated among the most "liveable" cities in the world, although people having to commute *into* and not simply *within* the city often have a different opinion. The most viable option to connecting low-density suburbs to core areas without long-distance car commuting is electric light railways, to which suburbanites connect through bike paths and park-and-ride. A large part of Holland consists of residential villages linked with city centers through dense railroad, extensive bike lanes, and large bike storage facilities at stations. Light railroad infrastructure can be built onto the median of existing highways, but funding often requires large public investments. Other technological solutions include smart grids covering the city and its periphery to recharge electric vehicles.

The links between low-density housing, the "subprime" mortgage market, and vulnerability to oil price hikes was illustrated by the 2007–8 financial crisis. The maintenance of low-density zoning rules, often a result of neighborhood homeowner associations, pushed both housing prices up and people further away from city centers. The result was a housing bubble fed by deceptively low-interest mortgages, exposing people to the double shock of rising interest rates and oil prices. Beyond city planning and transportation policies, a number of social movements have emerged to build "post-cheap oil" alternative communities, lifestyles, and livelihoods. These integrate notions of resilience, localism, and a low-carbon footprint. One recent example that has replicated itself with some success is Transition Towns, which seeks to foster local civil society innovation to reduce oil dependence. Started in 2005 in the UK, the initiative – now renamed Transition Network – had been taken up by community groups and municipal councils in nearly 400 towns in 26 countries by 2011. Activities are focused on increasing local sourcing of goods, including food, construction materials, and jobs. As shown in Figure 7.1, one of the long-term priorities for North American cities should be to increase population densities in urban areas: tripling density to about 8,000–10,000 persons per square kilometer would bring a fivefold reduction in GHG emissions from ground transportation.[6]

Preventing the oil curse
There is little doubt that oil will be around for decades, and the expectation is that oil prices will remain high, if volatile. It is thus crucial to mitigate the negative environmental and social impacts of oil extraction and to ensure that the producing

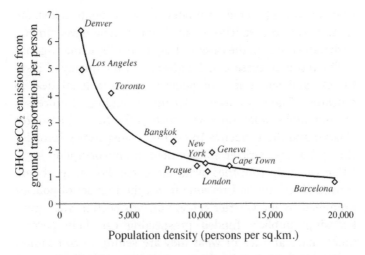

Source: Adapted with permission from C. Kennedy et al., "Greenhouse Gas Emissions from Global Cities," *Environmental Science & Technology* 43(19) (2009): 7297–7302. Copyright © 2009 American Chemical Society.

Figure 7.1 Urban population densities and ground transportation emissions per capita

countries escape the resource curse so that the next few decades of wealth transfer are not wasted for their populations. Addressing the resource curse will reduce supply and transit disruptions resulting from domestic unrest and outright conflict and from sanctions imposed by the international community on "rogue regimes." It will also help prepare producing countries for a post-oil context by diversifying their economies and opening their political institutions so as to attenuate the shocks of revenue decline. Better-governed oil-producing countries will more legitimately participate in international fora. Finally, tackling the resource curse can not only improve development outcomes but also prevent disruptions in oil production: there is good evidence that higher levels of corruption reduce production while political instability and economic sanctions can slow new field development, as demonstrated in the cases of Iraq, Iran, Libya, and Nigeria.

The resource curse is not a given, and the quality of institutions and soundness of policies matter a great deal to outcomes. There is now a better understanding of processes at work, and several initiatives, such as the Natural Resource Charter and the Extractive Industries Transparency Initiative (EITI), but also stricter enforcement of anticorruption legislation can help countries avoid the curse. Following the oil commodity chain and revenue flows, the first set of policies promoted by the Charter centers on prospecting and award licensing: publicly funded prospecting can help governments have an idea of what they are selling to companies. Public bidding of oil blocks is a must to ensure that returns are maximized through open competition and corruption risk minimized through transparent procedures that involve little discretionary power. Operations need to be properly regulated, with environmental and social impacts prevention and mitigation mechanisms to avoid conflicts with local communities and strict metering and cost monitoring to prepare for taxation. Tax collection needs to be based on competent evaluation, with independent verification of company payments and government receipts, as promoted by the EITI. Auditing all along the revenue stream is crucial, especially with regard to transfer mispricing on the tax assessment side and embezzlement on the part of officials on the expenditure side. Finally, revenues must balance allocations to savings, current expenditures, and long-term investments – with spending prioritizing sustainability, poverty alleviation, and long-term growth outside of nonrenewable resource sector.[7]

International efforts to avoid the resource curse have been put to the test in Chad. Taking place under a dictatorial regime in one of the world's poorest country, the Chad–Cameroon

Oil and Pipeline project was certain to attract both domestic and international criticism. Eager to reduce reputational risks, the Exxon-led project consortium obtained the backing of the World Bank in 2000. Leveraging its donor status, the World Bank obtained an agreement from the Chadian government to commit most of the revenues to poverty reduction programs and to accept independent revenue monitoring. The World Bank also oversaw an environmental impact mitigation program. The scheme has been held up as a pioneering effort and model for future oil development. Yet the scheme was soon confronted by the realities of a bankrupt and militarized regime that came under renewed attacks from Sudan-supported rebels in 2003 and 2006. The regime of Idriss Déby rescinded on the agreement with the Bank and the law on petroleum revenues it had passed, allocating more funds to defense. The World Bank attempted to put pressure on the government by suspending non-humanitarian aid to the country, but to no avail. By 2010, Chad produced about 120,000 barrels per day, generating around US$2 billion in government revenue, ten times the amount of taxes collected by the government before oil started flowing from the Doba fields to the Cameroonian port of Kribi. If the scheme demonstrated its limited benefits for the population, it proved sufficiently successful to sustain Exxon's tenure.

In Sudan, no such process came to support Canadian investments in the development of oil fields and the construction of a pipeline to Port Sudan on the Red Sea. Advocacy campaigns and the risk of delisting on the US stock market led the Canadian company Talisman to divest in 2003, selling its share to the Indian NOC, Oil and National Gas Corporation Videsh Ltd (OVL, ONGC's international arm). The Chinese NOC leading the consortium – CNPC – also faced criticisms, but while the Canadian government had conducted an investigation into allegations of Talisman's complicity in human rights abuses and war crimes, the Chinese government intervened repeatedly to protect its NOC and prevent sanctions from being imposed on the regime in Khartoum. The birth of South Sudan as a result of the 2011 referendum set new challenges to oil governance in Sudan, but also opportunities as both Northern and Southern governments have an interest in keeping the oil flowing. The Chadian and Sudanese oil projects demonstrate the motives and limits of governance interventions in poor and conflict-affected countries governed by autocracies.

Donor agencies and international NGOs can assist in addressing the resource curse. The Norwegian government plays a leading role through its Oil for Development program in terms of funding, capacity building, and technical assistance. Partnering with Revenue Watch Institute, a leading NGO on resource revenue accountability, this Norwegian program has helped run bidding processes and support local civil society organizations to reduce opportunities for corruption. The impacts of these programs alone are very often limited, as oil wealth too frequently insulates producer governments from both external and domestic pressure. A strong and independent local civil society is often required, while national champions among top bureaucrats and politicians can help supersede the vested interests of political, bureaucratic, and corporate circles. Even then, electoral cycles often disrupt the pace and direction of reforms, as suggested by the rollback in oil revenue transparency and accountability during the late rule of Nigerian President Obasanjo, who had been an early champion of the EITI. Addressing the resource curse is a major imperative: first, populations in many oil countries will benefit more from their oil wealth and see fewer economic and political distortions; second, stronger institutions and a diversified economy will facilitate the transition to post-oil that many countries are expected to experience in the coming two or three decades, improving the chances for long-term prosperity rather than debt and poverty; and third, by helping to lessen the risk of disruptions to production and supply, it will help to reduce price volatility.

Conclusion

Our account has sought to capture the emergence of a "new geopolitics" of oil. Conventional accounts of the geopolitics of oil situate oil at the center of a territorially based, zero-sum game in which states struggle over access to resources and markets. In contrast, we have stressed the network character of oil production, and the new realities that are reshaping its organization and geographies. In doing so, we have pointed to an apparently intractable challenge: efforts to sustain supply in the face of rising demand exacerbate the economic, social, and environmental problems already associated with capturing, producing, and consuming oil. There is, then, we conclude, a critical problem of governance. The world lacks an effective platform to negotiate the place of oil in a long-term energy future. The two main institutions, OPEC and IEA, remain largely hampered by their respective roles as producer and consumer clubs, and emergent structures like IEF and IRENA are also closely tied to producer roots. There are a number of ad hoc initiatives on key issues, such as revenue transparency with the EITI, but such fragmented approaches face a high risk of long-term failure when poorly institutionalized and only driven by voluntary participation. Their reliance on effective civil society organizations to bring about accountability for misused oil revenues, for example, does not account for the relative weakness of such organizations in authoritarian oil-rich states.

In the short-to-medium term, the challenge for actors all along the production network is to make oil better – that is, to improve oil's capacity to deliver social development, to disable its links to militarism and violence, to accelerate the decoupling of oil from greenhouse gas emissions, and to find ways to organize oil along lines that are fairer and more just for those who currently bear oil's costs. Making oil "better" might sound a modest proposition, but it is nothing of the sort. It recognizes that oil now consistently underperforms on broad social objectives and that ultimately it is society that grants firms and industries their "license to operate," a license that is conditional on perceived contributions to social goals. In the longer term, the task is to find ways to move beyond oil. This will involve action now to accelerate oil's exit from the transportation sector of the economy and curb energy demand. Given the proliferation of oil throughout modern life, policies to "disembed" oil will have broad range and reach, including policies on urban design, the funding of public transportation, the economic restructuring of oil-exporting countries, and the allocation and pricing of carbon.

Strategically, the choice between better oil and beyond oil is a false one. First, pursuing better oil need not undermine efforts to move beyond fossil fuels. Any desirable shift toward alternative fuels needs to be part of a broader transition toward economies that are more socially just as well as toward lower carbon, characterized in part by increasing the availability of energy services to the poor. Second, the most likely geopolitical scenario is that some countries will continue to take an early and precautionary path to a post-oil transition, while others – limited by their economic capacity or political ability to undertake such a shift – will remain at the mercy of a declining and problematic resource. The "great transition" beyond oil, in other words, will in practice be a divergence between the "oil-free" and the "oil-fueled." The good news is that such a partial and geographically uneven transition may reduce some of the supply constraints and market risks for the oil-fueled. The bad news is that it also risks taking off some of the pressure from oil consumers, producers, and other actors in the oil production network to improve oil's record. The most progressive countries should therefore not jettison oil – and their interest in better oil – too soon as their contribution here can make a significant difference. Last, but not least, many poor countries and communities will de facto move beyond oil: not as a result of active choices, but simply because they will be priced out. Such a forced move is unlikely to improve their energy security in the absence of collective efforts to build alternatives. For these reasons, we now need to commit to "better oil," while working toward a future "beyond oil."

Notes

CHAPTER I THE NATURE OF A POLITICAL RESOURCE

1 A largely disproven abiogenic (or abiotic) theory argues that petroleum comes from inorganic carbon. Another, the deep biotic theory, argues that some oil could come from the lifecycle of deep bacteria. M. Tucker, *Sedimentary Petrology: An Introduction to the Origin of Sedimentary Rocks* (Blackwell Science, 1991).

2 For work on energy surplus, see J. Martinez-Alier, *Ecological Economics: Energy, Environment and Society* (Blackwell, 1987); C. Hall et al. "Peak Oil, EROI, Investment and the Economy in an Uncertain Future," in *Biofuels, Solar and Wind as Renewable Energy Systems*, ed. D. Pimentel (Springer, 2008: 109–32); C. A. S. Hall et al., "Hydrocarbons and the Evolution of Human Culture," *Nature* 426(6964) (2003): 318–22; H. Haberl, "The Global Socioeconomic Energetic Metabolism as a Sustainability Problem," *Energy* 31(1) (2006): 87–99. G. Bridge, "Beyond Peak Oil: Political Economy of Energy Crises," in *Global Political Ecology*, ed. R. Peet et al. (Routledge, 2011).

3 On the risk of Saudi oil production collapse, see M. Simmons, *Twilight in the Desert: The Coming Saudi Oil Shock and the World Economy* (Wiley, 2005).

4 For example, M. Klare, "The era of Xtreme energy: life after the age of oil," www.tomdispatch.com/post/175127 (2009); see also M. Klare, *The Race for What's Left: The Global Scramble for the World's Last Resources* (Metropolitan Books, 2012).

5 Although geographically diversified by historical standards, global production remains dominated by huge formations in Saudi Arabia, other parts of the Middle East, Nigeria, and Russia. One in every 12–13 barrels produced worldwide comes from just two

fields, the Burgan field in Kuwait and Saudi Arabia's mammoth Ghawar field. For a commentary on historic shifts in the geography of oil production and consumption, see P. Odell, "The Global Oil Industry: The Location of Production – Middle East Domination or Regionalisation?" *Regional Studies* 31(3) (1997): 311–22. Reuters, November 21, 2011 "Saudi sees threat of shale oil revolution." On future unconventional oil production, see S. H. Mohr and G. M. Evans, "Long-term Prediction of Unconventional Oil Production," *Energy Policy* 38(1) (2010): 265–76.

6 Figures on oil consumption per capita are from the US CIA World Factbook. They need to be treated with caution, however, as they do not adjust for consumption in petrochemical refining and re-export: the equivalent figures for Singapore and the US Virgin Islands, for example, are 190 and 845, both of which host major oil refinery complexes. Hovensa's oil refinery on the US Virgin Islands – one of the largest in the world – was scheduled for closure in 2012.

7 T. Wang and J. Watson, "China's Carbon Emissions and International Trade: Implications for Post-2012 Policy," *Climate Policy* 8 (2008): 577–87. "Indonesia becomes net oil importer," *Alexander's Gas and Oil Connections*. August 9, 2005; quote is from J. Rubin, "Demand Shift," in *Carbon Shift: How the Twin Crises of Oil Depletion and Climate Change Will Define the Future*, ed. T. Homer-Dixon (Random House, 2009: 133–51).

CHAPTER 2 CAPTURING OIL

1 On the UN's role in the evolution of natural resource sovereignty, see N. Schrijver, *Sovereignty over Natural Resources: Balancing Rights and Duties* (Cambridge University Press, 1997). On the environmental and social history of oil in Veracruz in the early twentieth century and its role in Mexico's nationalization of American and Anglo-Dutch oil firms, see M. Santiago, *The Ecology of Oil: Environment, Labor and the Mexican Revolution, 1900–1938* (Cambridge University Press, 2007).

2 E. Palazuelos, "Current Oil (disorder): Players, Scenarios, and Mechanisms," *Review of International Studies* (2011); conditions in Siberia do not allow for a simple "shutting in" of production: see "Russia tells OPEC eyes swing producer role,"

Reuters, www.reuters.com/article/2008/10/22/us-opec-russia-idUSTRE49L20S20081022 (2010); "New oil war in Asia: Saudia Arabia vs. Russia," Al Arabiya News, www.alarabiya.net/articles/2011/06/29/155373.html. On oil and US–Middle East relations, see J. Nitzan and S. Bichler's explanation of a "weapondollar/petrodollar" coalition in *The Global Political Economy of Israel* (Pluto Press, 2002); figures on the erosion of spare capacity from J. Jesse and C. van der Linde, *Oil Turbulence in the Next Decade* (Clingendael International Energy Programme, 2008).

3 Eurasia Group, *China's Overseas Investments in Oil and Gas Production*, US–China Economic and Security Review Commission (2006); and X. Xu, *Chinese NOCs' Overseas Strategies: Background, Comparison and Remarks*, James A. Baker III Institute for Public Policy, Rice University (2007). On human rights and Chinese companies in Sudan and Myanmar, see M. Chen, "Chinese National Oil Companies and Human Rights," *Orbis* 51(1) (2007): 41–54. "PetroChina makes its debut as world's first trillion-dollar firm," *Guardian*, November 6, 2007; J. Jiang and J. Sinton, *Overseas Investments by Chinese National Oil Companies: Assessing the Drivers and Impacts*, International Energy Agency (2011).

4 "Agents" quote is from B. Mommer, *Global Oil and the Nation State* (Oxford University Press, 2002). China's oil imports nearly quadrupled between 2000 and 2010, making China the second largest importer after the United States. Over half the growth in oil demand over the next five years is expected to come from China.

5 For a discussion of whether the US needs a national oil company, see A. Jaffe and R. Soligo, *The International Oil Companies*, James A. Baker III Institute for Public Policy, Rice University (2007); V. Vivoda, "Resource Nationalism, Bargaining and International Oil Companies: Challenges and Change in the New Millennium," *New Political Economy* 14(4) (2009): 517–34; and R. Pirog, *The Role of National Oil Companies in the International Oil Market*. CRS Report for Congress, August 21, 2007.

6 E. Downs and S. Maloney, "Getting China to Sanction Iran," *Foreign Affairs* 90(2) (2011): 15–21. On the Alien Tort Act, see O. Murray, D. Kinley, and C. Potts, "Exaggerated Rumors of the Death of an Alien Tort: Corporations, Human Rights and the Remarkable Case of Kiobel," *Melbourne Journal of International Law* 12 (2011): 57–94.

7 Seven Sisters were Standard Oil of New Jersey (Exxon after 1972), Standard Oil of New York (Mobil), Standard Oil of California (Chevron), Gulf Oil, Texaco, Royal Dutch Shell, and Anglo-Persian Oil Company (BP). In 2007, the *Financial Times* listed the "New Seven Sisters" as Saudi Aramco, Russia's Gazprom, CNPC of China, Iran's NIOC, PdVSA of Venezuela, Brazil's Petrobras, and Petronas from Malaysia. Petroleum Intelligence Weekly, Ranking of Top 10 Oil Companies, December 2011.
8 Reserves replacement figures in previous section are from A. Jaffe and R. Soligo, *The International Oil Companies*, James A. Baker III Institute for Public Policy, Rice University (2007). The dynamic of cooperation and conflict between resource-holding states and resource-seeking firms is structured by three overlapping cycles: the price cycle, the project cycle, and the political cycle, see P. Stevens, "National Oil Companies and International Oil Companies in the Middle East: Under the Shadow of Government and the Resource Nationalism Cycle," *Journal of World Energy Law and Business* 1(1) (2008): 5–30; "ultimate prize" is from Dick Cheney (then CEO for Halliburton) in a speech in 1999, quoted in G. Muttitt, "Production sharing agreements: oil privatisation by another name?" Paper presented to the General Union of Oil Employees' conference on privatization, Basrah, Iraq, May 26, 2005.
9 For a discussion of "proprietorial" and "non-proprietorial" regimes, and the attempts by major oil importers to overturn nationalizations during the 1990s, see B. Mommer, *Global Oil and the Nation State* (Oxford University Press, 2002). For a comparison of different types of access agreements, see M. Likosky, "Contracting and Regulatory Issues in the Oil and Gas and Metallic Minerals Industries," *Transnational Corporations* 18(1) (2009): 1–42.
10 Concessions were the standard form of access agreement until the 1950s and provided international oil firms with highly favorable terms of access: concessions were very large (those in Iran, Iraq, Kuwait, and Saudi Arabia covered on average 88 percent of the country), and could be held for long periods of time (the average was 82 years). Financial payments were typically a lump-sum royalty and, until Venezuela introduced profit taxes in 1948 (subsequently replicated in the Middle East), included no link to the profitability of production. Companies were also given

a very large degree of managerial freedom in deciding where and when to produce, and how to price output. This set up tensions with the host state: it was a decision by the majors in the 1950s to cut oil prices that drove the governments of leading concession countries to form OPEC in 1960, and which gave encouragement to calls for nationalization. See Selected Readings section.

11 For an example of work by NGOs that seeks to draw attention of investors to the increasing reliance of IOCs on unconventional and "marginal oil," see L. Stockman, *Reserves Replacement in a Marginal World: Adequate Indicator or Subprime Statistic?* Report produced by Oil Change International, Greenpeace and Platform; "Exxon deal highlights oil reserves issue," *Financial Times*, February 16, 2011.

12 M. Minio-Paluello, *The Oil and Gas Bank: RBS and the Financing of Climate Change*, report produced by BankTrack, FOE-Scotland, Nef, People and Planet and PLATFORM, (2007); RBS "Our financing of the energy sector," RBS Sustainability Briefing Document, October 2010.

13 S. Mui and E. Landeros, *Oil Companies' Investments in Dirty Fuels Outpacing Cleaner Fuels by Fifty Times*, Natural Resources Defense Council. Available at www.arb.ca.gov/lists/lcfs2011/42-comments_of_nrdc_on_oil_industry_investments_lcfs.pdf (2011). "Extreme energy" is from Michael Klare (see chapter 1); "BP frozen out of Arctic drilling race," *Guardian*, August 25, 2010; M. Bradshaw, *Environmental Groups Campaign Against Sakhalin-2 Project Financing*, Pacific Oil and Gas Report, Spring (2005): 3–9. Figures for the Baku–Tiblisi–Ceyhan pipeline are from Platform, "The money behind the pipeline," Unravelling the Carbon Web, available at www.carbonweb.org/showitem.asp?article=40&parent=5&link=Y&gp=3.

14 See research by the Carbon Tracker Initiative, "Unburnable Carbon: Are the World's Financial Markets Carrying a Carbon Bubble?" (2011); see also Stockman, *Reserves Replacement* (n. 11 above).

15 See J. van Ypersele, "Climate Change and Fossil Fuel Depletion." Presentation at the 9th ASPO Meeting, Brussels, April 24, 2011. www.astr.ucl.ac.be/modx/index.php?id=69; The growing flow of oil into industrializing economies during the twentieth century flooded pollutant sinks across progressively larger spatial scales, from the challenges of urban photochemical smog associated

with suburbanization in the late 1950s to today's concern with global carbon dioxide accumulation: see B. Clark and R. York, "Carbon Metabolism: Global Capitalism, Climate Change, and the Biospheric Rift," *Theory and Society* 34(4) (2005): 391–428. For recent reflections on the impact of higher prices and efficiency on oil demand, see Deutsche Bank Global Research, October 4, 2009, The Peak Oil Market; IEA (2010) *World Energy Outlook 2010*; and Stockman, *Reserves Replacement* (n. 11 above).

CHAPTER 3 MARKETING OIL

1 On the barrel, see M. Downey, *Oil 101* (Wooden Table Press, 2009). The Fuel Quality Directive requires suppliers of fuel to report the carbon intensity of their fuels and reduce lifecycle greenhouse gas emissions by 10 percent by 2020; see D. Sperling and S. Yeh, "Toward a Global Low Carbon Fuel Standard," *Transport Policy* 17(1) (2010): 47–9. T. Zachariadis (ed.), *Cars and Carbon: Automobiles and European Climate Policy in a Global Context* (Springer, 2011). The proposed assigned value for bituminous sands is 107g CO_2 equivalent per megajoule of fuel versus an average of 87g CO_2 equivalent for crude oil, www.euractiv.com/climate-environment/eu-faces-tar-sands-industry-news-508140.

2 P. Odell, *Oil and World Power* (Pelican Books, 1986). Control of the majors in the US market was limited to transportation and refining: the "Seven Sisters" controlled only a third of upstream output with the remainder made up by thousands of smaller companies. Proration's influence on price stability therefore achieved what the majors alone could not, and was a source of tension between large and small oil-producing companies. B. Mommer, *Global Oil and the Nation State* (Oxford University Press, 2002: 56). R. Cook, "Pro-ration: the regulation of oil and gas." SPE Gas Technology Symposium, Omaha, Nebraska, June 1978. M. Huber, "Enforcing Scarcity: Oil, Violence and the Making of the Market," *Annals of the Association of American Geographers* 101(4) (2011): 816–26.

3 On Achnacarry and the "As-Is" Agreement, see J. Bamberg, *The History of the British Petroleum Company, Volume 2: The Anglo-Iranian Years, 1928–1954* (Cambridge University Press, 1994:

528–34). International oil companies came to see in OPEC an opportunity for an alliance around price, at the same time as they were disputing the changing terms of access to Middle East reserves. OPEC accounted for sufficient world production to exert control over supply, while its actions provided a convenient cover by which the international oil companies could distance themselves from rising prices to consumers. P. Odell, *Oil and World Power*, (Pelican Books, 1986). B. Mommer, *Global Oil and the Nation State* (Oxford University Press, 2002). J. Jesse and C. van der Linde, *Oil Turbulence in the Next Decade: An Essay on High Oil Prices in a Supply-constrained World*, Clingendael International Energy Programme, The Hague (2007).

4 D. Robinson, and F. Badin, "Does the Electric Car Have a Future?" *Oxford Energy Forum* 80 (2010): 13–19; M. Paterson, "Car Culture and Global Environmental Politics," *Review of International Studies* 26 (2000): 253–70; M. Huber, "The Use of Gasoline: Value, Oil and the 'American Way of Life,'" *Antipode* 41(3) (2008): 465–86; I. Rutledge, *America's Relentless Drive for Energy Security* (I. B. Tauris, 2005); E. Black, *Internal Combustion: How Corporations and Governments Addicted the World to Oil and Derailed the Alternatives* (St Martins Press, 2006).

5 OPEC, *World Oil Outlook* (2010); B. Fattouh, "Global Oil Demand Dynamics: Re-balancing the Debate," *Oxford Energy Forum* 80 (2010): 6–8; R. Fouquet, "The Slow Search for Solutions: Lessons from Historical Energy Transitions by Sector and Service," *Energy Policy* 38 (2010): 6586–96; IEA, *World Energy Outlook* (2010).

6 For a history of plastics and their remarkable proliferation in the twentieth century, see S. Freinkel, *Plastic: A Toxic Love Story* (Houghton Mifflin Harcourt, 2011). On efforts by Monsanto to secure peacetime markets for new plastics developed during the war, see S. Phillips, "Plastics," in B. Colomina et al. (eds), *Cold War Hothouses: Inventing Postwar Culture, from Cockpit to Playboy* (Princeton University Press, 2004: 91–123).

7 The control of the majors over the supply of oil was as high as 85 percent for areas outside Canada, the US, China, and the Soviet Union; cited in B. Fattouh, *An Anatomy of the Crude Oil Pricing System*, Oxford Institute for Energy Studies, WPM 40 (2011). On the growing gap between posted and actual prices, see D. Yergin, *The Prize* (Simon and Schuster, 1991).

8 R. Scott, *IEA: The First 20 Years, 1974–1994. Volume 1: Origins and Structure*, IEA (1994); B. Mommer, *Global Oil and the Nation State* (Oxford University Press, 2002); T. Van der Graaf and D. Lesage, "The International Energy Agency after 35 Years: Reform Needs and Institutional Adaptability," *Review of International Organisation* 4 (2009): 293–317. The EIA has released oil from its reserves on three occasions, most recently to offset loss of high-quality "sweet" crude from Libya during the Arab Spring of 2011; see "IEA drawdown marks major shift in oil price policy," *Financial Times*, June 23, 2011.

9 A significant "spot market" for oil first emerged at the end of the 1970s in the wake of the Iranian Revolution, which imposed significant restrictions on the amount of oil available to buyers under reference-price contracts, and where short-term sales of oil through Rotterdam provided some liquidity under very tight market conditions: Daniel Yergin, *The Prize* (Simon and Schuster, 1991). The long-windedness of BFOE reflects efforts by the price-reporting agency (Platts) to maintain a North Sea benchmark by adding new oil fields to ensure minimal volumes.

10 A. Turner et al., *The Oil Trading Markets 2003–2010*, Oxford Institute for Energy Studies, WPM 42 (2011); J. Parsons, *Black Gold & Fool's Gold: Speculation in the Oil Futures Market*, Center for Energy and Environmental Policy Research, MIT (2009); D. Domanski and A. Heath, *Financial Investors and Commodity Markets*, Bank for International Settlements (2007); B. Büyükşahin et al., "Fundamentals, Trading Activity and Derivative Pricing"; paper presented at the 2009 Meeting of the European Finance Association. While striking, comparisons of trading volumes with oil production (one analysis indicates a global figure as high as 19:1 in 2009) need to be treated carefully as the former is a stock variable ("snapshot") while the other is a flow variable measured over time: see R. Alquist and O. Gervais, *The Role of Financial Speculation in Driving the Price of Crude Oil*, Bank of Canada/Banque du Canada, Discussion Paper 2011-6. M. Labban, "Oil in Parallax: Scarcity, Markets and the Financialisation of Accumulation," *Geoforum* 41(4) (2010): 541–52.

11 The terminology of "commercial/noncommercial traders" seeks to distinguish commodity hedging behavior from speculation. See Alquist and Gervais (2011, cited n. 10). For a quantification of

the effect that speculation has on gasoline prices in the US, see R. Pollin and J. Heintz, *How Wall Street Speculation is Driving Up Gas Prices Today*, Political Economy Research Institute Research Brief (Amherst, University of Massachusetts, 2011). See also K. Medlock and A. Jaffe, *Who is in the Oil Futures Market and How Has it Changed?* James A. Baker III Institute for Public Policy, Rice University (2009). The number of NYMEX contracts for light sweet crude rose from around 600,000 in 2000 to over 3 million by the middle of 2008, with the bulk of this rise attributable to noncommercial traders, see OPEC (2010: 25), *World Oil Report*. On volatility and its relationship to price – so-called "oil vega" – see K. Moors, *The Vega Factor: Oil Volatility and the Next Global Crisis* (Wiley, 2011).

12 O. Noreng, *Crude Power: Politics and the Oil Market* (I. B. Tauris, 2007: xviii); F. Mohamedi, "China: a new model in overseas oil strategy," available at www.china.org.cn/opinion/2009-09/11/content_18509242.htm (2009).

13 J. Rubin, "Demand Shift," in *Carbon Shift*, ed. Homer Dixon, (Random House, 2009: 133–52). Paul Stevens comments on the rise of "value-based management" as a financial strategy in the oil industry since the 1990s and its implications for new capacity installation. The essence of this strategy is that "if the company cannot earn a rate of return on its capital at least as great as the equities in the sector and the market more generally, then it should return funds to the shareholders via dividends or share buybacks rather than investing itself," "Oil Markets and the Future," in *The New Energy Paradigm*, ed. D. Helm (Oxford University Press, 2007: 129). Stevens points out that in 2005 the six largest international oil companies invested $54 billion in new projects while returning $71 billion to shareholders via dividends and buybacks. See also A. Jaffe and R. Soligo, *The International Oil Companies*, James A. Baker III Institute for Public Policy, Rice University (2007). Share buybacks, as a proportion of capital outlay for the leading five supermajors, rose from 1% in 1993 to 37% in 2006 while expenditure on exploration fell in the same period from 13.8% to 5.8%. J. Jesse and C. van der Linde, *Oil Turbulence in the Next Decade: An Essay on High Oil Prices in a Supply-constrained World*, Clingendael International Energy Programme, The Hague (2007: 13).

CHAPTER 4 SECURING OIL

1 Iraqi armed forces invaded neighboring Iran in September 1980 to undermine its Islamic revolution and seize the oil-rich province of Khuzestan. Anxious not to see the Iran regime prevail, western and regional governments grudgingly supported Iraq, turning the Iran–Iraq war into an eight-year stalemate. The Iraqi regime of Saddam Hussein sought to regain wealth and prestige by militarily annexing Kuwait in 1990. Thrown out of the emirate within seven months by US-led coalition forces, Saddam Hussein finally came to a violent end as a result of the US-led invasion of Iraq in 2003. See D. Stokes and S. Raphael, *Global Energy Security and American Hegemony* (Johns Hopkins University Press, 2010).

2 On the geopolitics of natural gas, see M. J. Bradshaw, *Gas* (Polity Press, 2012). On oil and gas distinct diversification trends, see G. Cohen et al., "Measuring Energy Security: Trends in the Diversification of Oil and Natural Gas Supplies," WP/11/39, IMF (2011).

3 L. Hughes and D. Shupe, "Applying the Four 'A's of Energy Security as Criteria in an Energy Security Ranking Method," in *The Routledge Handbook of Energy Security*, ed. B. K. Sovacool (Routledge, 2011). Other renewables include geothermal, wind, and solar.

4 See M. Klare, *Rising Powers, Shrinking Planet* (Metropolitan Books, 2008); J. Colgan, "Oil and Resource-backed Aggression," *Energy Policy* 39(3): 1669–76; M. Ross, *The Oil Curse: How Petroleum Wealth Shapes the Development of Nations* (Princeton University Press, 2012).

5 About 60 countries in the world produce more than 50,000 barrels of oil per day, but nearly half remain net oil importers. E. Gupta, "Oil Vulnerability Index of Oil-Importing Countries," *Energy Policy* 36(3) (2008): 1195–1211; K. D. Jacoby, "Energy Security: Conceptualization of the International Energy Agency," *Facing Global Environmental Change* 4 (2009): 345–54; M. A. Delucchi and J. J. Murphy, "US Military Expenditures to Protect the Use of Persian Gulf Oil for Motor Vehicles," *Energy Policy* 36(6) (2008): 2253–64; R. J. Stern, "United States Cost of Military Force Projection in the Persian Gulf, 1976–2007," *Energy Policy* 38(6) (2010): 2816–25. Global oil stocks include two

billion barrels of commercial stocks and two and a half billion barrels in strategic stocks, about 52 days of consumption.

6 On the relative importance of income, see R. Kowsari and H. Zerriffi, "Three Dimensional Energy Profile: A Conceptual Framework for Assessing Household Energy Use," *Energy Policy* 39(12) (2011): 7505–17. Price elasticity for oil is about –0.09 (10% price increase reduces demand by 0.9%) in the short run and –0.31 in the long run, but the higher the price in absolute terms the greater the responses by consumers; see T. Havranek et al., "Demand for Gasoline is More Price-Inelastic than Commonly Thought," CUDARE Working Paper 1119, Berkeley (2011). Average households in OECD countries now spend about 5% of their income on transportation fuel, for a total of about 20% on energy.

7 On energy poverty in the UK, see B. Boardman, *Fuel Poverty: From Cold Homes to Affordable Warmth* (Belhaven Press, 1991). The fuel bill of 58 net fuel-importing countries increased by $60 billion, or 3.2% of GDP in 2007–8, about three times the 2006 domestic health budget of all low-income countries; see Statement by the Managing Director of the IMF, October 10 2008.

8 The price of gasoline in Iraq went from 1.5 cents to about 35 cents per liter between 2005 and 2007, with an informal market price of one dollar per liter; see www.fas.org/sgp/crs/natsec/RS22923. pdf. The 1989 "fuel riot" in Venezuela resulted in between 275 and 3000 deaths.

9 European countries heavily taxed transport fuel from the 1950s onward, in the case of France in 1951 to pay for roads and rearmament, and again in the context of the 1970s' oil crisis; see J. Dunn, "The French Highway Lobby: A Case Study in State–Society Relations and Policy," *Comparative Politics* 27(3): 275–95. On US public opinion about fuel taxes, see "New Poll Finds Little Support for Fuel Tax," *The Americano*, April 20, 2010; T. Friedman, "Who Is Afraid of a Gas Tax?" *New York Times*, March 1, 2006. Direct fuel taxes are more effective at reducing fuel consumption than fuel-efficiency incentives; see N. Wozny and H. Allcott, "Gasoline Prices, Fuel Economy, and the Energy Paradox" (MIT CEEPR, 2010); S. Li, "Gasoline Taxes and Consumer Behaviour" (Harvard and RFF, 2011). Reducing US oil consumption by half would result in a decline of oil

prices since the US consumes about 22 percent of global oil production. Arguments against higher taxation of automobility include: the freedom to choose (although market choice is structured by corporate decision making and strongly influenced by marketing); an anti-tax ideology (which tends to ignore large tax expenditures on car-related infrastructure); concern that taxes are economically inefficient and disproportionately hurt the poor (although the economic benefits of improvements in energy efficiency can be substantial and the distributional impacts of taxation depend on how tax receipts are allocated); and denial of significant environmental and social externalities (despite scientific evidence). See A. M. Bento et al., "Distributional and Efficiency Impacts of Increased US Gasoline Taxes," *The American Economic Review* 99(3) (2009): 667–99.

10 H. Wang, "China's Oil Policy and Its Impact," *Energy Policy* 23(7) (1995): 627–35. EIA *Energy Outlook 2011*. On Chinese NOCs and oil diplomacy, see Shaofen Chen, "Motivations Behind China's Foreign Oil Quest: A Perspective from the Chinese Government and the Oil Companies," *Journal of Chinese Political Science* 13(1) (2008): 79–104; Julie Jiang and Jonathan Sinton, "Overseas Investments by Chinese National Oil Companies: Assessing the Drivers and Impacts" (Paris: International Energy Agency, 2011). Chinese capping demand is suggested by FGE chairman Fereidun Fesharaki, cited in "Will China Cap Its Oil Demand?", *Oil and Gas Journal*, August 18, 2010. See X. Yan and R. J. Crookes, "Energy Demand and Emissions from Road Transportation Vehicles in China," *Progress in Energy and Combustion Science* 36(6) (2010): 651–76.

11 For human rights rankings, see CFIP at Carleton University. Human Rights Watch, *China's Involvement in Sudan: Arms and Oil*, November 24, 2003. Ben Geman, "BP Upped Ad Spending to $93M Over Spill," *The Hill*, September 1, 2010. The limits of CSR are discussed by J. G. Frynas, "The False Developmental Promise of Corporate Social Responsibility: Evidence from Multinational Oil Companies," *International Affairs* 81(3) (2005): 581–98. Saudi reaction to the 9/11 image problem is explained by J. Zhang and W. L. Benoit, "Message Strategies of Saudi Arabia's Image Restoration Campaign after 9/11," *Public Relations Review* 30(2) (2004): 161–7. See Andrew Nikiforuk, "The Fallacy of 'Ethical Oil,'" *The Tyee*, September 22, 2010. For an ardent

critique of the oil industry, see A. Juhasz, *The Tyranny of Oil: The World's Most Powerful Industry – and What We Must Do to Stop It* (Harper Paperbacks, 2009). For a corporate response putting the blame on government policies, see John Hofmeinster, *Why We Hate the Oil Companies* (Palgrave Macmillan, 2010).

CHAPTER 5 DEVELOPING THROUGH OIL

1 FAO, "The State of Food and Agriculture 2005 – Agricultural Trade and Poverty. Can Trade Work for the Poor?", ftp://ftp.fao.org/docrep/fao/008/a0050e/a0050e_full.pdf Table A4, p. 159. See D. A. Pfeiffer, *Eating Fossil Fuels: Oil, Food and the Coming Crisis in Agriculture* (New Society Publishers, 2006); J. Wright, *Sustainable Agriculture and Food Security in Era of Oil Scarcity* (Earthscan, 2008); D. Pimentel and M. Pimentel, *Food, Energy, and Society* (CRC Press, 2008).

2 See D. O'Rourke and S. Connolly, "Just Oil? The Distribution of Environmental and Social Impacts of Oil Production and Consumption," *Annual Review of Environment and Resources* 28 (2003): 587–617; CO_2 emissions based on IPCC and IEA data. M. Wu et al., "Water Consumption in the Production of Ethanol and Petroleum Gasoline," *Environmental Management* 44(5) (2009): 981–97; A. Price, "The 1991 Gulf War: Environmental Assessments of IUCN and Collaborators" (Gland: IUCN, 1994); Muhammad Sadiq and John Charles McCain, *The Gulf War Aftermath: An Environmental Tragedy* (Springer, 1993); "Oil Well Fires" section of the US Department of Defense Environmental Exposure Report (www.gulflink.osd.mil/owf_ii/). On marine oil pollution, see http://oils.gpa.unep.org/. US Statistics from the Pipeline and Hazardous Materials Safety Administration (http://phmsa.dot.gov/). Adam Nossiter, "Far from Gulf, a Spill Scourge 5 Decades Old," *New York Times*, June 16, 2010; Dirk Olin, "Exxon's Endless Lawsuit," *Portfolio.com*, March 23, 2009. Aging pipelines would come under greater corrosive stress from bitumen-based crude, a risk that Alberta's Energy Resource Conservation Board rejects: ERCB, "ERCB Addresses Statements in Natural Resources Defense Council Pipeline Safety Report" (2011); NRDC, "Tar Sands Pipeline Safety Risks" (2011).

3 Statistics from Baker Hughes, CIA World Fact book, EIA, Greenpeace, National Academies, World Health Organization, and M. R. Raupach et al., "Global and Regional Drivers of Accelerating CO_2 Emissions," *Proc. Natl. Acad. Sci. USA.* 104(24) (2007): 10288–93.

4 See W. W. Huebner et al., "Mortality Patterns and Trends among 127,266 US-Based Men in a Petroleum Company: Update 1979–2000," *Journal of Occupational and Environmental Medicine* 51(11) (2009): 1333–48; T. Sorahan, "Mortality of UK Oil Refinery and Petroleum Distribution Workers, 1951–2003," *Occupational Medicine* 57(3) (2007): 177–85. See S. Gower et al., "Development of a Health Effects-Based Priority Ranking System for Air Emissions Reductions from Oil Refineries in Canada," *Journal of Toxicology and Environmental Health, Part A* 71(1) (2008): 81–5. Health impacts of car use include road traffic injuries, cardiovascular diseases, diabetes, breast, lung and colon cancers, and depression: J. Woodcock et al., "Public Health Benefits of Strategies to Reduce Greenhouse Gas Emissions: Urban Land Transport," *The Lancet* 374(9705) (2009): 1930–43. On the costs of oil, see J. Hill et al., "Climate Change and Health Costs of Air Emissions from Biofuels and Gasoline," *Proc. Natl. Acad. Sci.* 106(6) (2009): 2077–2082; J. M. Ogden et al., "Societal Lifecycle Costs of Cars with Alternative Fuels/Engines," *Energy Policy* 32(1) (2004): 7–27; I. W. H. Parry et al., "Automobile Externalities and Policies," *Journal of Economic Literature* 45(2) (2007): 373–99. See M. Kaldor et al., *Oil Wars* (Pluto, 2007).

5 On media coverage of Exxon's profits, see http://moneymorning. com/2009/01/31/exxon-record-profit/. On Saudi earnings, see, www.imf.org/external/np/sec/pn/2009/pn09109.htm; www. europia.com/content/default.asp?PageID=412&DocID=25002 p. 73, source EUROSTAT and WoodMackenzie.

6 David Kocieniewski, "As Oil Industry Fights a Tax, It Reaps Subsidies," *New York Times*, July 3, 2010. On state oil companies fiscal relations, see Bernard Mommer, *Global Oil and the Nation State* (Oxford University Press, 2002).

7 John Perkins, *Confessions of an Economic Hit Man* (Berrett-Koehler Publishers, 2004).

8 See Mahmoud A. El-Gamal and Amy Myers Jaffe, *Oil, Dollars, Debt, and Crises: The Global Curse of Black Gold* (Cambridge University Press, 2009). See *Hard Lessons: The Iraq Reconstruction*

Experience, US Office of the Special Inspector General for Iraq Reconstruction, 2009.

9   For a recent review, see F. van der Ploeg, "Natural Resources: Curse or Blessing?", *Journal of Economic Literature* 49(2) (2011): 366–420.

10 C. G. Gaddy and B. W. Ickes, "Resource Rents and the Russian Economy," *Eurasian Geography and Economics* 46(8) (2005): 559–83; Y. Kim, *The Resource Curse in a Post-Communist Regime: Russia in Comparative Perspective* (Ashgate, 2003). On Saudi Arabia, see A. M. Jaffe and R. A. Manning, "The Shocks of a World of Cheap Oil," *Foreign Affairs* 79(1) (2000).

11 I. Kolstad and T. Soreide, "Corruption in Natural Resource Management: Implications for Policy Makers," *Resources Policy* 34(4) (2009): 214–26; B. Ige, "Abacha and the Bankers: Cracking the Conspiracy," *Forum on Crime and Society* 2(1) (2002): 111–17.

CHAPTER 6   GOVERNING OIL

1   See T. Cottier et al., "Energy in WTO Law and Policy" (World Trade Institute, 2010).

2   C. L. Cortese et al., "Powerful Players: How Constituents Captured the Setting of IFRS 6, an Accounting Standard for the Extractive Industries," *Accounting Forum* 34(2) (2010): 76–88.

3   B. Mommer, *Global Oil and the Nation State* (Oxford University Press, 2002, p. 178).

4   See "Hélène Pelosse: j'ai été contrainte de démissionner [I was forced to resign]," *Le Monde*, October 30, 2010. The US supported IRENA in part because of the UAE bid to host it; see Wikileaks, cited in A. Florini, "The International Energy Agency in Global Energy Governance," *Global Policy* 2 (2011): 40–50.

5   On Keystone and the tar sands, see A. Nikiforuk, "What the Keystone rejection really reveals," *The Tyee*, January 19, 2012; C. Hiar, "Higher spending doesn't prevent rejection of Keystone XL project," IWatch, January 25, 2012; F. G. Hayden, Conflicts in the Licensing Process of TransCanada's Keystone XL Pipeline, 2011, Economics Department Faculty Publications. Paper 74, http://digitalcommons.unl.edu/econfacpub/74; On the case of the tar sands' public relations machine and the Canadian government, see M. Price, "On the Trail of Ethical

Oil's Secrets," *HuffPost*, November 28, 2011; G. Dembicki, "Big Oil and Canada Thwarted US Carbon Standards," *Salon*, December 15, 2011; http://deepclimate.org/2012/01/13/ethical-oil-political-connections-part-1-conservatives-go-newclear/.

6 J. Barnett, "The Worst of Friends: OPEC and G-77 in the Climate Regime," *Global Environmental Politics* 8(4) (2008): 1–8; Abdalla Salem El-Badri, "OPEC Statement to the United Nations Climate Change Conference (Cop15) – Copenhagen, December 2009" (OPEC, 2009); statement on taxation is from "OPEC and the Environment," 2010, available from www.opec.org.

7 BP quit the GCC in 1996 and Shell followed in 1998. On API lobbying, see C. Carroll, "API Praises Congressional Action to Rein in EPA and Calls for President Obama to Work with Growing Bipartisan Coalition" (API, 2011). The oil industry spent $58 billion in the US between 2000 and 2008 on emission reductions; see www.api.org/ehs/climate/new/companiesaddress.cfm. A. Gillies, "Reputational Concerns and the Emergence of Oil Sector Transparency as an International Norm," *International Studies Quarterly* 54(1) (2009): 103–26.

8 V. Vivoda, "International Oil Companies, US Government and Energy Security Policy: An Interest-Based Analysis," *International Journal of Global Energy Issues* 33(1/2) (2010): 73–88. USA*Engage does not openly disclose its membership which extends far beyond oil companies; see www.usaengage.org/. On Iraq, see G. Muttit, *Fuel on Fire: Oil and Politics in Occupied Iraq* (Bodley Head, 2011); C. Avery, "Iraqi Oil Industry" (IAS Group, 2010). On US military spending in Iraq, see A. Belasco, "The Cost of Iraq, Afghanistan, and Other Global War on Terror Operations since 9/11," in *RL33110* (Washington, DC: Congressional Research Service 2011) – or US$ 856 billion (constant 2010). The main western companies in Libya are ENI, Wintershall, Total, Conocco-Phillips, Repsol-YPF, Hess, Suncor, and Occidental. The post-Gaddafi government stated that oil contracts will be reviewed but expected most to be honored.

9 S. Guriev et al., "Determinants of Nationalization in the Oil Sector: A Theory and Evidence from Panel Data," *Journal of Law, Economics, and Organization* 27(2) (2011): 301–23; G. Joffé et al., "Expropriation of Oil and Gas Investments: Historical, Legal and Economic Perspectives in a New Age of Resource Nationalism," *The Journal of World Energy Law & Business* 2(1) (2009): 3–23;

J. Stroebel and A. Van Benthem, "Resource Extraction Contracts under Threat of Expropriation: Theory and Evidence," *USAEE/IAEE Working Paper* (Department of Economics, Stanford University, 2010). Military presence includes permanent bases and defense agreements, as in the case of France in Gabon. For statistical evidence on the positive effect of aid on reducing expropriation risk, see E. Asiedu et al., "Does Foreign Aid Mitigate the Adverse Effect of Expropriation Risk on Foreign Direct Investment?" *Journal of International Economics* 78(2) (2009): 268–75.

10 Cited from M. Patterson, "Car Culture and Global Environmental Politics," *Review of International Studies* 26(2) (2000): 257.

11 Bush citation from A. Juhasz, *The Tyranny of Oil. The World's Most Powerful Industry – and What We Must Do To Stop It* (Harper Collins, 2007); R. Gramling, and W. R. Freudenburg, "A Century of Macondo: United States Energy Policy and the BP Blowout Catastrophe," *American Behavioral Scientist* (2011): 1–28. On MMS, see I. Urbina, "Inspector General's Inquiry Faults Regulators," *New York Times*, May 24, 2010.

12 The nine companies were BP, Coastal Corp (now El Paso Corp.), Conoco and Phillips (now ConocoPhillips), Enron, Goldman Sachs, J. Aron & Co, Koch Industries, Mobil (now ExxonMobil) and Phibro Energy (now a subsidiary of CitiGroup). See R. Bryce, *Pipe Dreams: Greed, Ego, Jealousy, and the Death of Enron* (Public Affairs, 2002); T. Slocum, "Oil Mergers, Manipulation and Mirages: How Eroding Legal Protections and Lax Regulatory Oversight Harm Consumers" (Public Citizen's Energy Program, 2007); E. Lipton, "Gramm and the 'Enron Loophole,'" *New York Times*, November 17, 2008; L. Fang, "How the Kochs' Shady Oil Speculation May Be Driving up Gas Prices," *ThinkProgress*, June 13, 2011.

13 On cycling policies, see J. Oucher and R. Buehler, "Why Canadians Cycle More than Americans: A Comparative Analysis of Bicycling Trends and Policies," *Transport Policy* 13(3) (2006): 265–79; J. Oucher et al., "Bicycling Renaissance in North America? An Update and Re-appraisal of Cycling Trends and Policies," *Transportation Research Part A* (2011): 451–75.

14 On China's international energy policy, see X. Xu, "Chinese Responses to Good Energy Governance," *Global Governance* 17(2) (2011): 161–5. On its regional policy, see L. Wang and

H. Li, "Cooperation and Competition of Oil and Gas Resources between China and Its Neighboring Countries and Its Impacts on Geopolitics," *Resources Science* 31(10) (2009): 1633–9.

CHAPTER 7 BETTER AND BEYOND: THE FUTURE OF OIL

1 On the rise of speculators, see K. B. III Medlock and A. Myers Jaffe, "Who is in the Oil Futures Market and How has it Changed?" (James A. Baker III Institute for Public Policy, Rice University, 2009). On recommendations, see for example J. M. Chevalier, "Oil Price Volatility" (Paris: Report of the Working Group on the Volatility of Oil Prices, 2010). The implications of the Dodd–Frank Act for oil trading are explained in M. Jickling and R. S. Miller, "Derivatives Regulation in the 111th Congress," in *R40646* (Washington, DC: Congressional Research Service, 2011). On the effects of price volatility on economic growth, see R. Sauter and S. Awerbuch, "Oil Price Volatility and Economic Activity: A Survey and Literature Review" (Paris: IEA, 2003); C. Blattman et al., "Winners and Losers in the Commodity Lottery: The Impact of Terms of Trade Growth and Volatility in the Periphery 1870–1939," *Journal of Development Economics* 82(1) (2007): 156–79. JODI was the main outcome of the 2000 International Energy Forum; see www.jodidata.org/.

2 On fuel efficiency improvements, see L. Cheah et al., "Factor of Two: Halving the Fuel Consumption of New US Automobiles by 2035," in *Reducing Climate Impacts in the Transportation Sector*, ed. D. Sperling and J. S. Cannon (Springer, 2009); S. Kobayashi et al., "Energy Efficiency Technologies for Road Vehicles," *Energy Efficiency* 2(2) (2009): 125–37. On the rebound effect, see K. A. Small and K. Van Dender, "Fuel Efficiency and Motor Vehicle Travel: The Declining Rebound Effect," *Energy Journal* 28(1) (2007): 25–51. On car life cycles and trade-offs of replacement, see M. Spielmann and H. J. Althaus, "Can a Prolonged Use of a Passenger Car Reduce Environmental Burdens? Life Cycle Analysis of Swiss Passenger Cars," *Journal of Cleaner Production* 15(11–12) (2007): 1122–34. Increasing fuel efficiency would have no negative impact on car safety; see M. Ross et al., "Vehicle Design and the Physics of Traffic Safety," *Physics Today* 59(1)

(2006): 49–54. For an example of a car-free school zone campaign, see www.walktoschool.org.uk/. On EU ban, see B. Waterfield, "EU to Ban Cars from Cities by 2050," *The Telegraph*, March 28, 2011. On urban access restrictions in Europe, see http://ec.europa.eu/transport/urban/studies/doc/2010_12_ars_the_european_traveler.pdf; B. Barrow, "Flying on Holiday 'a Sin,' says Bishop," *Daily Mail*, July 23, 2006.

3 J. Fargione et al., "Land Clearing and the Biofuel Carbon Debt," *Science* 319(5867) (2008): 1235–8.

4 On tail-pipe carbon capture, see C. W. Jones, "Technologies for CO_2 Sequestration," *Annual Review of Chemical and Biomolecular Engineering* 2(1) (2011): 31–52. On the range of fuel and power-train options, see M. Contestabile et al., "Battery Electric Vehicles, Hydrogen Fuel Cells and Biofuels. Which Will Be the Winner?", in *ICEPT/WP/2011/008* (Imperial College, 2011).

5 Major corporations already dominate the biofuel sector, such as Archer Daniels Midland, and lobby to protect this sector. On geothermal systems, see MIT, "The Future of Geothermal Energy. Impact of Enhanced Geothermal Systems (EGS) on the United States in the 21st Century" (Idaho National Laboratory, 2006). See J. Apps and K. Pruess, "Modeling Geochemical Processes in Enhanced Geothermal Systems with CO_2 as Heat Transfer Fluid," paper presented at the Workshop on Geothermal Reservoir Engineering, Stanford, January 31–February 2, 2011.

6 See source: www.bikesatwork.com/carfree/carfree-census-database.html. "Traffic entering Vancouver, 1986 to 2005," City of Vancouver, retrieved May 30, 2007. Commission on Oil Independence (2006), "Making Sweden an OIL-FREE Society," www.sweden.gov.se/content/1/c6/06/70/96/7f04f437.pdf. On the effect of zoning restrictions on the housing bubble and subprime crisis, see E. S. Mills, "Urban Land-Use Controls and the Subprime Mortgage Crisis," *Independent Review* 13(4) (2009): 559–65; H. Huang and Y. Tang, "Residential Land Use Regulation and the US Housing Price Cycle between 2000 and 2009" (Department of Economics, University of Alberta, 2010). See A. Haxeltine and G. Seyfang, "Transitions for the People: Theory and Practice of 'Transition' and 'Resilience' in the UK's Transition Movement" (Tyndal Centre for Climate Change Research, 2009); P. Newman et al., *Resilient Cities: Responding to Peak Oil and Climate Change* (Island Press, 2009). Critics point

out that while this approach may build greater resilience to high oil prices, it can increase vulnerability to other shocks, such as local weather events.

7 F. Al-Kasim et al., "Shrinking Oil: Does Weak Governance and Corruption Reduce Volumes of Oil Produced?" (U4, 2010). Natural Resource Charter, www.naturalresourcecharter.org/ and P. Collier, *The Plundered Planet: How to Reconcile Prosperity with Nature* (Penguin, 2010); M. Humphreys et al., *Escaping the Resource Curse* (Columbia University Press, 2007); I. Kolstad et al., "Mission Improbable: Does Petroleum-Related Aid Address the Resource Curse?" *Energy Policy* 37(3) (2008): 954–65.

Selected Readings

Oil is among the most storied resources. There are numerous accounts of the industry's history and the central and problematic role oil has come to play in economies of the global North and South. Here we highlight only a small selection. Readers seeking a more extensive presentation of the technical and financial aspects of the oil industry (chapter 1) will appreciate Morgan Downey's *Oil 101* (Wooden Table Press, 2009). For a historical and comparative perspective on the significance of oil and the machines it powers, see major contributions by Vaclav Smil: for example, *Energy at the Crossroads: Global Perspectives and Uncertainties* (MIT Press, 2005); *Energies: An Illustrated Guide to the Biosphere and Civilization* (MIT Press, 2000); and *Prime Movers of Globalization: The History and Impact of Diesel Engines and Gas Turbines* (MIT Press, 2010). A now "classic" treatment of the industry's history and main figures is Daniel Yergin, *The Prize: The Epic Quest for Oil, Money, and Power* (Free Press, 1991). Both Yergin's *The Quest: The Global Race for Energy, Security and Power* (Penguin, 2011) and Tom Bower's *Oil: Money, Politics, and Power in the 21st Century* (Grand Central, 2009) offer sequels. For a detailed account of Exxon, see Steve Coll's *Private Empire: ExxonMobil and American Power* (Penguin, 2012).

The state of global oil reserves has been a long-running concern. "Peak oil" articulates this concern as an imminent – and permanent – reduction in annual production due to geological constraints: see Colin Campbell and Jean Laherrère, "The

End of Cheap Oil," *Scientific American* (March 1998): 80–5; Kenneth Deffeyes, *Hubbert's Peak: The Impending World Oil Shortage* (Princeton University Press, 2008); and, for a more hyperbolic account, Richard Heinberg *The Party's Over: Oil, War and the Fate of Industrial Societies* (Clairview Books, 2005). For a biophysical analysis of the energy surplus from oil and its implications for economic and political power, see Charles Hall and Kent Klitgaard, *Energy and the Wealth of Nations: Understanding the Biophysical Economy* (Springer, 2011). For critical rebuttals of peak oil, see Leonardo Maugeri, *The Age of Oil: The Mythology, History, and Future of the World's Most Controversial Resource* (Praeger, 2006); and Robin Mills, *The Myth of the Oil Crisis: Overcoming the Challenges of Depletion, Geopolitics, and Global Warming* (Praeger, 2008). Duncan Clarke's *The Battle for Barrels: Peak Oil Myths and World Oil Futures* (Profile Books, 2007) argues that the future of oil will be determined "above ground" by geopolitics rather than "below ground" by geological limits. *Oil Panic and the Global Crisis: Predictions and Myths* (Wiley-Blackwell, 2010) by Steven Gorelick provides a detailed yet accessible assessment of oil reserves and the peak oil debate.

For an application of the global production network concept to oil (chapter 2) which provides links to the theory and history of the concept, see Gavin Bridge, "Global Production Networks and the Extractive Sector: Governing Resource-Based Development," *Journal of Economic Geography* 8(3) (2008): 389–419; see also Peter Dicken, *Global Shift: Mapping the Changing Contours of the World Economy* (Sage, 2010), chapter 8. Lisa Margonelli, *Oil on the Brain* (Random House, 2007), provides a great journalistic account. A fascinating analysis of the hybrid relationships between internationalizing NOCs and IOCs is undertaken by Nana De Graaff, "A Global Energy Network? The Expansion and Integration of Non-Triad National Oil Companies," *Global Networks* 11(2)

(2011): 262–83. The former Secretary-General of OPEC, Francisco Parra, offers an insider's perspective on politics between major oil exporters and importers between 1950 and 1990 in *Oil Politics: A Modern History of Petroleum* (I. B. Tauris, 2010). On the history of resource nationalism, see Paul Stevens, "Resource Nationalism and the Role of National Oil Companies in the Middle East: History and Prospects," *Journal of World Energy Law and Business* 1(1) (2008): 5–30. On the association of oil with the "body politic" and the politics of oil-fueled development in Venezuela, see F. Coronil, *The Magical State: Nature, Money and Modernity in Venezuela* (University of Chicago Press, 1997). Research by Amy Myers Jaffe and colleagues at the James Baker III Institute for Public Policy at Rice University examines the evolving relationship between IOCs and NOCs and its implications for the geopolitics of oil. For a systematic analysis of contemporary national oil companies, see David Victor et al. (eds), *Oil and Governance* (Cambridge University Press, 2012) and Valérie Marcel and John Mitchell, *Oil Titans: National Oil Companies in the Middle East* (Brookings Institution Press, 2006). On the impact of globalization on the changing character of (rentier) oil states in the Middle East, see Matteo Legrenzi and Bessma Momani (eds), *Shifting Geo-Economic Power of the Gulf: Oil, Finance and Institutions* (Ashgate, 2011). On the evolution of oil development in Venezuela, see Miguel Tinker Salas, *The Enduring Legacy: Oil, Culture, and Society in Venezuela* (Duke University Press, 2009), and Luis Giusti, "La Apertura: the Opening of Venezuela's Oil Industry," *Journal of International Affairs* 53(1) (1999): 117–28.

On embedding demand for oil within industrial societies (chapter 3), car culture and the political economy of automobility, see Matthew Paterson's excellent *Automobile Politics: Ecology and Cultural Political Economy* (Cambridge University Press, 2007). For a discussion of factors shaping car-centric cultures and strategies for changing course, see Daniel Sperling and Deborah Gordon's *Two Billion Cars: Driving Towards Sustainability* (Oxford University Press, 2009). On the petrochemical industry and plastics culture, see Susan Freinkel, *Plastic: A Toxic Love Story* (Houghton Mifflin Harcourt, 2011). For a rigorous theoretical account of the "production of scarcity" in the face of abundance, see Mazen Labban, *Space, Oil and Capital* (Routledge, 2008); on market-making, see work by Matthew Huber, including "Enforcing Scarcity: Oil, Violence and the Making of the Market," *Annals of the Association of American Geographers* 101(4): 816–25; and Paul Sabin, *Crude Politics: The California Oil Market, 1900–1940* (University of California Press, 2005).

For analysis of the evolution of oil pricing, see work by Robert Mabro including "The International Oil Price Regime: Origins, Rationale and Assessment," *The Journal of Energy Literature* XI (1) (2005): 3–20. Bassam Fattouh (and colleagues) at the Oxford Institute for Energy Studies provide detailed analysis of historic and contemporary pricing mechanisms and the influence of financialization: for example, "An Anatomy of the Crude Oil Pricing System," OIES Working Paper 40 (available via the OIES website). For an analysis of oil prices and their medium-term implications, see Jan-Hein Jesse and Coby van der Linde's *Oil Turbulence in the Next Decade: An Essay on High Oil Prices in a Supply-Constrained World* (Clingendael Institute, 2008). On the "tug of war" between producers and consumers over price and the role of OPEC within the global oil market, see Øystein Noreng, *Crude Power: Politics and the Oil Market* (I. B. Tauris, 2006).

The question of oil security (chapter 4) is traditionally viewed through the state-centric lens of international relations. The questions international relations poses remain central, but other perspectives on the (in)securities created around and through oil have emerged that unsettle the equation of security with a "national" frame of reference. *The Routledge Handbook of Energy Security* (Routledge, 2011), edited by Benjamin Sovacool, provides a broad and nuanced range of perspectives. Daniel Moran and James Russell's edited collection, *Energy Security and Global Politics: The Militarization of Resource Management* (Routledge, 2009), examines contemporary strategies of producer and consumer states and the emerging political challenges to the market-based allocation of oil. Discussion of energy security criteria and assessments can be found in Bert Kruyt et al., "Indicators for Energy Security," *Energy Policy* 37(6) (2009): 2166–81, and Andreas Loschel et al., "Indicators of Energy Security in Industrialised Countries," *Energy Policy* 38(4) (2010): 1665–71. The *New Energy Security Paradigm* of the World Economic Forum and CERA (2006) broadens the energy security concept at a policy level. John Mitchell, *The New Economy of Oil: Impacts on Business, Geopolitics and Society* (RIIA and Earthscan, 2001), remains one of the most encompassing discussions of the industry, emphasizing oil acceptability rather than availability alone. Kristian Coates-Ulrichsen, *Insecure Gulf: The End of Certainty and the Transition to the Post-Oil Era* (Columbia University Press, 2011), provides a detailed analysis of the sources of instability among GCC countries. For a critical analysis of the militarized approach of the US to oil security, see Garry Leech, *Crude Intervention: The US, Oil and the New World (Dis)order* (Zed Books, 2006), and Doug Stokes and Sam Raphael, *Global Energy Security and American Hegemony* (Johns Hopkins University Press, 2010). On the violence of neoliberalism and US decline, see Retort, *Afflicted Powers: Capital and Spectacle in a New Age of War* (Verso, 2005).

Michael Ross provides the most thorough analysis of oil dependence and development failure (chapter 5) in *The Oil Curse: How Petroleum Wealth Shapes the Development of Nations* (Princeton University Press, 2012) and covers much of the extensive literature on the "resource curse," including Thad Dunning, *Crude Democracy: Natural Resource Wealth and Political Regimes* (Cambridge University Press, 2008), and Terry L. Karl, *The Paradox of Plenty: Oil Booms and Petro-States* (University of California Press, 1997). Robert Engler's *The Politics of Oil: A Study of Private Power and Democratic Directions* (University of Chicago Press, 1961) is still one of the most influential critiques of the oil industry and its influence over society. Mahmoud El-Gamal and Amy Myers Jaffe take a detailed look at relationships between energy market cycles, Middle East geopolitics, and financial markets in *Oil, Dollars, Debts and Crises* (Cambridge University Press, 2010). On oil and food, see Dale Allen Pfeiffer, *Eating Fossil Fuels: Oil, Food and the Coming Crisis in Agriculture* (New Society Publishers, 2006); Julia Wright, *Sustainable Agriculture and Food Security in an Era of Oil Scarcity* (Earthscan, 2008); and David Pimentel and Marcia Pimentel, *Food, Energy, and Society* (CRC Press, 2008).

Joan Martinez-Alier (with colleagues at the Universitat Autònoma de Barcelona) has developed an influential framework for assessing the ecological distribution conflicts associated with extractive economies (based in part on the experience of oil); see *The Environmentalism of the Poor: A Study of Ecological Conflicts and Valuation* (Edward Elgar, 2002); see also the EJOLT project (www.ejolt.org). Anthropologists, geographers, and political ecologists have explored the ways in which livelihood strategies, corporate activity, and state institutions combine in different ways along the oil production network: *Crude Domination: An Anthropology of Oil* (Berghahn Books, 2011), edited by Andrea Behrends and other researchers at the Max Planck Institute for Social Anthropology; also Tobias Haller et al. (eds), *Fossil Fuels, Oil Companies, and Indigenous Peoples* (Lit Verlag, 2007). On extractive conflicts in Latin America, including oil and gas, see Anthony Bebbington (ed.), *Extractive Industries, Social Conflict and Economic Development: Evidence from South America* (Routledge, 2012); for an anthology of work on environmental justice and oil and gas development in Russia and the Caspian, see Julian Agyeman and Yelena Ogneva-Himmelberger (eds), *Environmental Justice and Sustainability in the Former Soviet Union* (MIT Press, 2009); see also Michael Bradshaw, "A New Energy Age in Pacific Russia: Lessons from the Sakhalin Oil and Gas Projects," *Eurasian Geography and Economics* 51(3) (2010): 330–59.

Michael Watts has theorized oil's multiple creative/destructive political economies, drawing upon the appalling environmental and social record of oil in the Niger Delta, and the dire implications of a petro-state's "failed modernization" for those who live around, through, and despite oil: see, for example "Petro-Insurgency or Criminal Syndicate?" *Review of African Political Economy* (114) (2008): 637–60; "Empire of Oil," *Monthly Review* 58(4) (2006): 1–16; "Anatomies of Community," *Transactions of the Institute of British Geographers*, 29 (2004): 195–216; and "Petro-Violence: Community, Extraction, and Political Ecology of a Mythic Commodity," in Nancy Peluso and Michael Watts (eds), *Violent Environments* (Cornell University Press, 2001): 189–212. For an incisive critique of representations of violence and criminality in oil production areas, see the works of Anna Zalik, such as "Protest as Violence in Oilfields: The Contested Representation of Profiteering in Two Extractive Sites," in S. Feldman et al. (eds), *Accumulating Insecurity* (University of Georgia Press, 2011). For a wide-ranging indictment of the violence of oil-based "development," see Peter Maas, *Crude World: The Violent Twilight of Oil* (Knopf, 2009). On oil, the "resource curse" and armed conflicts, see Philippe Le Billon, *Wars of Plunder: Conflict, Profits and the Politics of Resources* (Hurst and Columbia University Press, 2012). For a nuanced analysis of opposition to petroleum in Ecuador and the complex imbrications of oil with class, regional, and national identities, see G. Valdivia, "Governing Relations Between People and Things: Citizenship, Territory and the Political Economy of Petroleum in Ecuador," *Political Geography* 27(4) (2008): 456–77; and Suzana Sawyer, *Crude Chronicles: Indigenous Politics, Multinational Oil, and Neoliberalism in Ecuador* (Duke University Press, 2004). For a captivating account of the politics of tar sands development in Alberta, see Andrew Nikoforuk's *Tar Sands: Dirty Oil and the Future of a Continent* (Greystone Books, 2010).

Global Energy Governance: The New Rules of the Game (Brookings Institution Press, 2010), by Andreas Goldthau and Jan Martin Witte, discusses options for improving energy security through better governance (chapter 6). On the re-politicization of energy policy, see Dieter Helm (ed.), *The New Energy Paradigm* (Oxford University Press, 2007). Readers interested in the evolution of the International Energy Agency can turn to the IEA's former legal counsel Richard Scott's *The History of the International Energy Agency: The First 20 Years*, and a subsequent volume by Craig Bamberger available on IEA's website. Sylvia Karlsson-Vinkhuyzen's "The United Nations and Global Energy Governance," in *Global Change, Peace and Security* 22(2) (2010): 175–195, provides a detailed account and explanations for the slow progress of energy governance through the UN system, especially the reluctance of member states to forgo sovereign energy policy. The role of the G8 in global energy governance, its articulation with energy-related organizations, and explanations for a performance below expectations is provided in Dries Lesage et al., *Global Energy Governance in a Multipolar World* (Ashgate, 2010). Jon Skjaerseth and Tora Skodvin provide one of the most detailed enquiries into oil companies' engagement with climate policy in *Climate Change and the Oil Industry* (Manchester University

Press, 2003). Suzana Sawyer critically deconstructs a Chevron media campaign in "Human Energy," *Dialectical Anthropology* 34 (2010): 67–75.

For an entry to the growing literature on post-oil transition (chapter 7), see Peter Newman, Timothy Beatley, and Heather Boyer on strategies for decreasing vulnerability to oil shocks in *Resilient Cities: Responding to Peak Oil and Climate Change* (Island Press, 2009). Opportunities for China in relation to transport policy are discussed in Kelly Gallagher, *China Shifts Gear: Automakers, Oil, Pollution, and Development* (MIT Press, 2006). For proposals that seek to cut off carbon at source and "keep the oil in the soil," see Nnimmo Bassey, *To Cook a Continent: Destructive Extraction and the Climate Crisis in Africa* (Pambazuka Press, 2012); and Pamela Martin, *Oil in the Soil: The Politics of Paying to Preserve the Amazon* (Rowman and Littlefield, 2011). In *Sustainable Fossil Fuels: The Unusual Suspect in the Quest for Clean and Enduring Energy* (Cambridge University Press, 2005), Mark Jaccard sketches a climate-consciousness energy future in which oil has a substantial role.

Index

Page numbers in **bold** refer to a table, a figure or a box.

Abacha, President 147
Abu Dhabi National Oil Company
 40
abundance 3, 69, 74–82, 126
Abyei **95**
acceptability, social 3–4, 119–21
access agreements 41, 60–2, 161
 bilateral agreements 61, 91, 94,
  161, 168, 170, 178–9, 185,
  187
 China **44**
 concessions 28–9, **59**, 76, 209
 multilateral agreements **91**, 179,
  184, 187
 production sharing agreements
  (PSAs) 29, 58–60, 169,
  175
 see also contracts
accessibility 3, 55–60, 99, 100,
  104–11, 166
 to marketing 24, 51, 73, 75–6,
  83, 84, 85, 99
accidents 100, 130–1, 133
 Alaska 129, 131
 Deepwater Horizon, platform 14,
  46, 62, 121, 129, 130, 172–3,
  183
 oil spills 46, 121, 129, 130, 131
 traffic 134, 138
accountability 125, 144, 148, 160,
  166, 202, 203

acid rain 131–2
acquisition 19, **28**, 29–30, 44–5,
  49, 53–4
advertising 159, 194
affordability 3, 99, 104, 111–18,
  122, 150, 151, 153, 157, 182
Afghanistan 93, 151
Africa 26, 53, 60, 109, 184
Africa, North 17, 56
 sub-Saharan 58–60
 West 17
Africa Oil 53
"Age of Plenty" 3, 33, 70, 77, 83,
  101, 154, 194
agriculture 126, 133, 143, 149, 195
air quality 20, 27, 112, 129, 133,
  134, 194
air travel 8, 20, 71–2, 193
Alaska 15, 57, 60, 129, 131, 140
Albert, Lake **95**
Alberta 13, 42, 121, 129, 141, 164,
  165, 195
al-Falih, Khalid 15
Algeria **40, 142**, 145, 170
Al-Jazeera 176
alternative energy sources 34, 80,
  94, 98–101, 195
 affordability and availability 79,
  157
 environmental impact 100, 101,
  120, 151–2, 165, 186, 196

alternative energy sources (*cont.*)
  governance 164, 165, 179, 184,
    185, 188, 194–8, 204
  governments, national 186, 196
  investment 63, 184
  nuclear energy 80, 98, **99**, 100,
    101, 196
  renewable energy 120, 162, 164,
    174, 195
  transportation 101, 102, 172,
    179, 195
  and United Kingdom 164, 198
  and United States 98, 164, 174,
    185
American Petroleum Institute 165
"American way of life" 78, 185
Amoco Cadiz, tanker 129
Anglo-Persian Oil Company 76,
  209
Angola 107
  exploration 15, 59
  and governance 168, 176
  and inequality and poverty **142**,
    147
  and national oil companies
    (NOCs) 45, 168
  and oil revenues **140**, **142**, 147,
    148
  and social development 32, 125,
    136, 149
Apertura Petrolera 58, 60
Arab Heavy (crude oil) **14**
Arabian Light Crude 83, 84, **108**
Arab Spring 105, **108**, 213
Arctic 13, 47, 53–4, **57**, 61, 121, 129
  and energy security 93, **95**
  and environmental impact 131,
    132, 164
Argentina **95**, **142**
Asia 25, 186
  consumption 20, 26, 34
  demand for oil 27, 79, 80, 82,
    90, 178, 189

national oil companies (NOCs)
    54, 99
  and refineries 51, 107
Asia, Central 60, 109
Asia, East 17 *see also* China
"As-Is" Agreement 76
ASTM International 73
Athabasca oil **14**
Atlantic, South 61
Atlantic Ocean **95**, 131
Atyrau-Dushanzi pipeline
    109
Australia **16**, **95**, 164
authoritarianism 141, 144, 146,
    150, 185, 203
availability 3, 26, 33, 102, 151, 154,
    180, 183, 187
  alternative energy sources 79,
    157
Azerbaijan **95**, **140**, **142**, 187

backstream phase **36**, 37, 188
Bahrain 105
Bakken shale, North Dakota 15
Baku-Tiblisi-Ceyhan pipeline 63,
    164
Baltic Sea **95**
Bangladesh 110
banks 63–4, 147
Barents Sea **95**
barrels 73, 129
Beaufort Sea 47
"Big Oil" *see* international oil
    companies (IOCs)
bilateral agreements 61, 91, 94,
    161, 168, 170, 178–9, 185,
    187
bin Laden, Osama 146
biodiesel **57**, 132
biodiversity 121, 122, **134**
biofuels 63, 98, **127**, 132, 133, 185,
    195, 224
Bisphenol A 81

bitumen 7, **16**, 61, **64**
  Canada 12, 13, **14**, 15, **16**, **64**
    and energy security 120, 121,
      122
    and environmental impact
      74, 132, 195
    and environmental impact 120,
      121, 122, 130, 132
    and carbon emissions 74,
      183, 195, 211
    production costs **57**, 63, 99
    Venezuela 13, 132
Blair, Tony **148**, 166
blockades 106, 121
Bonny Light (crude oil) **14**
Bosphorus/Turkish Strait 51
bottles, Sqezy 81
boycotts, consumer 121
BP **40**, **44**, 48, 49, 63, 169, 209,
      222
    and environmental impact 165,
      221
    Deepwater Horizon, platform
      14, 46, 62, 121, 129, 130,
      172–3, 183
BP Oil Spills Response Plan 173
Brazil 14, 45, **91**, **142**, 182
    and governance 161, 162, 177
    unconventional sources **16**, 61
Brent Blend (crude oil) **14**, 86, **108**
British National Oil Corporation
      (BNOC) 42
Brunei **95**
Brzezinski, Zbigniew 93
Burma (Myanmar) 48, 109, 110
buses 78
Bush administration 184

Cabinda, Angola 147, 149
Cadillacs 78
Cairn Energy 53
California 47, 74, 112, 123
Cameroon 94, **95**

Canada **142**, 185, 201–2
  bitumen 12, 13, **14**, 15, **16**, **64**,
      121, 122, 123
    and energy security 120, 121,
      122
    and environmental impact
      74, 132, 195
    and energy security **95**, 121, 122,
      123
    and environmental impact 74,
      81, 132, 172, 195, 197
    ownership of oil reserves 41–2,
      95
cancer 132, 133
capacity 19, 47, 50, 51–2, 55, 92,
      105, 107, 114
    spare capacity 42–3, 52, 74–82,
      89, 175, 182, 189
car industry 79, 116, 159, 171, 194
car licensing 119
car use 71–2, 78, 118–19, 133,
      171–2
    and environmental impact 172,
      195
    fuel efficiency 101, 112, 116–17,
      188–9, 192–4
    and health issues 134, 219
    ownership 20, 79, 197
    and United States 78–9, 133,
      173, 192, 197
carbon credits 66, 67
carbon emissions 19, 183
    carbon cycle 6, 65–7
    and environmental impact 129
    and bitumen 74, 183, 195,
      211
    and climate change 6, 27, 33,
      64, 65–7
    reduction 22, 120, 151, 166–7,
      180, 194–8
    carbon capture 20, 37, 66,
      67, 100, 119, 121, 167, 194,
      195

carbon emissions (*cont.*)
  reduction (*cont.*)
    carbon trading 66, 67, **134**,
     184
    and governance 21–2, 74, 80,
     157, 185, 187, 188, 204
    and nongovernmental
     organizations (NGOs) **64**,
     66
carbon sinks 66, 67
Cardenas government 38
Carter Doctrine 93
Caspian Sea 51, 58, **59**, **95**
Caucasus 105
Celebes Sea **95**
Center for American Progress 174
Center for Responsive Politics 173
Central African Republic 113
Chad 59, 103, 132, 200–1
Chad–Cameroon pipeline 132,
  200–1
Chavez administration 60, 113
chemical engineering 81, 151
Cheney, Dick 109
Chevron **40**, 45, 48, 49, 57, 78,
  175, 209
China
  access agreements **44**, 91,
   178–9, 187
  and Africa 109, 184
  consumption 12, 17, 19, 43,
   117–18
  and demand for oil 17, 19, 37,
   42–3, 123, 182, 191, 208
  and economic development
   100, 118, 128, 177
  and energy security 31, 94, **95**,
   103, 109, 110, 112, 116–18
  and environmental impact 19,
   100
  and governance 85, 161, 162,
   176, 178–9
  and human rights **44**, 118

  and inequality and poverty 136,
   142, 149
  national oil companies (NOCs)
   24–5, 43–5, 184, 202
  and oil revenues **142**, 158
  production 12, 19, 117–18
  and taxation **115**, 118, 193
  and unconventional sources 13,
   16
  and United States 19, 106
China Seas 61, 93, **95**, 187
Chinese National Offshore Oil
  Corporation (CNOOC) 25,
  44, 45
Chinese National Petroleum
  Company (CNPC) *see*
  PetroChina (CNPC)
Chukchi Sea 47
civil society organizations 25–6,
  33, 48, 66, 119, 146, 160–7,
  178, 202, 203
civil war 106, 145, 149
Clarke, Duncan 158
climate change
  and carbon emissions 6, 27, 33,
   64, 65–7
  and energy security 98, 99,
   118–21
  and governance 20–2, 62, 154,
   164, 166
Clinton administration 114
coal 8, 80, 98, **99**, 100, 101
coal tar 81
coal-to-liquids technology **14**
Cold War 178
Colombia **142**, 164, 185
colonialism 128
combustion 8
Commodity Exchange Act **174**
Compagnie Français des Pétroles
  76
companies 23–5
  and energy security 48, 104, 121

and environmental impact 33,
    62, 121, 154, 159, 165, 183
and gas, natural 25, 61, 153
and governance 33, 62, 120,
    154, 155, 158–9, 160–8, 170,
    175–6
and human rights 53, 121, 159,
    183, 201–2
integrated oil companies 23–4,
    30, 40, 44, 48–62, 76, 83,
    84
and national governments 37,
    79, 84, 139–40
    and corruption 47, 139, 170
    and governance 155, 166,
        167–8, 170, 172–5
    and resource-seeking 28, 55–7
nonintegrated (independent)
    49, 52–4, 56, 58, 60, 75, 84
and oil revenues 136, 137, 138,
    139–40, 167–8, 170–1
and price of oil 83, 212
resource-holding companies
    see national oil companies
    (NOCs)
resource-seeking companies see
    international oil companies
    (IOCs)
and social development 62, 121,
    183
and stock markets 40, 42, 44
transnational corporations
    (TNC) see national oil
    companies (NOCs)
see also competition;
    international oil companies
    (IOCs); national oil
    companies (NOCs)
compensation 132, 137, 170
competition 3, 35, 68, 181, 200
    between companies
        access to markets 25, 73,
            75–6, 83, 84, 85
    access to reserves 25, 28–9,
        55, 56, 60, 104
    between national governments
        17, 22–3, 30, 37, 45, 58, 171
    between national governments
        and companies 41, 45, 49,
        75–6, 99, 103, 123, 153, 160
concessions 29, 59, 76, 209
congestion charging 194
Congo 16, 95, 125, 149, 176
ConocoPhillips 49, 58, 61, 221,
    222
construction industry 79
consumerism 34, 119
Consumer Protection Act 148, 190
consumers 77, 111, 119, 120, 121,
    138, 155, 158
consumption 12, 13, 17, 19, 21, 22,
    28, 36, 37, 128
    Asia 20, 27, 34
    China 12, 17, 19, 43, 117–18
    growth 18–19, 79, 149, 158
    United States 12, 16–17, 31, 135,
        216–17
contracts 86, 148, 168, 170–1, 174,
    175, 184, 190, 221
    contractual agreements 59, 110,
        138, 145
    service contracts 28–9, 44, 56,
        58, 60, 169
    see also access agreements
corporate social responsibility
    (CSR) 121, 159
Correa, President 134
corruption 25, 91, 139–40, 143–9,
    153, 170, 178, 199–200
    and governance 47, 144, 148,
        153, 159, 164, 175, 200, 202
Coryton, UK 97
cracking technology 52, 80–1
crime, violent 97
Cuba 113, 184
cycling 172, 197

Dana Petroleum 45
debt 128, 139, 141, 142–3, 145, 146,
       149, 151
decolonization 38–9
Deepwater Horizon, platform 14, 46,
       62, 121, 129, 130, 172–3, 183
deep-water resources 9, 13–14, 57,
       59–60, 61, 63, 132, 172–3
deforestation 132, 133
demand destruction 22, 80, 92,
       188, 191
demand for oil 16–22, 77–80
   and consumers 77, 138, 155, 158
   control 17, 155, 188, 191–4
   reduction 22, 80, 88, 92, 99,
       184, 188, 191
   and environmental impact
       79–80, 182, 192
   growth 89, 92, 102, 123, 191, 203
   and International Energy
       Agency (IEA) 80, 102
   and Organization for Economic
       Cooperation and
       Development (OECD) 42,
       79–80, 123
   and price of oil 17, 74, 79–80,
       90, 92, 190
   and production 183, 187, 189–90
   see also individual countries
democracy 144, 149, 153
Denmark 95
dependency 32, 143, 188, 193–4,
       196, 204
depletion 10, 66, 107, 127, 154,
       178, 182
deregulation 172–5, 184, 190
derivatives 86, 87, 89, 174
devaluation 108, 139, 151
development, social and economic
       28, 177, 180–1, 186, 187,
       199–200
   economic 32, 61, 79, 125–6, 152,
       182, 187

and governance 144–9, 155,
       158–9, 160, 167
and price of oil 23, 88, 142–3,
       144–5, 150, 171, 181–2
social 19, 20, 25, 27, 32, 79–80,
       94, 125–52
   and companies 62, 121, 183
   and environmental impact
       19, 98, 119, 128–35, 204
   and governance 167, 200–1,
       204
   see also individual countries
Devon Energy 54
diesel 8, 20
diplomacy 118, 167, 169
direct cash payments 140
"dirty oil" *see* bitumen; shale oil
disasters *see* accidents
disasters, natural 96, 160
diversification 17, 57–9, 62–3,
       109, 142, 143, 199
dividends 90, 136
DNO, company 53
Dodd-Frank Wall Street Reform
       148, 190
downstream sector 36, 37, 51–2, 54
"drill, baby, drill" 46, 157
Dubai–Oman, crude oil 86
"Dutch disease" 143
Dutch East Indies 105

Eastern Siberia–Pacific Ocean
       pipeline 91, 109
East Timor 95
ecosystems 129, 131, 133
Ecuador 60, 130, 134, 136, 142, 188
Edmonton–Kitimat pipeline 109
education 113, 127
Egypt 110, 142
EITI (Extractive Industries
       Transparency Initiative)
       122, 148, 163, 166, 167, 176,
       200, 203

electric vehicles 78, 196–7, 198
electricity 80, 100, 127, 186, 195,
    196
Elf 42
elites, ruling 125, 136, 143, 145,
    146, 147
embargoes 43, 93, 105, 106, 107,
    108, 139, 144, 158, 168–9
Emissions Trading Scheme 22, 185
EN228 standard 73
Energy Charter Treaty 103, 161,
    163, 184, 185
Energy Information Agency 102
energy returns 9, 99, 127
energy security 17, **28**, 31, 93–124,
    154
    and companies 48, 104, 121
        and international oil
            companies (IOCs) 120, 123
        and national oil companies
            (NOCs) 97, 184
    and environmental impact 94,
        97, 98, 99, 118–21
    and governance 94, 119, 156,
        177
    and inequality and poverty
        97–8, 100, 111, 113, 164
    and investment 17, 45, 85, 191
    and marketing 45, 77, 96–7,
        112, 120, 121, 160
    and military intervention 17,
        99, 105–6, 110
    and national governments 22–3,
        46, 96–7, 120, 155, 156, 205
    and Organization of Petroleum
        Exporting Countries
        (OPEC) 30, 77, 93, 107,
        108, 212
    and price of oil 51, 70, 104, 107,
        111–13, 189
    and production 74, 92, 184, 187,
        199–200
    and taxation 114, **115**, 216

and unrest 105, 166, 199
    see also individual countries
energy surplus 9, 32, 33, 34, 75–7,
    127, 196
engines 8, 78
English Channel 131
enhanced oil recovery 187
ENI company 40, 41, 49, **49**, 59, 221
Enron **174**, 222
environmental impact
    and alternative energy sources
        100, 101, 119, 151–2, 165,
        186, 196
    and Arctic 131, 132, 164
    and car use 172, 195
    and carbon emissions 6, 27,
        32–3, **64**, 65–7, 74, 129,
        183, 195, 211
    and climate change 6, 27, 32–3,
        64, 65–7, 119–22
    and companies 33, 62, 121, 154,
        159, 165, 183
        and international oil
            companies (IOCs) 131, 165,
            177, 178, 221
    and demand for oil 79–80, 182,
        192
    and energy security 94, 97, 98,
        99, 118–21
    and governance 20–2, 154, 184,
        204
        and civil society 26, 33, 164,
            167, 188
        and financial institutions
            63–4, 201
        and national governments
            22–3, 28, 33, 46, 48, 62,
            188, 196
    and unconventional sources
        74, 122, 181
greenhouse gases (GHG) 19,
    36, 37, 98, 119, 133, 196,
    198, **199**

environmental impact (*cont.*)
  greenhouse gases (GHG) (*cont.*)
    and governance 74, 119, 154,
      165, 204
    and poor quality oils 13, 183
    and hydrocarbon chain **28**, 32–3
    and nongovernmental
      organizations (NGOs) 61,
      62, **64**, 66, 154
    and Organization of Petroleum
      Exporting Countries
      (OPEC) 166–7, 188
    pollution 27, 32–3, 112, 130,
      138
      air 27, 33, 99, 112, 129, 133,
        134, 194
      water **14**, 26, 27, 33, 99, 101,
        130, 131–2, 133
    and production 19, **36**, 37, 46,
      81–2
    and social development 19, 98,
      119, 128–35, 204
    see also accidents; *individual*
      countries
environmental sustainability 123,
  157, 178
Equatorial Guinea 120, 141, **142**
Equator Principles 64
"equity oil" **44**, 52, 60, 84, 91, 118,
  123, 158
Essar Energy 52
ethanol 63, **127**, 132, 195
Europe 17, 20, 185–6
  demand for oil 25, 37, 74, 78,
    79, 191
  and environmental impact 131,
    186
  and price of oil 20, 193
  and taxation 20, 30, 114, **115**,
    216
European Bank for Reconstruction
  and Development (EBRD)
  64

European Council 161
European Emissions Trading
  Scheme 171
European Transport Commissioner
  194
European Union (EU)
  and energy security 103, **108**
  environmental standards 22,
    74, 81, 123
EU–Russia Energy Dialogue 103,
  185
exploration 13–15, **28**, 35–6, 46–7,
  53–4, 58–9, 60, 104,
  129–30, 200
expropriation 168, 170, 175
"extreme energy" **14**, 61, 63, 99,
  132, 183
Exxon 24, **40**, 48, 49, 58, 61, 136,
  201, 209
  and environmental impact 131,
    165
  and national governments 41,
    50, 169, 170
  and unconventional sources 61,
    63
Exxon Valdez, tanker 129, 131

Fahd, King 146
Falkland Islands **95**
Fall Blau campaign 105
fee-for-service 56
Firestone Tire 78
fishing industry 131
Florida 47
food production 127, 135, 195
food security 98
Foreign Corruption Practices Act
  47, 148, 175
foreign policy 107, 167, 168–71
fossil fuels 7–9, 80, 98, **99**, 100,
  101
  see also gas, natural; oil,
    crude

fracking **14**, 101
Framework Agreement on Energy
     157, 178
Framework Convention on Tobacco
     Control 194
France 42, 103, 106, 136–7, 169,
     171, 216, 222
fuel efficiency 101, 112, 115–16,
     119, 166, 188–9, 192–3
Fuel Quality Directive 74
fuel sources *see* alternative energy
     sources; fossil fuels
Fukushima power plant 100
futures market 2, 73, 83, 86, 87–8,
     89–90

G8 166
G20 164, 179, 190
Gabon 103, 222
Gaddafi, Colonel 113
gas, natural 5, 6, 98, **99**, 143
   as alternative to oil 8, 20, 79,
       80, 100–1, 102, 195
   and companies 25, 61, 153
gas stations 129, 136, 158, 184
gasoline 7
   and price of oil 116, 137, 216
       and taxation 114, **115**, 193
   production **14**, 73, 81
   and transportation 8, 20, 78,
       116, 195, 216
Gazprom **40**, **59**, 209
General Motors 78
geopolitics 27–33, 93–4, 155, 185
geothermal energy 196
Germany 100, 105, 170
Ghana **95**, 102
Ghawar field 207
Global Climate Coalition (GCC)
     163, 165, 221
Global Gas Flaring Reduction
     initiative **163**, 166
Global Witness 25, **148**

governance 153–79, 203
   and alternative energy sources
       164, 165, 179, 184, 185, 188,
       194–8, 204
   and carbon emissions 21–2, 74,
       80, 157, 185, 187, 188, 204
   and climate change 20–2, 62,
       154, 164, 166
   and companies 33, 62, 119–20,
       154, 155, 158–9, 160–8, 170,
       175–6
     international oil companies
         (IOCs) 153, 169, 173, 177
     national oil companies (NOCs)
         159, 175, 178, 187, 201–2
   and corruption 47, 144, **148**, 153,
       159, 164, 175, 200, 202
   and energy security 94, 119,
       156, 177
   and environmental impact
       20–2, 154, 184, 204
     and civil society 26, 33, 164,
         167, 188
     and financial institutions
         63–4, 201
     and national governments 23,
         28, 32–3, 46, 48, 62, 188,
         196
     and unconventional sources
         13, 74, 123, 181
   and governments, national 23,
       28, 32–3, 46–8, 62, 160–7,
       188
   and human rights 25–6, 47, 48,
       63–4, 121–2, 164, 165–6,
       167
   and inequality and poverty 167,
       189, 200
   and International Energy
       Agency (IEA) 160–4,
       177–8, 203
   and marketing 160, 173, **174**,
       176, 179, 183, 184, 185, 190

governance (*cont.*)
   and military intervention 144,
      184, 222
   and oil revenues 176, 179, 190,
      200, 203
   and Organization of Petroleum
      Exporting Countries
      (OPEC) 160, **163**, 166–7,
      176, 177, 203
   and price of oil 144–5, 147, 162,
      171–5, 188, 189–91
   and social and economic
      development 144–9, 155,
      158–9, 160, 167, 200–1, 204
   and transparency 147–8, 159,
      162, 164, 189, 190
   Extractive Industries
      Transparency Initiative
      (EITI) 121, 148, **163**, 166,
      167, 176, 200, 203
   see also individual countries
governance deficit 155–60, 182
governments, national
   and alternative energy sources
      186, 196
   and companies 37, 47, 55–7,
      79, 84, 139–40, 155, 166,
      167–8, 170
      and corruption 47, 139, 170
      and governance 155, 166,
         167–8, 170, 172–5
      international oil companies
         (IOCs) 29, 55, 168,
         169–70, 175
      national oil companies
         (NOCs) 24, 39, 144, 167,
         168–9, 175, 183
   and competition 17, 23, 30, 37,
      45, 58, 171
      and companies 41, 45, **49**,
      75–6, 99, 103, 123, 153, 160
   and energy security 23, 96–7,
      120, 155, 156, 205

   and environmental impact 23,
      28, 32–3, 46–7, 48, 62, 188
   and governance 23, 28, 33,
      46–8, 62, 160–7, 188
   and oil reserves 23–4, 25, 28–9,
      38–9, 96–7, 191
   and oil revenues 136–41, 144,
      145, 155, 170, 175, 196, 200,
      201, 209
   and price of oil 83, 84, 190, 205
   and production network 37–48,
      62
   and social development 62, 79
"government take" 138, 140–1
Gramm, Phil and Wendy **174**
Grand Mosque, Mecca 93
Grangemouth, Scotland 52
Greece **95**
greenhouse gases (GHG) 133, 196
   and governance 74, 119, 154,
      165, 204
   and inequality and poverty 19,
      98, 119
   and poor quality oils 13, 183
   and population density 198,
      199
   and production 19, **36**, 37
Greenland 61, 63, **64**
Green Revolution 126–7
Green River Formation, United
      States **14**
grievance 144–9
Guantanamo naval base 110
Guinea 59
Gulf of Aden 93, 105
Gulf of Guinea 14, 61, 93, **95**, 102,
      107
Gulf of Guinea Commission 176
Gulf of Mexico 14, 15, 46, 54, 60,
      61, 130
Gulf Oil 168, 209
Gulf War 102–3, **108**, 130, 146,
      169, 215

Guyana 94, **95**
Gwadar–Kashgar pipeline 109

habitat loss 26, 32
Haiti 106
Halfaya oil field **44**
health and safety 23, 46, 120, 133,
    153, 184
health issues 2, 79–80, 81–2, 97,
    127, 132–3, 134, 135, 219
heating oil 20, 80, 87, 101, 112,
    113, 196
home ownership 78, 198
Human Development Index (HDI)
    141, **142**
human rights 62, 97, 99, 118–21,
    132
  and China **44**, 118
  and companies 53, 120–1, 159,
    177, 183, 201–2
  and governance 26, 47, 48,
    63–4, 121–2, 164, 165–6,
    167
Human Rights Watch 140
Hydrocarbon Law 60
hydrocarbons 6–7, 27–33, 80,
    195–6
hydrogen 6–7, 195
hydropower 98, **99**, 100, 101, 196
hydroskimming technology 52

ICE Futures Europe **174**
independent producers *see*
    companies
India **12**
  and companies 25, 41, 43, 177
  demand for oil 85, 123, 182, 191
  and economic development 128,
    142
  and energy security 100, 109,
    112, **115**
  and governance 161, 162
Indian Ocean 110

indigenous populations 47, 133–4,
    164, 178
Indonesia 19, 57, **59**, **95**, **142**, 149,
    187
industrialization 143, 149
INEOS Group 52
inequalities, social 97–8, 111,
    112–13, 125–52, 198–203,
    216
  and energy security 97–8, 100,
    111, 113, 164
  and environmental impact 19,
    98, 119, 204
  and governance 167, 189, 200
  and oil revenues 25–6, 34, 97–8,
    134, **142**, 143, 148, 151, 201
infrastructure, oil-related 46, 61,
    96, 107, 109, 132, 164
  see also pipelines
infrastructure, transport 78–9,
    127, 133, 138
innovation 99, 121, 184, 185–6,
    193, 198
insurance 166, 170
Intercontinental Exchange (ICE)
    87, **174**
internal combustion engine 8, 78
International Court of Justice (ICJ)
    94
International Energy Agency (IEA)
    24, **44**, 85, 166
  and demand for oil 80, 102
  emergency oil reserves 85, 109,
    213
  and governance 160–4, 177–8,
    203
  and price of oil 70, 85–6, 88, 189
International Energy Business
    Forum (IEBF) 162
International Energy Forum (IEF)
    162–4, 176, 179, 203
international financial institutions
    (IFIs) 63–4

internationalization 34, 122, 178
international oil companies (IOCs)
    24–5, 48–62, 70
  and access 55–60, 209
  and energy security 120, 123
  and environmental impact 131,
    165, 177, 178, 221
  and governance 153, 169, 173,
    177
  and national governments 24,
    29, 30, 49, 55, 56, 168,
    169–70, 175, 209
  and national oil companies
    (NOCs) 45, 49, 50, 99,
    162, 178, 191
  and production 30, 75–6, 181,
    212
International Organization for
    Standardization 73
International Organization of the
    Securities Commission
    190
International Petroleum Council
    (IPC) 163
International Renewable Energy
    Agency (IRENA) 162, 163,
    164, 176, 203, 220
interventionists 156, 157
investment
  alternative energy sources 63,
    184
  and energy security 17, 45, 85,
    191
  lack of 77, 82, 90, 92, 96
  in new regions 9, 43, 102
  and price of oil 70, 77, 189, 190
  and production 17, 51–2, 53,
    58–9
Iran 157
  and companies 44, 49, 56, 61,
    209
  and energy security 95, 108, 114,
    115

oil reserves 11, 12, 39, 42, 44,
    50, 184, 209
  and oil revenues 91, 114, 136,
    139, 140, 142, 144, 145, 176
  and taxation 115, 193
  and production 11, 12, 187, 200
  and social development 125,
    136, 149
  and inequality and poverty
    111, 142, 144
  and United States 47, 49, 84,
    93, 103, 108, 110
Iran–Iraq war 110, 130–1, 145, 215
Iraq 157
  and energy security 77, 109, 114,
    200, 216
  oil reserves 12, 44, 50, 56, 209
  and oil revenues 114, 139, 176,
    216
  and social development 125,
    136, 141, 149
  and United States 102–3, 105,
    108, 110, 119, 141, 151, 169,
    215
  and warfare/unrest 183, 184
    invasion of Iraq 102, 110, 119,
    215
    invasion of Kuwait 102, 105,
    106, 108, 110, 130, 146, 169,
    215
Iraq National Oil Company 40
Iraq Petroleum Company 41
isolationists 156, 157
Israel 77, 95, 108
Italy 41
Ivory Coast 95, 176

Japan 12, 43, 95, 104, 105, 108,
    164, 184, 191
"Jeddah Meeting" 189
jet fuel 8, 20
Joint Organizations Data Initiative
    (JODI) 112–13, 162, 190

Jordan 115
Juhasz, Antonia 173–4

Kapuscinski, Ryszard 125
Kashagan oil field 59
Kazakhstan 16, 91
    access 59, 60, 109, 175
    and national oil companies
        (NOCs) 44, 45, 187
    and social development 125, 142
Kenya 17
kerosene lamps 72, 134–5
Keystone XL pipeline 165
Kissinger, Henry 85, 139
Koch Industries 174, 222
Korea National Oil Company 25,
    41, 45
Kurdistan 53, 149
Kuwait 12, 41, 50, 56, 142, 207,
    209
    invasion of 102, 105, 106, 108,
        110, 130, 145, 184, 215
Kuwait Petroleum Corporation
    39, 40
Kyoto Protocol 118–9, 166

land use 133, 171, 172
Latin America 17, 26, 44–5, 60,
    79
Latvia 95
Lavera, France 52
Law of the Sea Tribunal 94
leasing 172–3
Lebanon 95
liberalization 57–9, 156, 157, 184,
    185, 186, 187–8
liberals, economic 156
Libya 47, 125, 142, 157, 170, 200
    Arab Spring 103, 107, 108, 186,
        213, 221
    and companies 39, 40, 84
    and energy security 106, 113
    and oil revenues 140, 142

Libya NOC 39, 40
liquefied natural gas (LNG) 100
Lithuania 95
loans-for-oil 91
lobbying 120, 159, 165, 171, 172,
    173, 179
localism 198
Lockerbie bombing 170
Los Angeles 79, 132
Low Carbon Transition Plan 184
low-density polyethylene (LDPE) 81
low-income communities 132, 134
low-income countries
    and energy security 104, 205
    and governance 162, 166, 175
    and social and economic
        development 113, 128, 132,
        139, 150, 187
lubricants, mechanical 1, 7
Lukoil 40, 50
Lycra 81

Madagascar 64
Maine 112
Malacca Strait 50–1, 110
Malaysia 41, 95, 142
Mali 104
Malvinas Islands 95
manufacturing industry 112, 149
marketing 2, 26, 69–92, 119–20,
    182
    access to 25, 51, 73, 75–6, 83, 84,
        85, 99
    and companies 25, 40, 42, 44
    and energy security 45, 77,
        96–7, 112, 120, 121, 160
    futures market 2, 73, 83, 86,
        87–8, 89–90
    and governance 160, 173, 174,
        176, 179, 183, 184, 190
    over-the-counter markets 87,
        190
    spot markets 83, 86–7, 90, 213

marketing (*cont.*)
   and United States 120, 185, 190
   see also price of oil
markets, distance to 8, 56
Mattei, Enrico **49**
mechanization 9
media coverage 129, 176
Mediterranean 93, **95**
Mercatus Center **174**
methane 7, 101
Mexico 38–9, 41, 77, **142**, 144, 162,
   170, 185
Middle East 10, 11, 17, 27, 50, 56,
   109, 191, 206–7
   and nationalization 15, 41, 56, 60
   production costs 15, 56
midstream phase **36**, 37, 50–1
migrant workers 134
military intervention 186, 187, 204
   and energy security 17, 99, 106,
   110
   and governance 144, 184, 222
   and United States 115, 185
      Gulf War 102–3, **108**, 130,
      146, 169, 215
      invasion of Iraq 102, 110, 119,
      215
military technology 81
Minerals Management Service
   (MMS) 46, 172, 173
Mobil 76, 209, 222
mobility, personal 71–2, 79, 113,
   118–19
modernity 72
modernization 32, 79, 126, 128
Mommer, Bernard 161
monopolies 50, 157
Monsanto Company 81
Morocco **16**
mortality 133, 134, 135
mortgages 198
multilateral agreements **91**, 161,
   178–9, 184, 185, 187

National City Lines 78
National Foreign Trade Council
   168
National Iranian Oil Company
   (NIOC) 39, **40**, 41, 50, 209
nationalization 15, 38, 41, 46,
   60–2, 84
   and international oil companies
   (IOCs) 24, 30, 49, 56, 209
   and oil revenues 144, 145, 170,
   175, 209
national oil companies (NOCs)
   39–46
   and energy security 97, 184
   and governance 159, 175, 178,
   187, 201–2
   and governments, national 23,
   39, 144, 167, 168–9, 175,
   183
   and international oil companies
   (IOCs) 45, **49**, 50, 99, 162,
   178, 191
   and production 24–5, 29, **40**,
   56, 60
   transnational corporations
   (TNC) 25, 26, 29, 45, 60,
   63–5, 183
   see also individual countries
National Oil Company of Japan 43
National Oil Company of Libya **40**
National Oil Corporation 39
National Petrochemical and
   Refiners Association 74
National Resource Charter 200
NATO (North Atlantic Treaty
   Organization) 73
natural gas liquids (NGL) 101
neoliberalism 58
Netherlands 107, **108**, 143, 186,
   197–8
New York City 197
New York Mercantile Exchange
   (NYMEX) 87, 89, 214

Niger Delta 93, 107, 131, 136, 147, 149, 164
Nigeria 44, 131, 200, 206
    and energy security 94, 95, 107, 114, 121
    and nationalization 15, 57–8, 59–60
    and oil revenues 140, 142, 143, 144, 145, 147
    social and economic development 125, 145, 149
    and inequality and poverty 48, 111, 113, 136, 142, 143, 144, 147, 202
Nigerian National Petroleum Corporation 40, 57
Nissen 197
nongovernmental organizations (NGOs) 62, 202
    and environmental impact 61, 62, 64, 66, 154
    and human rights 48, 53, 61, 165–6
North America 61, 79
North American Free Trade Agreement (NAFTA) 108, 161, 176, 184
North Dakota 15
North Sea 42, 57, 60, 143
Norway 61, 142, 202
    and energy security 95, 114, 115, 196–7
    and national oil companies (NOCs) 15, 41, 42
    and oil revenues 32, 138, 140, 142, 150
    and taxation 114, 115, 141, 196–7
Norwegian Pension Fund 42
nuclear energy 80, 98, 99, 100, 101, 196
nuclear proliferation 100

Obama administration 114, 119, 165
Obasanjo, President 202
Occidental 84, 221
oil, crude 5–9
    benchmark 14, 69, 83, 86, 108
    conventional sources 5, 10–11, 14, 56, 57, 60, 82, 153
        in unconventional places 14, 61, 63, 99, 122, 132, 183
    "equity oil" 44, 52, 60, 84, 91, 117–18, 123, 158
    formation and composition 2, 5–6, 7, 206
        density 7, 8, 9, 14, 101
        quality 2, 11–13, 26, 34, 72–3, 120, 183
    heavy oil 12, 13, 14, 16, 51, 57, 58
        see also bitumen
    light oil 14, 20, 51, 58, 83, 84, 108
    unconventional sources 5, 14, 15–16, 102, 153, 180
        deep-water 9, 13–14, 57, 59–60, 61, 63, 132, 172–3
        and environmental impact 74, 121, 122, 123, 130, 132, 181, 183, 195, 211
        and governance 13, 74, 123, 181
        production costs 57, 82, 99
        see also bitumen
Oil and Natural Gas Corporation (ONGC) 25, 41, 53, 201
Oil for Development program 202
oil products 80–2
oil reserves 9–16 see also individual countries; oil, crude
    accessibility 3, 99, 104–11, 166
    and companies 25, 29, 40, 53, 55–60, 104
    acquisition 19, 44–5, 49, 53–4

oil reserves (*cont*.)
  availability 26–7, 33–4, 101–4,
    151, 154, 183, 187
  unconventional sources 102,
    180
  emergency 85, 105, 109, 213
  and governance 176, 186
  and national governments 23,
    29, 38–9, 96–7, 191
  ownership 22–5, **28**, 30, 38–9,
    41, 55, 60, 137, 157
  reserve replacement 54–5,
    61
oil revenues 74, 158, 201
  accountability 125, 144, 148,
    160, 166, 202, 203
  and companies 136, 137, 138,
    139–40, 167–8, 170–1
  and governance 176, 179, 190,
    200, 203
  and governments, national
    136–41, 144, 145, 155,
    170, 175, 196, 200, 201,
    209
  and inequality and poverty
    25–6, 33, 97–8, 134, **142**,
    143, 148, 151, 201
  revenue distribution **28**, 32–3,
    59, 77, 135–52, 166,
    209
  and taxation **28**, 141, 192, 196,
    200
  and transparency 144, 147–8,
    166, 178, 202, 203
oil spills 46, 129, 130, 131
  deliberate **108**, 129
oil supplies *see* energy security
oil wars 93–4, 103–4
  see also Iraq; Nigeria; Sudan
Oil Watch 25
Oklahoma 75
Oman **142**
OMV, company 50

Organization for Economic
    Cooperation and
    Development (OECD) 19,
    20, **21**, 42, 45, 79–80, 85,
    123, 178
Organization of Petroleum
    Exporting Countries
    (OPEC) 10, 23, 30, 41, 43,
    187
  and energy security 30, 77, 93,
    107, **108**, 212
  and environmental impact
    166–7, 188
  formation of 23, 46, 76–7,
    84–5, 209
  and governance 160, **163**,
    166–7, 176, 177, 203
  and price of oil 15, 70, 84, 85–6,
    88, 92, 189, 209, 212
  and surplus capacity 77, 93
  and United States 42, 107, **139**
Orinoco Delta, crude oil **14**, 58, 60
Outer Continental Shelf Deep
    Water Royalty Relief Act 172
outsourcing 19
over-the-counter markets 87, 190
ownership **28**, 30, 38–9, 41, 55,
    60, 137, 157
  foreign 58, **59**
  see also companies;
    governments, national

Pacific City Lines 78
Pacific Gyre 131
Pacific Ocean 131
Pakistan 109, 110
Palestine **108**
Panama Canal 110
partnership, strategic 17, 184, 185,
    187
Paterson, Matthew 171
Peak Oil Task Force 186
Pearl Harbour 105

Pemex 130
pension funds 140, 141, 150
People and Planet movement **64**
Perkins, John **139**
Persian Gulf 11, 93, **95**, 102–4,
    108, 110, 130–1, 154, 185,
    186
Peru **64**, 170
pesticides 81
Petrobras 29, **40**, 54, 183, 209
PetroCanada 41–2
petrochemicals 7, 81–2
PetroChina (CNPC) 40, **44**, 52,
    118, 119–20, 187, 201, 209
    as integrated oil company **40**, 50
    as transnational company 25,
        29, 183
petrodollars 138, **139**, 150
Petroleos de Venezuela SA
    (PdVSA) 39, **40**, 41, 50, 58,
        60, 209
PetroleosMexicanos (Pemex) **40**, 41
Petroleum Act (1934) 38
petroleum coke 9
Petroleum Exchange **174**
Petronas **40**, 41, **44**, 209
PetroPlus 97
Philippines **95**
Phillips Petroleum 78
pipelines 96, 109, 117, 129, 131–2
piracy 105
plastics 81, 127, 131
Platform movement 26, **64**
Platts 86, 213
politics, domestic 171–5
pollution 130, 138
    air 27, 32–3, 99, 112, 129, 133,
        134, 194
    bags, plastic 81
    water **14**, 26, 27, 32–3, 99, 101,
        130, 131–2, 133
population density 198, **199**
population displacement 97

Port Sudan 201
Portugal **108**
"posted prices" 76, 84
poverty *see* inequalities, social;
    resource curse
President's Working Group on
    Financial Markets **174**
price elasticity 112, 115, 216
price of oil
    affordability 3, 99, 104, 111–18,
        122–3, 150, 151, 153, 182
    and consumers 111, 138, 158
    and demand for oil 17, 74,
        79–80, 90, 92, 190
    and economic development
        22–4, 88, 142–3, 144–5, 150,
        171, 181–2
    and energy security 51, 70, 104,
        107, 111–13, 189
    and energy surplus 34, 75–6
    and gasoline 114, **115**, 116, 137,
        193, 216
    and governance 144–5, 147, 162,
        171–5, 188, 189–91
    and governments, national 83,
        84, 190, 205
    and International Energy
        Agency (IEA) 70, 85–6, 88,
        189
    and investment 70, 77, 189, 190
    and marketing 2, 69–92, 112,
        190
    and oil revenues 135, 144–5, 147
    and Organization of Petroleum
        Exporting Countries
        (OPEC) 15, 70, 84, 85–6,
        88, 92, 189, 209, 212
    and production **10**, 15, 29–30,
        96, 187, 190
    and taxation 19–20, 114, **115**,
        136–7, 158, 171–5, 190, 192,
        193
    see also marketing

price reporting agencies 86–7
price shocks 88, 96, **108**, 150–1, 186, 190, 198
privatization 39, 58, 156, 157, 169
production **10**, **12**, **28**, 29–30
    China **12**, 19, 116–18
    control of supply 30, 74, 76, 92, 99
        see also Organization of Petroleum Exporting Countries (OPEC)
    and demand for oil 183, 187, 189–90
    and energy security 74, 92, 184, 187, 199–200
    and environmental impact 19, **36**, 37, 67, 81–2
    gasoline **14**, 73, 81
    geography of production 15, 17, 21, 206–7
    and governance 158, 172–5, 200
    and international oil companies (IOCs) 30, 75–6, 181, 212
    and investment 17, 51–2, 53, 58–9
    and Iran 11, **12**, 187, 200
    and national oil companies (NOCs) 24–5, 30, **40**, 56, 60
    and price of oil **10**, 15, 30–1, 96, 187, 190
    and Saudi Arabia 11, **12**, 187, 189
    subsidies 113, 138, 158, 184, 185
production costs 15, 19, 56, **57**, 61, 67, 137, 153
    unconventional sources **57**, 82, 99
production network 35–8, 51, 62–7, 181–2, 183, 185, 188, 203
production sharing agreements (PSAs) 29, 58–60, **91**, 169, 175

proration 75–7, 211
Publish What You Pay 25, 164

Qatar 41, 107, **142**, 176
Qatar Petroleum **40**

railroads 171, 197
Rajasthan 53
Reagan administration 172
recession, economic 19, 90, 116, 128, 191
Red-Line Agreement 75–6
refineries 97, 107, 132
refining 2, 29–30, **36**, 37, 137, 172–3, 195
    capacity 19, 47, 50, 51–2, 55, 92, 105, 107, 114
reformers **156**
renewable energy 120, 162, 164, 165, 166, 167, 174, 195
Repsol-YPF 45, 50, 221
Republican party 46, 157, 173
Reserves/Production Ratio 10–11
resource curse 25–6, 32, 140–9, 152, 188, 198–203
resource nationalism 29, **59**, 60, 99, 181
revenue distribution **28**, 32, **59**, 77, 135–52, 166, 209
Revenue Watch Institute 25, 202
Rhodesia **108**
roads 129, 133, 134, 171, 172, 184, 197
Roosevelt, President 170
Royal Bank of Scotland 63, **64**
royalties 46, 84, 172, 184, 209
rubber, synthetic 81
Rumaila oil field **44**
Russia
    demand for oil **12**, 182
    energy security 31–2, 93, **95**, 109, **115**
    and governance 64, 162, 175

oil reserves 13, 15, **16**, 58, 60,
    64, 206
  and oil revenues **115**, **140**, **142**
  production **12**, 17, 43, 58, **59**, 77,
    91

sabotage 97, **108**, 129, 130, 131
Saddam Hussein **108**, 146, 169
Sakhalin 2 **59**, 64
sanctions 47, 105, 118, 157, 199
São Tomé 59
Saro-Wiwa, Ken 121
Saudi Arabia 19–20, 130
  energy security 105, 106, 114,
    115
  and governance 162, 175, 176
  oil reserves 11, **12**, 13, **14**, 41, **44**,
    56, 207, 209
  oil revenues 32, 86, 136, **139**,
    142, 145–6
  production 11, **12**, 42–3, 50, 187,
    189
  social and economic
    development 32, 125, 136,
    142, 145–6
  and United States 52, 121
Saudi Aramco 24, 39, **40**, 41, 50,
    52, 187, 209
savings 190, 200
secession 94, 149
Securities and Exchange
    Commission (SEC) **14**, 55,
    148
security, energy *see* energy security
security, food 98
security, national 23, 155
seismic activity **14**, 130, 131
Serbia 106
service contracts 29, **44**, 56, 58,
    60, 169
"Seven Sisters" *see* international
    oil companies (IOCs)
shale gas 101

shale oil 13, **14**, **16**, 16, **57**, 61, 99
share-buybacks 90, 214
Shell 24, 209
  and environmental impact 64,
    221
  and governance 76, 165
  and marketing 48, 76
  and Nigeria 57, 59–60
  oil revenues 40, 49
  production 40, 52, 61, 63
  production sharing agreements
    (PSAs) 41, 57, 59
  and Russia **59**, 64
shipping 8, 15, 50, 129
shipping lanes 106, 110, 131
Siberia 147
Sinopec **44**, 45, 50
Sittwe–Kunming pipeline 109
solar power 196
Somalia 53
Sonatrach company **40**
Soros, George **148**
South Africa 100, **108**, 162
South Korea 43
South Sudan 47, **95**, 149, 157, 202
sovereign wealth funds (SWF) 97
Soviet Union 25–6, 49, 84, 145
spare capacity 42–3, 52, 74–82,
    89, 175, 182, 189
speculation, financial 62, 88–91,
    153, **174**, 182, 189
spot markets 83, 86–7, 90, 213
Sri Lanka 110
stability, political 89, 96, 111, 145,
    157
Standard Oil 24, **49**, 72, 209
Standard Oil Blue Barrel (bbl) 73
Standard Oil of California *see*
    Chevron
Standard Oil of New Jersey 41,
    76, 209
Standard Oil of New York *see*
    Mobil

standardization 69, 71–4
Stanlow refinery 52
Statoil 42
steam power 8, 78
storage 36, 37, 50–1, 52, 75
Strait of Hormuz 50, 106, 108
Strait of Malacca 50–1, 110
subsidies 98, 113, 138, 158, 184,
    185
subsistence 111
Sudan/South Sudan
    and governance 157, 168, 202
    and human rights 47, 48, 53,
        118
    oil reserves 45, 61, 95, 183
    oil revenues 59, 142, 147
    and social development 142,
        147, 149, 202
Suez Crisis 110
sulfur 7, 13, 51
"supermajors" see international oil
    companies (IOCs)
supertankers 15, 50, 129, 130–1
supply gap 82, 183
supply risk see energy security
Suriname 94, 95
sustainability 26, 127, 158, 161,
    166, 177, 179, 181, 200
    environmental 122, 157, 178
SUVs 78, 118–9
Sweden 196
swing producers 42, 43, 77
Switzerland 100, 108, 147

Taiwan 95
Talisman Energy 53, 201
tar sands 13, 109, 120, 122, 129,
    130, 164, 165, 183
Task Force on Commodity Futures
    Markets 190
taxation 114–17, 171–5, 216–17
    and companies 84, 138
    and energy security 114, 115, 216

and environmental impact 22,
    167, 196
and gasoline 114, 115, 193
and governments, national 23,
    30, 48, 79, 196, 200
and oil revenues 23, 28, 135, 141,
    192, 196, 200
and price of oil 20, 114, 115,
    136–7, 158, 171–5, 190, 192,
    193
windfalls 143, 150, 151, 170, 190
see also individual countries
terrorism 47, 105, 119, 121, 146,
    170
Texaco 209
Texas Railroad Commission 75, 76
Thatcher government 42
THINK, company 197
Three Gorges dam 100
Timor Sea 95
Torrey Canyon, supertanker 131
Total 42, 44, 48, 49, 61, 97, 221
tourism 112, 131
traders, noncommercial 89–90,
    213, 214
Transition Towns Movement 184,
    198
transnational corporations (TNC)
    25, 26, 29, 45, 60, 63–5, 183
transparency
    and governance 147–8, 159,
        162, 164, 189, 190
    Extractive Industries
        Transparency Initiative
        (EITI) 121, 148, 163, 166,
        167, 176, 200, 203
    oil revenues 144, 147–8, 166,
        178, 202, 203
transportation 79, 80, 149, 171 see
    also car use
    alternative energy sources 101,
        102, 195
    alternatives to cars 172, 179

fuel efficiency 101, 112, 115–16,
188–9, 192–4
public 78, 192, 197, 204
transportation of oil 36, 37, 50–1,
101, 109, 127
transportation fuels 8, 20
see also gasoline
Trudeau government 41
Tullow Oil 53
Tupperware 81
Turkey 95
Turkish Petroleum Company 76
Turkmenistan 95

Uganda 64, 95, 102
UN Commission on Sustainable
Development 166
unemployment 145–6
UN-Energy 163, 166
UN Framework Convention on
Climate Change (UNFCCC)
22, 46, 65, 66, 163, 167,
188
United Arab Emirates 17, 41, 50,
95, 142, 162, 176
United Kingdom 17
and energy security 103, 105,
106, 110
and environmental impact 19,
64
and governance 164, 165–6,
169, 171, 172, 184, 186, 198
oil reserves 15, 38, 41, 42, 95
and oil revenues 138, 140, 142,
147, 166
United Nations 108, 161, 162, 179
United States
and alternative energy 98, 164,
174, 185
consumption 12, 16–17, 31, 135,
216–17
demand for oil 16, 25, 37, 42,
78–9, 191, 192

and energy security 45, 46–7,
93, 95, 98, 109, 112, 113,
119
and foreign affairs 31, 105,
108, 110
and taxation 114, 115, 115–16
and environmental impact 46,
159, 175, 184, 185, 192, 197
and foreign affairs 31, 77, 110,
185
and Afghanistan 93, 151
and China 19, 106
and Iran 47, 49, 84, 93, 103,
108, 110
and Iraq 102–3, 105, 108, 110,
119, 141, 151, 169, 215
and Japan 105, 108
and military intervention
102–3, 108, 115, 130, 146,
169, 185, 215
and Saudi Arabia 52, 120–1
and governance 157, 159, 164,
184, 185, 190
and domestic politics 171,
172–5
and foreign policy 168–9, 170
and human rights 47, 165–6
subsidies 184, 185
and marketing 120, 185, 190
oil reserves 38
and oil revenues 139, 140, 142,
158
and Organization of Petroleum
Exporting Countries
(OPEC) 42, 107, 139
production 12, 52
social and economic
development 113, 135, 142
and economic development
126, 149, 151, 171
and taxation 114, 115, 116–17,
135, 138, 173–4, 184, 185,
192

United States (*cont.*)
  and transportation 8, 78–9, 133,
    173, 192, 197
  and unconventional sources 13,
    14, 16
Unocal 45
unrest 99, 105, 106, 107, 144, 145,
    184, 199, 216
upstream phase 36, 37, 43, 49, 54
urban planning 79, 194, 197, 204
USA*Engage 168, 221
US African Command
    (AFRICOM) 102
US Air Force 73
US Alien Tort Claims Act 48
US dollar 77, 108, 139, 151, 189
US–UK Voluntary Principles 163

V8 engine 78
value 28, 30–1, 135, 214
Vancouver 197
vehicular access 118
Venezuela 32, 175
  and companies 39, 45, 58, 209
    Petroleos de Venezuela SA
      (PdVSA) 39, 40, 41, 50, 58,
      60, 209
  and energy security 113, 114, 115,
    216
  and inequality and poverty 114,
    142
  oil reserves 12, 39, 41, 58, 60
  and oil revenues 114, 115, 140,
    142, 216
  and unconventional sources 13,
    14, 16, 132

Vietnam 19, 93, 95, 151
Voluntary Principles on Security
    and Human Rights 121,
    166
voluntary schemes 165–6

walking 172, 174, 194
warfare 135, 204
waste 75, 113, 130
water 14, 26, 27, 32, 99, 101, 130,
    131–2, 133
weather events 69, 105
West Texas Intermediate (crude
    oil) 14, 86, 87
windfalls 143, 150, 151, 170, 190
wind power 196
women 143
World Bank 63, 166, 201
World Health Organization
    (WHO) 134, 194
World Petroleum Congress (WPC)
    163
World Summit on Sustainable
    Development (WSSD)
    166
World Trade Organization (WTO)
    157
World Wars 105, 110, 170
WTO (World Trade Organization)
    178

XTO 61

Yasuni–ITT initiative 134, 188
Yemen 111, 149
Yom Kippur War 77, 108